TREADING A DELICATE
TIGHTROPE

TREADING A DELICATE
TIGHTROPE

*A principal balancing between education and
political change during turbulent times*

by

Mike Burton

Published in South Africa on behalf of the author by
NISC (Pty) Ltd, PO Box 377, Makhanda, 6140, South Africa
www.nisc.co.za

ISBN: 978-1-920033-83-5 (softcover)
ISBN: 978-1-920033-84-2 (ePub)
ISBN: 978-1-920033-91-0 (pdf)

Cover design: Advanced Design Group
Photographs: Peter King & Andrew Stevens – pages 1, 6, 16, 31, 49, 91, 96, 102, 103, 104, 115, 130, 153, 161, 173, 174, 191, 198, 219, 222 and cover images; Bisho Private College Trust – pages 40, 45, 50, 53, 55, 59, 78; All Saints College Development Trust from *Out of the Fire: Where schooling worked in times of crisis, All Saints College, South Africa 1986–1996* – pages 116, 126

CONTENTS

Acknowledgements

I would like to acknowledge the help, encouragement and friendships that I received in producing this book. At the top of my list is Mike Schramm who accepted the responsibility of mentoring me through the process of professional publishing.

Four people helped me in the process. Crispin Sonn produced such an insightful foreword; Russel Bradfield was with me from the start; Dave Muller used the word persevere more than once; and Vrij Harry assisted me in the early stages of preparing the manuscript.

Finally, to my wife Noreen for sticking it out with me when times got really tough and shouldering the burdens that I neglected at home, and then for encouraging me to "write it down", and my children Andrew, Simon and Debbie for their understanding and loyalty throughout.

FOREWORD

ALL SAINTS COLLEGE was a courageous project, undertaken at a time in the history of our country when the risk of failure of such a project was high despite the obvious need for its success.

The events that played out at All Saints during the mid-1980s to early 1990s was a representation of the trauma that the country was about to experience. More lives were lost in the struggle for liberation between 1986 and 1992 than at any other period in the history of South Africa.

In a compelling manner, this book illustrates the complexity of the All Saints project - the noble but politically naive approach to the project by its founders, given the political environment, as well as the courage of the founders to take on a project of this nature during the death throes of apartheid.

All Saints and its story play out as a symbol of a wider society going through a fundamental social, political and economic transition. This was all happening while the majority of the white population was oblivious to the fundamental changes taking place in the country, only emerging to get a glimpse of events through the jaundiced lens of the public news broadcaster, the South African Broadcasting Corporation (SABC).

Traditional western private school education, Christian National Education, Apartheid education and radical liberation theory (freedom before education) were clashing as artificial barriers held up by apartheid fences and boundaries were forcibly being broken by angry black youth.

A Eurocentric approach and an Afrocentric approach to authority and education, which was held in place by an effective police state, were set to collide in a most dramatic way.

With the clarity of hindsight, despite the obvious social and political challenges faced by a project of this nature, All Saints was a success by virtue of the students it graduated who went on to make a significant difference in society, the teachers it attracted and the beacon of transformation it turned out to be.

At a personal and human level, recollecting some of the events I am familiar with, is exciting and heart racing stuff. At a more academic and somewhat impersonal level, it presents learnings and insights that serve as a, "must read" for the many who claim "We did not know what was going on!"

This book is a necessary and cathartic experience for Mike Burton and the

Burton family. In as much as this book is Mike's story, I can well imagine the impact the All Saints experience must have had on the Burton nuclear family. So, for them and successive generations of Burtons, this is a necessary bit of work.

For the All Saints alumni and family this book is equally necessary. Like the story told of many other private schools, this is a unique one that will serve as a reminder that there were brave men and women, white and black, who were willing to take risks when risks were often rewarded with death, detention or rejection. Mike Burton, Noreen Burton, Peter King, Ben Tengimfene, Quentin Hogge, Raj Kurup and Andrew Stevens are examples of such people.

There were learners who were transported from multi-generational township neighbourhoods to a school with facilities many had not considered accessible to them.

Yet, access to great facilities was actually the least of many students' concerns. The bigger challenge was believing that white people actually cared that they got a good education, that they be prepared for the new SA that awaited them and were vested in their success.

For me All Saints was an adventure. It was located in a part of the country I had never travelled to prior to enrolling at All Saints. I had been very active in the anti-apartheid movement as a student and learner and came from a political and ANC-aligned home. I suspect the same applied to many students who came from Gauteng and other parts of the country.

Upon reflection, All Saints' complexity was hidden in the diverse lives and experiences of learners who came to the college.

In most cases, learners were politically aware, in some cases politically trained and coached, and in other cases politically naive and even reactionary. The latter group were enrolled at the college to complete their secondary education and pursue a life out of poverty for themselves and their families. Politics was marginally interesting and, in many cases, just an inconvenience.

The politically aware and active students fell into different groups.

Group one was the group whose identity and history was closely linked to the struggle. Some of them lost siblings in armed conflict with apartheid forces. These learners would wear their political badges with pride and would distinguish themselves from other learners politically. Politics to a large extent defined them and how they wished to be seen in the world. At the time South Africa was caught in the political cauldron and it was hard to escape it.

A second group of learners felt tremendous guilt at being at All Saints and betraying the call for *Liberation before Education*. This guilt would play out in unpredictable ways which these students themselves could often not understand as they navigated their own emotions, consciences and youthful ambitions.

A third group of students wished to build a reputation at All Saints as politically savvy, future leaders. Their engagements were often self-serving and dangerous for the institution. They would often not survive the scrutiny of honest and considered political discourse and interrogation, and resorted to the threat of violence and populist rhetoric.

Putting these students in plaid pants and on a golf course where they and their families were previously only allowed as caddies, on squash courts or cricket pitches, and teaching them classic Latin, would only serve to raise their suspicion about the white teachers' attempts to resocialise them into being an 'acceptable' citizen and a betrayal of what they wished to be known for. If the founders were guilty of one thing, it was the extent to which they underestimated the maturity, pent-up anger and confidence of the learners they were seeking to attract to the college.

The only white person many students had had contact with was someone who represented a form or authority in South Africa, a policeman, a rude civil servant, a lawyer or a doctor. The expected re-socialisation of learners in relation to race and hierarchy was meant to be quick and intense.

Bringing black learners into contact with white people who cared about their success and well being was as big a surprise for learners. It was often met with suspicion and distrust, fuelled by the self-serving nature of some students, and teachers who had little training and experience in environments like this was, in hind sight, an opportunity waiting to be exploited.

Richard Todd's vision was noble and an idea whose time had come. The paradigm he chose to move from in executing his ideals was fundamentally flawed and the book deals with this well and exhaustively.

It calls to mind the warning, "*go to people where they are, and respect them for who they are, don't assume they want to find happiness in who you are*".

I had the good fortune of knowing Richard Todd and knew him as a confident capable person who was willing to take on a challenge head on. However, the paradigm he chose to approach this project from was founded in old colonial traditions whose time in Africa had expired. His stubborn tenacity was the basis of his success but also turned out to be his greatest challenge.

Bringing all these students together under one roof with the assumption that the incredible educational opportunity afforded us would be sufficient to douse the struggle flames or at least suspend them until we finished our time at the college, was ill considered. The motive was to prepare learners for the new South Africa that awaited them and anglicising them in the process was not going to happen.

Many of us were taught that every platform was a potential site of struggle. It was a place to advance the battle for liberation. This zeal in the hands of young people who felt they had nothing to lose and nothing to gain until the system was destroyed, was at the root of the rebellion against authority at All Saints. Expecting black learners to suspend their suspicion because a few kind-hearted progressive white people asked it of them, directly contradicted their life's experiences of white people.

In this, I believe, lies the big insight and lesson that through trial and error, willingness to take risks and follow his instincts, Mike makes a big breakthrough. The paradigm shift happens here and the lessons for many of us as we confront the rapid pace of change today, is still very relevant: co-create the rules, offer transparency, build trust, ensure everyone is held accountable to the same standards and norms, be willing to stand brave in defence of the agreed rules, and be committed to a process that may change these rules if they are inappropriate. This is democracy at work and a lesson in itself.

This was the lesson of All Saints College which the pages that follow will reveal. I am grateful to Mike for writing a story that needs to be told.

Crispin Sonn — Constantia, Cape Town, May 2021

PREFACE

THE 1980s were characterised by the most intense explosion of civic and student unrest the country had ever known. In response, President PW Botha adopted a total strategy entailing the co-ordination of military, political and developmental policies. So many in the white community of South Africa did not know what was happening on the other side of apartheid's separation line when a national state of emergency was declared in 1986. I was one of them. My story is a memoir and personal journey into the thick of things, if you like, during this particularly turbulent time. All of it actually happened. It is a story of crossing apartheid's formidable dividing line.

Journey with me and experience what I went through at that volatile time as I relate it to you. To start I have chosen the year 1991 to convey the stakes of the storyline. Like a volcano, things exploded overnight where once friendly faces were spewing hatred, much of it directed against me at a deeply personal level. Why this happened and how calmness was regained is a perplexing theme continuing throughout the journey.

When 1986 came, I was unprepared for most of the harrowing events that then unfolded. They just suddenly landed on my shoulders forcing me to react there and then. The events in this story happened over thirty years ago when South Africa's apartheid system was uncoiling towards its inevitable demise.

I have now had plenty of time to reflect on what happened and am ready to share. When I say that I was unprepared and that events took over, the litmus test would be that everyone including my family who knew me before I crossed that line on that precarious tightrope, would find it difficult to reconcile the before with the after. That I should stand in front of a huge crowd and raise my fist and shout out amandla! This wasn't the me that they knew or even I knew.

So, what happened and why did events change me?

Much of my story entails backgrounds and people connections. I grew up and was schooled in a results-dominated society and to my mind I had succeeded within this background. I was a qualified teacher with post graduate degrees from Rhodes University and Oxford University. I ticked the boxes to the extent that I was trusted with growing a non-racial school as the principal. I had been drawn into this role by a person very important to my story. He is Richard Todd whose mind and vision crossed the apartheid line, but he could not physically step over the line himself. He was bound and represented the corporate community and the all-important old school-tie connection from where he sourced the necessary funding. Ultimately our paths had to diverge as I made the choice to cross the line.

It was Franklin Sonn who showed me the way. He was the first to open my eyes to a different way of doing things. This new way was process-dominated whereby people are drawn into decision making. In other words, a democratic process. To appease the students who came from the other side of the apartheid divide, I needed to join them and walk with them and with the struggle community. It was not an easy line to cross and it came with its dangers. Franklin Sonn's advice was that if I was to succeed, I needed to recognise and understand the two different approaches to leadership, namely the western results-driven way and the African process-driven way, and then to draw the best of both into a new blend. This was a microcosm of the broader South African challenge.

The end of my story after all the trials and tribulations, highs and lows, is reached when Nelson Mandela comes to the college and face to face, I can share with him what we are doing in this corner of the country as a relevant school model for the new South Africa. The All Saints model produced significantly successful results at secondary school level and more importantly tertiary education throughput.

But thirty years on, education continues with the same challenges today that we faced back then. I would like to think that the lessons learned then, if embraced today, would go a long way to reconciling South Africa's different educational offerings.

What are the lessons learned?

A key lesson learned is about how to work together with people towards a common goal. A goal that is not for financial gain but a goal that is largely intrinsic in its sense of achievement. For teachers to teach because we understand and want to experience the results of education's real purpose not because it's just a teaching job.

Another is to recognise that a successful school community is successful because of the co-constructive energy of all its people harnessed for its progress that includes teachers, students, governors, parents and communities. It's all about building the right attitude of each stakeholder. The ownership of education in a school should be a shared ownership where every participant can have a say in how it is expressed.

Michael Burton — Nahoon, 2021

Abbreviations and Acronyms

ANC	African National Congress
AZAPO	Azanian Peoples Organisation
AZASM	Azanian Students Movement
AZASO	Azanian Students Organisation
BCB	Border Cricket Board
BSCU	Border Schools Cricket Union
BSSSU	Border Senior Schools Sports Union
CASAC	Community and Student Affairs Committee
COSAS	Congress of South African Students
COSATU	Congress of South African Trade Unions
DET	Department of Education and Training
IB	International Baccalaureate
INSET	In-Service Education and Training
ITEC	Independent Teachers Enrichment Centre
JMB	Joint Matriculation Board
JMC	Joint Management Centre
LEAF	Leadership and Education Advancement Foundation
MaST	Management and Skills Training
MCC	Marylebone Cricket Club
MDM	Mass Democratic Movement
NADEL	National Association of Democratic Lawyers
NDS	National Democratic Struggle
NEC	National Education Conference
NECC	National Education Crisis Committee
NETF	National Education and Training forum
NEUSA	National Education Union of South Africa
NGO	Non-Governmental Organisation
NOSC	National and Olympic Sports Congress
NSC	National Schools Cricket
NUSAS	National Union of South African Students
OUCC	Oxford University Cricket Club
PAC	Pan Africa Congress
PASO	Pan African Students Organisation
PSP	Primary Science Project
PTSA	Parent, Teachers, Students Association
RETF	Regional Education and Training Forum

RSEP	Regional Science Education Program
SAAIS	Southern African Association of Independent Schools
SACC	South African Council of Churches
SACOS	South African Council on Sport
SADF	South African Defence Force
SADTU	South African Democratic Teachers Union
SANSCO	South African National Students Congress
SARFU	South African Rugby Football Union
SASSCO	South African Senior Schools Congress
SRC	Student Representative Councils
UDF	United Democratic Front
USSASA	United Schools Sports Association of South Africa
UWC	University of the Western Cape
YWCA	Young Womens Christian Association

part one

ERUPTION

chapter 1
Rejection

"Now try to imagine who else was stuck in the conundrum: being in school and hungry to learn, but sceptical of the White man and refusing to be 'brainwashed'.

"What's even more intriguing is that I initially perceived the school and its administration with eyes jaundiced by conspiracy theories and suspicion"

— Putuma Gqamana PhD (Student 1987–88)

I T IS A FATEFUL DAY in August 1991 when passions erupt amongst the students of the college. They burst away from a national call for peaceful protest and defiance against apartheid, and turn their fury on me and the staff of our college. Why?

The day starts so well but ends so badly. It is a crisp and cloudless early Monday morning on 19 August 1991 when I leave my home on the campus, humming a tune while Chips, our little Jack Russell dog, frisks in the grass next to the path looking for field mice. Such a wide and open view stretches out in front of me. The rolling grasslands look serene all the way to the green and misty blue of the Amatole Mountains, secure like a distant promise. Not far from me two blue cranes leap and stretch and crouch in their magical mating dance. It is a special early morning start to the day.

Trees have just been planted by students to mark National Arbor day, and Chips and I make our way slowly through the newly planted walkway to my office. It is the start of another brisk spring day and the sun is barely up. I can see two students walking energetically up towards me from the residence. This is unusual as our students normally drift ever so slowly up to the college. They call out to me. They are Teboho Monaheng, chairman of the Students' Representative Council, and Tando Bonga. When they catch up, they ask:

"Sir, may we use the phone to contact the office of the Congress of South African Students (COSAS) to get information about the forthcoming National Mass Action Week?"

"Certainly guys. We would all like to know how our school might become involved in the call for a campaign of defiance against apartheid. Come with me."

Cell-phones have not yet entered the market and social media is not yet known. Little about the defiance call from the Mass Democratic Movement (MDM) has been publicised. This type of news is not displayed in apartheid-controlled newspapers, but it is public knowledge that some form of resistance is brewing.

This is an important and perplexing matter. I think to myself that by supporting the students' quest I can be properly informed about what might be expected of us.

Together we walk the two hundred metres to the administration block and I take them to the telephone in my office. Unfortunately, they cannot make contact so I give them permission to use the telephone back in the dining hall. All the other students are waiting for information before coming to classes which normally start at eight o'clock.

At eight the teachers gather in the staff room wondering why no students are to be seen. Impatiently we all wait as time ticks slowly by. I have tried to explain what is going on but after an hour of waiting the teachers become annoyed and suggest that I should go down to the hall to find out what is happening and chivvy the students up.

Just then we see a small delegation ambling up from the hall, obviously not in any hurry to start classes. They ask to meet with all of us in the staff room. First, they politely thank us for our patience and they then present the week's mass action schedule. We are invited to participate in a church service and a demonstration peace march at the end of the week. Teachers mumble amongst themselves and respond differently, but the consensus outcome relayed to the students is that we wish to consult with parents and community structures before committing ourselves to their suggestion. Perhaps we are missing an opportunity to support what the students are offering so as to show that we are united in our anti-apartheid stance?

However, at our induction five years back, we were cautioned not to get mixed up in politics and this is still weighing on most of us. We have been told that our focus should be the classroom where we feel most comfortable, so several teachers are nervous about stepping out into a demonstration peace march and exposing ourselves in support of any mass protest action. In addition, the marches appear to be devoid of white participants and most of our teachers are white.

I have sent Sindisile McLean to investigate the situation on our behalf and he comes into the staff room to brief us. He is the secretary of the regional African National Congress and recently he has joined our staff as a liaison officer. Sindisile tells us that COSAS has not asked students to stay away, so they shouldn't be avoiding classes. Yet our students still do not come for lessons and send us a message demanding a continued break. So, after a short discussion with the staff, we recognise that we must abandon any idea of teaching for the day.

We seem to be very much in the dark so I phone a parent member of the Parent, Teachers, Students Association (PTSA):

"Hello Nomonde, I hope that you are well. Our students are boycotting classes and we need to understand why. Please would you call the other parent members of the PTSA and I will collect the teachers and invite the student members so that together we can learn what is happening."

"Hello Mr Burton. This is news to us too so we will definitely attend the meeting at six o'clock this evening."

It seems that a class boycott is not in line with COSAS or national expectations and yet our students are staying away. Perhaps something else is happening.

*   *   *

Later in the morning boys and girls are seen moving from the dining hall *en masse* into the Girls' Residence that can only be interpreted by us as some sort of confrontational act of defiance. It seems to be a calculated move to break college rules as well as an overt attempt to neutralise the girls in case they reduce the momentum that appears to be gathering.

What is going on?

The students laze around the common room in the residence and watch TV at full blast. Peter King, who is the warden of the residence, goes into the room and asks them to turn the TV down and demands that the boys leave. He advises them that they are damaging the staff-student relationship and trust. He is clapped and jeered as the students ignore his ultimatum and lounge back on the sofas in non-compliant defiance. Things are not looking good.

In the evening three parent members of the PTSA drive onto the campus and join the three academic PTSA staff members who are already waiting in the staff room. Together we now wait for the meeting to start, but no student representatives are with us. This won't work without them. Just as we are about to give it up and go home, two students stroll slowly into the staff room to present apologies and to inform us that matters are now out of control in the residence.

What do they mean by "out of control"?

There is a sense of foreboding in the staff room because the two students are not responsive. In fact, they look decidedly sullen. There is an unmistakable air of antagonism. Still, nothing can be resolved in a meeting without student representatives so when the two leave us staff and parents start talking.

Mr Ngebulana suggests *"We the parents should go down to the residence to find out directly what is happening. They will talk to us."*

We all feel that this might work as parents should gain the respect and co-operation of the student body. We agree and before the parents set off, they say that they will let us know the outcome before returning home.

The two teachers with me, May Swana and Raj Kurup, are bewildered. What should we do next? After some tentative discussion I recommend that matters are now out of our hands, since the parents have taken the initiative to meet with the students. There is no point in all three of us sitting around and waiting any longer. The other two retire to their homes while I stay and wait alone for the parents to return to give me their report. I walk from the staff room to my office, switch on the light and wait. And wait. And wait. I cannot help nervously trying to unravel what is happening down in the residence. I dare not move away so I just sit waiting anxiously. It grows darker and time ticks slowly by.

While we have experienced student resistance before, we have usually known the cause and have been able to address the grievances successfully. This time round I can only second guess, and that cannot happen because I can't even come up with a first guess.

Eventually, after an interminable wait and as midnight approaches, I can see the three parents getting into their cars down at the residence, but they drive on the road right below and past my office without making any attempt to stop and report anything to me. I don't understand why because the lights in the office are shining brightly. Perhaps it's because they have seen that the lights are off in the staff room at the other end of the building where we first met. For me it has been an arduous and nerve wracking wait for nothing. I am left no closer to understanding what is happening. There's no point in waiting any longer, so I lock up and make my slow, disappointed way back to my house at the top end of the campus in the dark.

We learn later that just as the parent delegation was about to leave, the students surrounded Mr Gubuza, demanding that he call a meeting the next day for parents and students without the 'authorities' of the college. They have grievances and look to the parents for guidance without the teachers.

I feel that somehow that the teachers and I have been cast as enemies and perhaps even oppressors. Who knows?

*   *   *

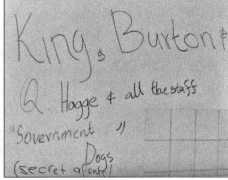

Shocking graffiti - some of which was obscene and personalised – displaying the vehemence of the perpetrators

Early the next morning we are shocked to find the college's administration buildings and residences spray-painted in bright pink with graffiti messages of a frighteningly malicious nature. A lot of it is deeply offensive and loaded with personal attacks on me. It is a bitter pill to swallow. How can student leaders be pleasant and supportive one day, then be part of such brutal spite towards me and our institution the next? What information or disinformation, have they uncovered? It seems they have been led to believe there is some sinister conspiracy against them and that this treachery is somehow instigated by the authorities of All Saints led by the principal.

This is so deeply shocking and unexpected that I am horror struck. What is meant by *Government Dogs – secret agents*? How come I am portrayed as a *double snake* that *kills*? What have I done? These accusations go to my very core and I feel a need for time out. How is the rest of the staff reacting? What can I possibly do, as we all seem under direct threat?

Because I am no nearer to knowing the cause of this bitterness, I am filled with righteous anger. But I feel powerless to react, even though I as the head represent the authority of our institution.

I am perplexed and have a deep knot in my stomach. I just don't know what to do.

*   *   *

Around mid-morning the students emerge from the residences displaying placards and performing the characteristic political resistance toyi-toyi march with the intimidating 'huff-huffing' war dance shuffle. Toyi-toyiing usually begins with the stomping of feet and breaks into spontaneous chanting that can include previously created or improvised political slogans or songs during protests. One of the placards accuses All Saints of being a Joint Management Centre (JMC); another warns *Beware JMC Agents*. I have no idea what a JMC is. Sometime later Peter King briefs us all that JMC is a Joint Management Centre, which is part of the state security system and is deeply offensive to the liberation resistance movement.

Other placards proclaim *Private Schools are dangerous*, *To hell with LEAF Poison is here to frustrate* and *All Saints not a Solution*. The students huff-huff, chant and dance in protest along our campus ring road and out the front gate onto the main road to Bisho (now called Bhisho), the Ciskei capital some four kilometres away.

This is totally out of our control or understanding and I feel that something must be done soon. However, I'm at a loss of what I can do to defuse things. I cast my mind around to find someone to help us. Eventually I decide to phone a prominent local former headmaster, Gideon Sam, who is better versed in this type of student confrontation than I am. Gideon is a trustee on our Board. I ask him for advice. I also make sure that the other trustees are made aware of what is happening. They too may be able to help. Even though the students have rejected me, I feel that it is my responsibility to them and their parents to follow their march, so as to monitor movements and, if necessary, try to make sure that no harm befalls any of them. I run this by Gideon and he agrees that it is the responsible path.

I quickly walk back to my house, get into my car and drive carefully up to the back of our protesting demonstrators. As they approach the outskirts of Bisho, the procession is stopped by a white police vehicle. It's time for me to pull over a way back and peer through my windscreen. They are talking animatedly. After a short while the protest continues through the housing area of Bisho and on to the Bisho Business Village. There a plain-clothes police presence blocks them once more and forces them to stop. From my vantage point some way back, I can see two casspirs (mine-resistant vehicles usually manned by two soldiers in the cab and carrying 12 additional troops and equipment). They are speeding towards the scene. Clearly the police are coming out as they recognise something amiss is happening. This is not looking good. Now I really don't know what to do other than to hang back and observe, although I feel in the pit of my stomach that I must do something to prevent any possible violent outcome, I decide to follow these troop-carrying vehicles to the taxi rank. To my alarm I see them collecting more troops, guns, riot shields and masks. They then rapidly drive around the car park area of the shopping mall towards the students. I am really anxious so I back track towards the students to reach them ahead of the armed security forces. My aim is to alert them to the danger building up around the corner. As I drive up to the students, I can only think to flick my car's headlights on and off in an attempt to warn them, but they don't understand what I am trying to do so they gesticulate rudely at me.

The casspirs arrive suddenly, troops form ranks and the phalanx advances. The students scatter amongst the houses. They are followed but fortunately no one is caught or injured. Somehow they all make their way back to the college. Clearly they want nothing to do with me and they do not need my help. I drive back past several groups of students who gesture angrily at me.

We learn later that the students believed that I had organised the military block and confrontation. To them this was the damning proof that I am collaborating with the armed forces of the apartheid state.

*   *   *

What to do next? Sindisile Maclean suggests that we should seek advice at the office of the African National Congress (ANC) in nearby King William's Town (now Qonce), and should share the events of the day with ANC members there.

It soon becomes apparent that the All Saints students have abandoned their original intention and have embarked on a wild-cat strike with little reference to the national movement. They appear to have found something else much more immediate and significant about which to vent their anger. Their actions are now directed away from the wider anti-apartheid struggle and towards All Saints College and its umbrella body, the Leadership and Education Advancement Foundation (LEAF). Our students are convinced that All Saints College is a façade for a deeper, more sinister conspiracy: that we are a Joint Management Centre in cahoots with President PW Botha's Total Onslaught strategy.

How did they ever come to this conclusion?

*   *   *

Following the march debacle, the parents arrange to meet with the students back at the college in the early evening. Peter King joins me and we wait in my office in the administration block for the promised report-back from the parents. The meeting ends near midnight and once again parents drive past the office and off the campus without briefing us. It is all very baffling but then Peter and I notice a student walking on the veranda just outside the office window in the gloom. Suddenly a mass of agitated students emerges from the darkness and surges panting through the open office door towards us.

In shock Peter and I step backwards. There is yelling and jostling and shouts of *"Let's move in"*. This is frightening and serious. In horror we realise that we are possibly in mortal danger and there is very little time to react. Wild-eyed students pour into my office and surround the two of us. This is possibly going to escalate into something vicious. Peter and I try to act as calmly as we can under the circumstances. I raise my hands and show my palms trying to calm everybody. Mercifully, some order emerges from the chaos and Ignatius Mabuza shouts out:

"We the student body demand to search the administration building."

There is no point in confronting the invading students in their present unpredictable mood. Peter and I are also horribly outnumbered. I try to instil some sort of order by addressing Ignatius by name and asking that ten or twenty students be nominated to carry out the search. My request is shouted down from a number of the highly charged intruders. They mill around the office and start searching randomly by roughly opening up filing cabinets and stripping files. Peter King calls out that rather than confiscating originals they should use photocopy documents. This too is ignored. It is extremely difficult to guess what is going to happen next, but for the moment they are ignoring Peter and me, and are scavenging through what documents they can find in the office.

A message somehow gets out to the resident academic staff that Peter and I are under an aggressive siege. Several teachers then arrive and take up positions to support us and to observe the search which has moved on into other quarters of the administration building. The student search eventually loses momentum in the early hours of the morning and we suggest that surely by now they have found what they are looking for. The raiders decide to drift off with armfuls of papers, leaving the ravaged office all awry.

After a brief chat with the perplexed teachers who have joined us, we all recognise that nothing more can be achieved at this hour of the morning. We are in shock and exhausted, mentally and physically. It has been so unpredictable and taxing that my throat feels like a rasp. I feel breathless. I need to break away, so we decide to lock up, go home and come together in the staff room around seven thirty later in the morning to gather our wits. We can then decide what we can possibly do. None of us understands why this insurrection is happening or where it is heading.

At dawn I realise that I must phone Richard Todd in Cape Town. He is the director of our college. As the principal I must inform him of the invasion and what is happening. Clearly we are experiencing a serious breach. The students have forcefully entered the office and other areas of the administration block and violated the confidentiality of the college's administrative records in a criminal fashion. Surprisingly Richard has little to say. He gives no comment or advice on what could or should be done. I cannot help feeling that he is harbouring a personal grudge against me, perhaps about how I am managing his college and that somehow I am the cause of this outbreak of insubordination. I perceive that in his mind I should be able to control what is happening and not just go with the flow. In other words, show them who is boss and in charge!

Soon after my phone call to Cape Town I meet the academic staff in the staff room and we discuss the events of the students' confrontational march to Bisho, the late evening invasion of the administration block and the removal of documents during the night.

A short while after we gather and Mr Gubuza, the *ad hoc* parent chairman, arrives to give the staff his report. I am obviously very distressed and disappointed by the way the parents abandoned us the previous night and I tell him so in front of all. He does not seem too concerned. Clearly, he has other things on his mind and it is evident that he has sided with the students in their mob aggression. He is not at all friendly towards the teachers. Mr Gubuza rationalises that the occupation and removal of documents are part of a fact-finding strategy. He tells us that many accusations were levelled at the staff during the parents' meeting with the students before the incursion. The parents then told the students to find proof to support their allegations.

At this point I can feel my blood pressure rising and I cannot contain myself any further. I object angrily that it was extremely reckless and irresponsible to suggest this to the students while their emotions were running so high. It is nothing short of incitement for parents to give an unpredictable and potentially dangerous student body virtual carte blanche to confront Peter King and me and invade our offices. I am incensed at Mr Gubuza and the other parents for leaving the campus without even briefing or forewarning me or anybody else.

The situation on the campus is dangerously unpredictable. I feel it necessary to call in the services of the Red Alert Security Company to protect personnel and college property. I even take the precaution of driving my family and caravan to safety in the nearby King William's Town caravan park. I have no idea of how violent this insurrection can become.

*   *   *

The next morning Sindisile Maclean collects and brings the regional COSAS leadership onto the All Saints campus with the aim of using them to find out what is going on with our students. In the presence of teachers, he briefs the delegation on the events. By this stage we are virtually certain that the national action call has been hijacked by opportunists on our campus and that something far more sinister is taking centre stage. Pambili Booi, the All Saints COSAS leader, later confirms that this is what is happening. He says that there are some serious educational issues which are considered to be relevant to the mass action. The COSAS representatives withdraw as they have been side lined and indicate that they cannot help us.

Later in the morning the All Saints students once more move en masse into the administration offices and invade our college secretary's office while Joan Schmidt is there. They make hundreds of photocopies of documents supposedly supporting their accusations. The academic staff hovers over them and even helps them to manage the machine, but we remain entirely in the dark about what they are looking to uncover and what is in their minds. They are not sharing anything with us. Clearly someone has shared some dangerous subversive disinformation with them and the students have reacted immediately by becoming violently mutinous.

chapter 2
Flashpoint

"You don't have to see the whole staircase, just take the first step."
— Martin Luther King Jr

AFTER THE INITIAL SHOCK of the student mutiny, the turmoil continues into the next day. Steps are taken in an attempt to restore order before events get violent and entirely out of hand. But our attempts are thwarted and we are left bewildered and still in danger.

It is Thursday, four days into the insurrection. After a quick session with the staff I call for an emergency trustees meeting. We decide to connect with Crispin Sonn, a former All Saints student who is at Cape Town University. He is the son of Franklin Sonn, our Trust chairman. Crispin listens to what's going on and offers to collect a number of alumni of mostly University of Cape Town students to come to All Saints, a trip of one thousand kilometres, overnight. He suggests that the alumni will talk to and hopefully pacify the rampaging students by sharing the true mission of All Saints College and LEAF with them. Crispin is not doing this because of my asking him to. He feels strongly that the students at the college are misinformed and he believes that his group of alumni might be able to sway them.

The teachers and I agree that it's time to call for a meeting of all parents since the PTA members have abandoned us. Throughout the day there is no formal contact between students and academic staff. We use our time to meet as a staff team. Using a flip chart, we draw up a memorandum outlining our position in reaction to the situation and reaffirming our commitment to the ideals of the college. The outcome is a list of conditions to present to the students before we will agree to go back to teaching again. Our demands are for a public apology, a written statement recognising the bona fides of all employed by LEAF, the return of all documents and property removed during the student invasion of the administrative building, and an agreement to follow accepted channels for future grievances.

We feel violated and we are still alarmed at the unexpected hostility which may flare up again at any moment. The aggressive and hateful behaviour displayed towards us burns us deeply, so any form of forgiveness and reconciliation is far from our thoughts at this stage. We are outraged, and yet we still do not know exactly what has caused the students to turn on us so suddenly and so vehemently. If they would only enlighten us, we might yet sympathise with their cause. However, being kept in the dark, we still feel threatened. At the same time, we express our outrage at the inexplicable actions of the loose-cannon parents.

At last, the parent-student meeting that has been in session all evening invites me in an hour before midnight on Friday. This is five days after the students started their rampage. Perhaps we might now be getting somewhere, but I am still quaking in my boots. It soon becomes clear to me that parents are backing the students and might even be orchestrating events. Peter King has just given me a written report that he has recorded from what he overheard. He taped a number of inciting statements made by one parent, Rev Dr Solomon Abram during a gathering in the residence earlier in the day. Slowly and carefully, I read them all:

"We must expose the evil things that they have tried to do here."

"Even Russian newspapers must print this story." (Implying that it must be heard all over the world?)

"Students who come here in 1992 must not have to go through the same things that you have."

"When you go to classes tomorrow, you must be united."

"We must not allow them to divide us."

"They will offer you sweets and chocolates... don't accept them."

Just exactly what is he up to? What evil things? What chocolates? Why Russian newspapers? I cannot grasp what this is all about.

*   *   *

Very early on Saturday morning the team of alumni from Cape Town arrives at the campus entrance in a kombi. It has been an arduous drive through the night. They have come to help, but their position is soon compromised at the entrance gate and they are prevented from getting close to us or the student body by a group of aggressive students who have waited for them in ambush. How did they know? The alumni are whisked off to the dining hall where a full meeting of students is in sway.

I have just been made aware of the alumni team's arrival and capture. A short while later I am in the administration block when Richard Todd also

13

arrives from Cape Town to join me in my office. He has been instructed to come to All Saints by Franklin Sonn so that he can take stock, offer support and protect his institution. Richard and I do not have much to say to each other after I have shared that Crispin and his colleagues have been hijacked and are in the dining room probably being grilled. In fact, I am feeling most uncomfortable with the arrival of Richard in my office. I see him as like a school inspector reserving the right to watch and be critical of the goings-on without offering any assistance. The events unravelling are stressful enough without accommodating an uncommunicative person in my space. Little do I realise that he is planning to slip away.

Eventually a raucous noise bursts out from the dining hall. I go to the window of the office looking down on the campus and can see the alumni group emerging through the door. They are being noisily frog-marched up towards the office. Without realising that Richard is no longer in my office, I walk outside the office door and out onto the balcony above the road to look down at the scene unfolding below.

The procession with the captives being held roughly and shoved up front gathers on the road just below the office. I'm not sure what to do as no one is saying anything. They are just standing, panting and staring aggressively while there is resignation and even fear on the faces of the captive alumni. The intensity of passion is vividly displayed in the students' hostile body language as they hold the shaken alumni in front of me. Suddenly I am taken off guard as a small group comes rushing up the stairs onto the veranda and crowds next to me. I get a sick feeling and am shaking like a leaf, it is difficult not to show panic and take some form of evasive action. One student in particular, Simphiwe Tom, moves up right next to me until his shoulder is nearly touching mine. His body is trembling and he has a wild look on his face. This is menacing, and the thought even crosses my mind that I might be knifed at such close quarters.

I learn much later from Simphiwe, when he is an undergraduate student at Rhodes University, that some students had openly declared that they were going to kill the principal then and there, because they were convinced that I was an agent of the apartheid government. Simphiwe and a few other local Xhosa students have rushed ahead and positioned themselves around me so as to protect me in case an attack is triggered. With all the passion displayed around me, understandably I mistake their wild looks as something hostile.

My heart is beating ninety to the dozen as I decide to push past Simphiwe and walk down the stairway away from the protection of my office to the agitated student group gathered in the road and stand right up in front of them. Thinking about it now, it was a provocative thing to do and it surely could have ended in disaster for me. To this day I don't know what prompted me to make this move in the heat of the moment.

Simphiwe's group follows me down the steps and still keeps close to me. It is a frightening and unpredictable engagement. I can only stand unprotected in the mêlée and silently pray that I am not baiting some rash action towards me by someone in the crowd. Everything unfolding around me is unpredictable and menacing. The situation is on a knife's edge.

I take a quick look around me for Richard Todd who I thought was in my office with me when the rush came from below and the students stormed up to the administration block. I really need him at this moment, but he is nowhere to be seen. Disappeared. Gone. It seems that he has left me to fend for myself.

In front of me all the alumni students are being forcibly manhandled and are standing in a line just two metres in front of me. One of them, Matshele Koko, is clearly under duress and forced to say:

"I am a spy and I was sent by Mr Burton and there is no place for me here."

This moment marks the climax of animosity and the confusion deflates after Matshele makes his confession. The alumni team is then hurried off into their kombi and they drive slowly away down the road and off the campus.

Without a word, the leaders of the insurgence then walk back to the residences. After milling around aimlessly for a while, the remaining students disperse quietly. Simphiwe and the small group that had rushed up the stairs towards me are still in close proximity and are still wild-eyed. The storm abates, yet moments earlier I felt this confrontation might just get out of control with tragic consequences. I have said nothing and have just witnessed the events as they unfolded in front of me. It has all been so sudden and traumatic.

Now I am left standing alone. Richard Todd is not around. So I walk slowly up the stairs back into my empty office, collapse into my chair and exhale audibly. I sit motionless for some time just looking out of the window. Outside it looks eerily calm now but it is not how I feel. I am all churned up and I need to regain my composure and think around what has just happened.

How did things build up to this frightening climax the day after the student march to Bisho, and what is yet to happen? How am I, now sitting in this office, going to go about resolving the situation as a competent headmaster should do? I am all alone. I feel exhausted. I get up slowly, walk out of the admin block, make my way up to the reservoir at the top of the campus and sink onto the plinth at the base of the tank. For a while I feel that I do not want to move on. It has all been too much for me to absorb and I am feeling the after-shock of having been so exposed and unprotected during some really traumatic events. The ending might so closely have been tragic and led to my demise. It has been a day of darkness and foreboding. I just don't want to leave this reservoir, a place of tranquillity that looks out over the soothing panorama of rolling countryside. It belies the drama that has just happened below.

It is dusk when I eventually wander down to my home and am about to walk up to the garden gate when a frightening spectre appears out of the gloom. I step back in fear but find that it is the smiling face of Anderson Diko, our college printer, who has been waiting for me. He tells me that a group of students is planning to attack my home during the night and he intends keeping a sentry vigil. He won't hear of any comfort that I offer and says that he would rather sit it out and patrol around the house.

An unsung hero is someone who does a great deed but receives little or no recognition for this. Anderson Diko is one such unsung hero and a true friend. He keeps vigil through the night at our front gate, accompanied by our little Jack Russell dog. It must have caused him a great deal of discomfort and yet he does not make this public. He just does it, and he keeps a lonely watch armed with a formidable knobkerrie.

I learn later that Anderson did chase off some boys who were creeping up in the darkness. His aggressive presence took them by surprise. They fled into the night and didn't come back.

Anderson Diko our college printer and member of the service staff. It is poignant that he put himself selflessly between me and the students

chapter 3

Connecting

"Do not drown in your own emotions. Take a breather, regain your
strength, do not let what worries, control you."

— Leon Brown

I T HAS BEEN TWO DAYS OF harrowing experiences. After some off-campus
deliberation we seek a positive way forward. I have met an antagonism that
will later play out against me – at the next meeting of the Board of Trustees.

Late in the afternoon, I and a few teachers, together with Richard Todd,
meet with the alumni group who have waited for us at the nearby Amatola
Sun Hotel rather than return to Cape Town. There is so much to discuss. We
are living through an unpredictable nightmare with rumours that the students
intend to burn the college in the name of the struggle. Somehow, we have to
regain equilibrium. On the recommendation of Crispin and the alumni group,
advice from the National Education Crisis Committee (NECC) is sought. In
our meeting, we agree that the way forward is to ask the NECC to convene a
meeting with community structures in nearby Zwelitsha township tomorrow.
The alumni group who have helped me with this suggestion then leave to drive
back to Cape Town. They have, at great personal sacrifice, exposed themselves
to unforeseen danger and helped us to connect with a legitimate facilitating
structure, the NECC. We wave goodbye and settle in to plan the way forward.
We need to see how this move will play out.

Richard is quiet. It is clear that he is unhappy. The antagonism that has just
erupted on his showpiece college needs some form of acceptable justification
that he can report to the LEAF Trust and to the funders. He also needs to
find a scapegoat. He targets me with his opening remarks, saying that I should
make firm decisions, be the captain of the ship and not to use so much time
and energy in consultations. He states that he dislikes the structures of the SRC
and PTSA that we have developed at All Saints. He adds that he does not like
that we have built a culture of democracy and that *"all and sundry"* are part of

our decision making at All Saints. It is anathema to him that even the agendas of our staff meetings are drawn up by staff members in rotation who then go on to chair the meetings. In fact, our meetings have evolved into participatory discussions. This is not the manner of traditional schooling where staff listen to the principal, who is in charge. If his aim is to create division amongst us, Richard's criticism gains no traction.

Richard and I are clashing and the tension between us is getting close to breaking point. I am sure that the issue of the difference in our strategies of handling conflict has not yet run its course and things are bound to boil over at some stage. I sense that I will have to face the music later. After all, Richard Todd is the director of LEAF and he wants me to establish his kind of firm control. But although he is reserving the right to be critical, he is not offering any positive suggestions for a way forward. After this meeting Richard takes his sombre leave of us and returns to Cape Town.

It is extremely vexing for me to grapple with a crisis not yet resolved and to have an antagonistic boss barking at my heels. What makes it particularly hard for me to accept is his open personal criticism of me in front of others while it is still fresh in my memory that he inexplicably disappeared in the face of imminent danger at the office doorstep. He never confides why he moved away from the action.

*   *   *

Back at All Saints after the impromptu meeting at the hotel, my task now is to update the remainder of the staff and gather them all in to accept an appeal to accompany me to Zwelitsha tomorrow for the next round. It is obvious that a number of them feel uncomfortable about this idea. They start to raise objections and are clearly resistant. Richard has already stated his opposition to teachers moving off campus and into a township in pursuit of support to break the impasse on the campus. Some consider it to be both foolhardy and dangerous that white people should venture into a township, especially as the motivation can be construed as being political at a time when political meetings are banned and aggressively raided by security forces.

I don't wish to force anyone to come with me to Zwelitsha but the next day it is pleasing to find a very good staff turnout in support of what will prove to be a pivotal meeting. We drive to the venue in our school minibus. I sense that our mood is one of apprehension and I too am unsure that this step will yield a positive outcome, given the rebellious students and their parents on the one hand, and our umbrella body, LEAF, and its director, Richard Todd, on the other.

After disembarking and being shown our places in a full community hall, we meet representatives from a wide range of structures brought in by the NECC which include COSAS, the PTSA of Forbes Grant School, the Pan African Students Organisation (PASO), the South African National Students' Congress (SANSCO), the South African Democratic Teachers' Union (SADTU), and the Azanian Students Movement (AZASM). For many of our staff, attendance at this meeting feels perilous. All these organisations are still banned by the ruling National Party at this dangerous time during a declared state of emergency. This meeting could easily be considered subversive and could be invaded by security forces at any time.

After being welcomed, I am invited to state our case, which I do by declaring that I respect those present and that I recognise them as the legitimate progressive structures in the liberation struggle. I then point out that the actions of the All Saints College students is mystifying to me and the teachers. We have no idea what the problematic issues are. Thus we anticipate that if there is anything that we are doing wrong, we need to be told what it is. The meeting is then told that parents have reported to us that the students are now prepared to come back to classes. I explain that the staff is not ready. We have been confronted, insulted and offended, and need a proper understanding of why students have turned on us and become so aggressively abusive before we can consider reconciliation and closure of the matter. I go on to deny any connection with a JMC or any collusion with state security, which is the only real accusation we have picked up from the students' actions. I emphasise that the students hijacked a legitimate national call of protest against apartheid that was supported by me and the academic staff. We do not understand why matters then went awry. I conclude by saying that All Saints College's policy of community interaction has meant that the college's resources have been widely used in the region and yet the students have openly declared that their agenda is to burn and destroy the college in the name of the struggle. Since they claim to align their actions with the national struggle, they need to learn that this is not what the defiance campaign is calling for. Either that or the staff and I need to learn that we are somehow out of line.

A way forward is decided at the meeting. A delegation from the two major student organisations, PASO and COSAS, will immediately go to All Saints to assess the situation with their constituencies. A report back is set for the same time and place on the following evening.

The time drags by slowly through the next day until we make our tentative way back to Zwelitsha in the evening. What are we going to hear? Will it be another step downwards or is there perhaps a tiny positive light at the end of this dark tunnel? We are still so unclear about what is happening to us and are even more anxious about what we might be doing by going back to Zwelitsha township.

After the usual introductions and pleasantries, the leader of the NECC opens the meeting with a remarkable and surprising statement:

"Mr Burton, you and your staff have nothing further to worry about."

This is so direct and unexpected. I am on the edge of my seat. He goes on to say that the PASO and COSAS delegations tried to talk to our students on the campus but were told that the students did not want assistance or interference from what they termed 'outside' organisations. The delegations were sacked ignominiously without being able to find out anything.

It dawns on me that the ramifications of this statement are huge. The outcome of connecting with these organisations in order to resolve our crisis is that the staff and I have now gained important allies while the All Saints students have isolated themselves. The anti-apartheid struggle structures led by the NECC are now recognising the legitimacy of our concerns and are ready to support us to find a solution.

Then, ten days after the initial flare-up a delegation of students comes to my office to inform me that they have heard from the NECC. They accept with immediate effect the conditions that are set and that the SRC and the PTSA have been re-instated. They denounce chaos and want to go back to classes as soon as possible.

My reply is that this is not going to happen as we, the staff, have set some pre-conditions before we will consider that normality and mutual respect have been restored. We have been needlessly trodden on and have experienced damaging hatred. We now need some breathing space to regroup and gather our own emotions.

*   *   *

In his first action since leaving us following the Amatola Sun discussion, Richard Todd decides to instigate a court interdict against Mr Gubuza for coming onto the All Saints College campus and removing confidential documents from the property. It is his opinion that Gubuza is a key instigator of the insurrection. I inform Richard that I am fully supportive of his move because of my own misgivings about the role Gubuza appears to be playing. In my opinion Gubuza is a dangerous person. I am certain that this parent has been leading the action and using the students as pawns. He has taken all the stolen and copied documents and has not even shared them with the parent constituency. He intentionally abandoned me when my office was invaded late at night, withheld all the information and gave us no feedback.

The next step is that a special NECC committee attempts to break the deadlock between staff and students by calling a meeting with both the SRC and staff. However, the deadlock prevails. The SRC will not divulge anything to do with their week of action as the representatives claim that they do not have a mandate to do so. Their assertion is that the student body has done nothing wrong. The meeting considers that the only viable option is to bring forward the end of the term. The SRC is in favour of this, but the student body with its leading agitators is not. They do not want to bring the holiday forward as they say this will disunite them. Their uprising will lose momentum. The students claim that there were no leaders in their insurrection, only a united student body.

My decision, supported by the staff, is to send all of them home as soon as possible. The local parents are in favour of an early holiday too, but it is clear that the students still have unfinished business. Although I think it may cause another flare up, I make it clear that food will no longer be provided by the college, as the college is deemed to be closed. I strongly believe that the students need to learn there are consequences for illegal acts such as the seizure of confidential documents, theft of computer disks and money as well as the unlawful perusal of private personal documents, let alone daubing insulting and intimidatory graffiti slogans on the property.

*　　*　　*

One important thread that emerges from all this angst comes from Mluleki George, a prominent leader of the United Democratic Front (UDF). He feels that All Saints College is too vulnerable to the wrong elements, and that the college should be more community based and stop drawing students from as far away as Johannesburg. He wants to talk to Richard Todd and Franklin Sonn about these issues. In his opinion, All Saints College needs to be more relevant to the local community, but this flies in the face of Richard's grand vision of a national initiative with satellite campuses around the country. He is clearly peeved that his flagship, All Saints Senior College, appears to be steering towards the rocks with me at the helm and unable to change course. He sees me as a wrecking ball damaging his dream rather than supporting it.

A parents' committee arrives at the college the next day with lawyer Mike Smith from the National Association of Democratic Lawyers (NADEL). After a meeting in the boys' residence, a delegation of four parents comes to my office to inform me that a Committee of Nine has been formed, documents will be returned and the students' case will be tabled for resolution.

At midday that day, the Committee of Nine convene a meeting with lawyer Mike Smith, the SRC, me and four other academic staff. The two items on the agenda are soon confirmed. They are the return of documents and early closure for the term. Prominent in the Committee of Nine is Solomon Abram. After the meeting closes, he starts to talk loudly and adversely about the situation whilst we are still gathered. I interrupt him and say that the meeting is now over and that the most important thing is that the documents need to be returned before we can move forward. Abram is angry with me and gesticulates:

"This is bad history. You are making bad history!"

I have really had enough of this man:

"Mr Abram you were stirring things by exposing malicious conspiracies to students in the residence so as to incite them; the bits about evil things done at All Saints, that Russia should be informed and not accepting chocolates. What you said in the Residence to the students has been overheard and recorded, so I would quieten down if I were you."

Shaken, he calls out: *"Can't we even have a private meeting in this place?"*

*   *   *

An investigative commission is established and I am asked to nominate three commissioners to represent the college and its Trust. This is a window of opportunity for me to put my stamp on things and even if this means flying in the face of Richard Todd and LEAF. So I choose not to consult with Richard Todd. Instead I phone Mluleki George and after a short discussion I ask:

"Comrade George, please would you nominate commissioners for us, who recognise the value of our school and will represent a broad base of community structures in our region so that All Saints' bona fides will not ever be questioned again."

I know that I am putting my neck into the noose. It will antagonise Richard as I am now openly surrendering LEAF control of All Saints in favour of seeking legitimacy through alliance with anti-apartheid structures. Even though I know there will be serious consequences for me, I believe that this is the right and only course to take. A decision without sanction from the LEAF director is a red rag to a bull and I accept I will be called to account at some later stage. But the explosion of recent events is still raw in my mind and I am still hurt that Richard had abandoned me to the dangers of the moment when it came to the crunch. So now I feel released from his control and recklessly free to do what I consider is best.

As representatives for All Saints, Mluleki George nominates Penrose Ntlonti (who was later to becomes the secretary of the South African National Civics Organisation in the Eastern Cape), Reverend Bongani Finca (a prominent leader of the South African Council of Churches (SACC)) and Isaac Roji (of the South African Communist Party).

The appointed chairman of the commission is John Smith, a lawyer at Smith and Tabata. The terms of reference include investigating fully the specific grievances and accusations of the students and the response of the principal and staff to these matters. The commission is to draw up a comprehensive report of its findings and issue recommendations where appropriate.

The commission is thorough and it works carefully through all the students' grievances placed before it. It is required to investigate fully the specific grievances or suspicions held by students, and the accusations made by them which precipitated their actions during the last two weeks of term; the specific actions of students over this two-week period; to hear the response of the principal and staff on these matters; to issue as a matter of extreme urgency a full and comprehensive report on their findings; and to issue recommendations where appropriate that will be made public prior to the start of the final term. All parties are bound to accept the findings of the Commission.

The Commission orders Richard Todd to explain the funding support given by the President of Ciskei, Lennox Sebe: a payment of R200 000 made on 22 August 1984, and again on 3 April 1985 an amount of R150 000, both paid to the Bisho Private College Trust. This information was the spark that led to the student insurrection. It is an astounding revelation.

chapter 4
Disclosure

"Before you can see the light, you have to deal with the darkness."

— Dan Millman

THE EPIPHANY FOR ME is when the students divulge for the first time to the Commission that they had received information that large amounts of money from President Lennox Sebe and the Ciskei Government had been paid directly to Richard Todd at the very start of his All Saints College project. This had suggested to them that the Ciskei government continued to be actively involved in the management of the college and was therefore influential in its policy decisions. This 'revelation' had led to their rebellion because it appeared to prove to them that we were and possibly continued to be funded by the apartheid government's JMC programme.

In an instant I understand the students' reaction. They believed that the information they had uncovered showed that LEAF, All Saints College, I and all the staff were not what we claimed to be. To them we were, in fact, something far more sinister. I also now understand why they wrote ugly personal graffiti on college walls and doors. It is because they see me as a secret agent of the apartheid regime. They feel threatened and have a need to tell the world. They chose to do this with a march off the campus to make their point publicly. My distress that parents had abandoned me now also makes sense. They were inveigled into believing the conspiracy plot.

It is clear that this early funding revelation unveils everything about the insurrection. The only trouble is that it is not altogether true. It is true that Richard Todd received large sums of money in 1984, but what the students inferred from this is not true.

Neither I nor any staff member knew anything of that initial financial transaction. As Richard did not think that it was any of our business, he had never revealed anything to us about seed-funding made two years before we were employed. Consequently, all along we had been unaware and I had been

24

denying knowledge of this substantial amount of money. I now can understand why I have been the personal target of student vehemence. To them I am a liar. To them, being the principal, I must have known about it.

* * *

When the commission finally publishes its conclusions, it reports that all the student accusations are unfounded and without any substantive evidence.

The SRC then submits a written unconditional apology and the staff recommits to making up lost classroom time.

* * *

The teaching staff and I still need to expunge all the hurt that we have endured. We do this individually by writing down our private reflections on what positive things have come out of the insurrection and its aftermath. Then we talk about it in the staff room. Sharing our thoughts and getting the nightmare episode off our chests for the time being is cathartic for each of us.

Some of the views expressed are that if crises are opportunities for growth, then this is no exception. One teacher points out that some of the debilitating rumours against us such as secret funding from government and being part of a JMC have been exorcised. Another feels that the relationship with the surrounding communities has been strengthened because we drew and can continue to draw on their involvement so as to resolve conflict. We all agree that our tolerance, honesty and openness have been displayed throughout the crisis period. We can feel good about ourselves. We held up, and I commend staff for this. We agree to use this experience as an opportunity to grow by re-examining our commitment to the umbrella body LEAF and its director, to our college and most importantly to our students. I gain most confidence in that the staff stuck it out with me, despite perhaps feeling very insecure in doing so. We have remained unified and retained our integrity.

A telling comment, however, is that we have been painfully reminded that not all are ready to work together in a constructive spirit to build All Saints as a non-racial, democratic community. In other words, we have simply learned that we have enemies. In a roundabout sort of way we see this as positive, because it rids us of our missionary naivety and strengthens our resolve to persevere. We all pick ourselves up and are ready to tackle the challenge of reconnecting with our students and making up for lost time. We have purged the hurt that we have endured by openly sharing our feelings with each other. The most positive aspect has been our steadfastness in sticking together and seeing the crisis through to the end.

The examination results at the end of the year turn out to be the best to date!

*   *   *

I feel that my trials are now over for a while. The student rebellion is over and the cause has been exposed. Proper teaching is restored at All Saints, but we do not know what the future still has in store for us. We have solved the impasse by reaching out for support, and have done all we can to secure the immediate future for All Saints College in a turbulent political environment. However, it has been done mostly with the disapproval of the director and founder of the college.

I know my future as college principal is now threatened. I anticipate being described as ineffective in dealing with the crisis, which I should have nipped in the bud. None of the trustees has yet been informed that the cause of the insurrection was Richard Todd's non-disclosure of substantial amounts of money paid to him by the Ciskeian Government in the two years before the staff arrived and the college opened its doors. If the Board of Trustees are not informed about and understand this, I feel I will surely be removed from my post.

I reflect that if Richard Todd points the finger of blame at me for being unable to prevent the uprising, he cannot hide from the fact that the reason for the flare-up is of his doing. The Commission has uncovered the truth and we can get back to our job of teaching and learning. But it is not over. All indications suggest there is more to come.

chapter 5

Cauldron

"A man does what he must – in spite of personal consequences, in spite of obstacles and dangers and pressures – and that is the basis of morality."

— Winston Churchill

AN OMINOUS STORM CLOUD of expectation hangs over the table. The All Saints Senior College Board of Trustees sits grim-faced, anticipating an ugly drama. The riotous events of the past few weeks have left the college reeling. This is a crucial meeting. It is to be make or break.

My future as college principal is under threat and subsequently the very future of the college is in the balance. I have cared deeply for this school of hope, born five years ago in the Ciskei, a designated homeland in fractured apartheid South Africa. But my recent memories are raw. Overnight, once friendly students have turned to spitting words of hatred, scrawling ugly obscenities on walls, and threatening my life.

The central players on the Board of Trustees are divided. For too long now the director and I have been in disagreement. It cannot continue like this. I swallow nervously. After all, I am only an ex officio member of the Board without a vote. A defining decision has to be made. Something or someone has to capitulate if there is to be a future for the college. I feel that my head is on the block. Will the Board of Trustees, to whom I am accountable, understand?

If members of the Board of Trustees do not understand, I will be sacked ignominiously. The status quo is balancing on a delicate tightrope.

As executive director and founder of the college, Richard Todd is incensed that his vision, for which he has won national acclaim, has been seriously threatened through student anarchy and insurrection. The future of his College appears to be disintegrating. He blames me by pointedly alleging that the crisis could have been averted had it been properly managed. He reports that I have completely mishandled the situation. I have not followed his management style which is to show them who is boss. I will have to take responsibility for the state of affairs and face the music.

The mediator and key player at the table is Franklin Sonn, the charismatic education leader in the mass democratic struggle against apartheid. He is the Chairman of the Board. It is his responsibility to break the impasse and to steer the meeting to an appropriate resolution.

This is 1991 and political resistance in South Africa is reaching its climax as apartheid is visibly crumbling. All indications suggest it is going to collapse completely in the near future. It was in this cauldron of external political conflict, five years previously, that the non-racial All Saints Senior College was born: for me it has been five years of treading a difficult and dangerous path with the staff and students – though there have been moments of success and signs of hope in our collective search for meaningful education in stressful times. Now the board of trustees is sitting in judgement that could possibly prematurely end it all. So many futures are in the balance.

Why did the students rise en masse in uncontrolled fury, hell-bent on destroying the college? It seemed illogical and inexplicable. What are the issues? Who is to blame? Will the trustees believe that I have mismanaged the situation?

How is it that two people – who have shared the responsibilities of establishing and managing a ground-breaking, and in so many ways, a successful pioneering college – have taken such divergent paths?

It wasn't always like this.

*   *   *

The meeting reaches its climax when the chairman asks the director to explain what he means by my completely mishandling everything. His reply is that I have handed All Saints over to the ANC and have stepped beyond my mandate as the college principal. This is when Franklin Sonn says in a calm and no-nonsense manner:

"Michael Burton did the only thing possible to get the students to return to classes. He engaged the relevant community structures to defuse the situation. All Saints Senior College is now much stronger than it has ever been before and it is now recognised as a peoples' school engaged in the struggle."

He asks Richard what he would have had me do and the reply is that I should have sacked the ring leaders right at the start if I had shown any gumption. It is clear that Franklin Sonn is exasperated, so he asks:

"What is the end of the road Richard?" And he repeats: *"What is the end of the road?"*

Richard is stunned and does not answer. Franklin goes on:

"Just exactly how was he to do that? How was he to physically remove the ring-leaders if they were not revealed to him? If he had called in any security forces you could kiss your college good-bye."

*　　*　　*

The outcome of this definitive meeting gives me the full support and approval of the Board of Trustees – with the exception of Richard Todd. I am congratulated for the manner in which I have led the staff, gained the backing and acceptance of the community and defused the mass action. Despite my apprehension at the start of the meeting, I have now been exonerated. The stage is set for All Saints College to take its place in the forefront of the reconstruction for the nascent post-apartheid South Africa. The end-of-year examination results should vindicate everything that has been done at the college this year, despite facing such a level of hostility and mayhem. I feel so much better.

Both sides – the staff and students – have learned valuable lessons for the future. But the insurrection has wrung a whole lot out of me and I know that Richard Todd is not going to accept the situation without retaliating at some stage.

part two

CRAFTING THE VISION

chapter 6
Synchronicity

"A meaningful coincidence of two or more events where something other than probability is involved."

— Carl Jung

FIRST MET Richard Todd in 1966 when I was studying for my teacher's diploma at Rhodes University, and carrying out my teaching practice at St Andrews College, where he was a schoolmaster. We had become good friends as I had just been picked to play cricket for the Eastern Province XI against the touring Australian cricket team, and he was a cricket enthusiast. He made my teaching practice enjoyable by introducing me to other cricket devotees among the staff members. He had even invited me to a social evening at his home, and during the cricket match against the Australians at St George's Park, he had brought along some learners to meet me and get my autograph. When I said good-bye and thanked Richard at the end of the two-week teaching practice, I little thought of how our paths would cross again in the future.

After I gained my teaching diploma at Rhodes, I studied further at Oxford University in England, and Noreen and I were married and started our family. We returned to our homeland, Zimbabwe (then still Rhodesia), and both started teaching. In the 1970s the country was totally engaged in the bush war. Towards the end of the 1970s I was teaching at the residential Plumtree School in Matabeleland on the Botswana border, located 100 kilometres from Bulawayo, the nearest urban centre. The school occupies an isolated and, at the time, dangerous spot. When Noreen and I recognised that the tensions and the very real danger all around threatened our young family, it was time to think about leaving. Our children were Andrew aged six, Simon aged four and Debbie, a little mite just one year old. Their future in Zimbabwe was looking increasingly bleak.

Noreen and I were not sure of our own teaching futures, as rumours abounded that white people could have their career opportunities blocked to make way for black teacher advancement. We started to make plans to leave our homeland and relocate to South Africa. Life had become tough and uncertain. It was a threatening time and it was clear to us that we were living in dangerous circumstances on a daily basis. All teachers at the school had to teach with an FN rifle close at hand in the classroom. We were even required to hold the weapon at the ready when out on the sports field, umpiring sporting practices and inter-school cricket matches.

We did once experience an attack on the school property by a group of seventeen insurgents (at the time, we called them "terrs" – terrorists – whereas the rest of the world recognised them as freedom fighters). On this occasion, extreme good fortune favoured the learners and the school, as the invaders mistimed their attack. Their intention had been to strike at morning tea-break when the boys usually gathered at their hostel verandas to collect their morning tea and sandwiches. But Plumtree School had two teaching timetables, one for winter and one (with an earlier start) for summer, and the terr intelligence got the season wrong. Their attack happened while classes were still in session a short distance away. Nobody was on the veranda of Lloyd House just across the road when all hell broke loose as AK-47 rifles peppered the building with a cacophony of rapid firing. Poor matron! She was all alone in her room on the upper level and was bewildered as her peaceful morning of sorting laundry was shattered with sharp cracks, thuds, and whining, as bullets screamed around. The firing went on for around five to ten minutes. Then the attackers melted away into the adjoining bush. Paratroopers arrived (too late) and hurriedly followed the spoor.

It was a massive wake-up call for us at the school, as the war was literally on our doorstep. Our community was now on maximum alert. As their housemaster at Milner House, I was required to equip prefects and senior boys with their cadet .303 rifles in the evenings and to drill them to be ready. Safety was uppermost in the minds of everyone at this outpost school, adjacent to the railway station, and close to the Botswana border.

*   *   *

As the war heated up, I realised that I was involved in defending a lost cause at great personal risk. My role had always been a passive one of safeguarding and protecting, but there was still the continuous threat of being attacked. There were minimal resources available for training in self-defence, and as back-up to come to our assistance. Although we had not been directly in the line of fire at any time, Noreen and I finally and firmly believed it was time to emigrate from Rhodesia as the country started shedding its colonial liability so as to embrace a new era as the liberated Zimbabwe. But where in the world should we go? I had very positive responses to my enquiries from Australia because of my Oxford University scholarship and qualifications. I even considered Papua New Guinea as an exotic destination but, in the end, we decided to settle just south of the Limpopo River. This decision was taken because we feared for our parents, who were set on staying in the new Zimbabwe. We did not want to go too far away from them in case they might need help.

We resolved to move towards the end of 1978 and I posted off an application to the Private Schools Association for a teaching job in South Africa. It had to be a private school because in Rhodesia my O-level second language subject at school had been French and not Afrikaans. To teach in a public school in South Africa at the time, one had to have a standard level of competence in Afrikaans.

Woodmead College, in the "mink-and-manure" belt on the northern rural-urban fringe of Johannesburg, responded positively to my application. Towards the end of the year, I was contacted by the founder and headmaster, Mr Steyn Krige, and invited to an interview. I boarded the plane in Bulawayo in a whirl of apprehension and hope. This was going to be a big step.

Steyn Krige met me at the airport and drove me past mine dumps and dense skyscrapers on our way to the school in the north-west of the urban sprawl. How different this was from the extensive open expanses of rural bushveld surrounding Plumtree. Already in my mind I was uneasy. I asked myself whether the Burton family would be able to fit into this concentrated urban environment of southern Africa's principal city. Mr Krige was very friendly and our initial conversation in the car was positive and encouraging. My hopes of an appointment were high. The school's campus was not in the city, which was a plus. Being on the outskirts of the conurbation, the panorama was wide. After the interview, I was offered the post of teacher in charge of Geography at Woodmead College.

There was one important drawback, as there appeared to be no primary school nearby for our children to attend. Mr Krige suggested that I contact the headmaster of a very successful preparatory school that was not too far away. I used his telephone and made an urgent appointment to meet the headmaster that afternoon, before I to flew back home to Rhodesia.

*   *   *

This school was St Peter's Preparatory School in Rivonia. Unbeknown to me, the headmaster was the very same Richard Todd with whom I had become acquainted in my university practical teaching days at St Andrew's College. We were both taken aback at this second encounter. He was warm and welcoming and offered me not only places at the school for our two boys but also teaching posts for Noreen and me. I accepted his offer on the spot. For the next few years Noreen and I taught little boys at St Peter's Preparatory school under the firm, authoritarian and capable headship of Richard Todd. I felt very guilty about reneging on Steyn Krige's invitation to join Woodmead College staff, as it looked very much as if I had used his offer as a stepping stone to find something better. At least Richard did the honourable thing and reimbursed Woodmead for the cost of my return flight from Bulawayo.

*   *   *

Richard Todd was the Headmaster of St Peter's Preparatory School on the outskirts of Johannesburg from 1971 to 1980. In this time he turned a small farm school into a leading suburban preparatory school. I soon learned that he was very versatile and skilled at the helm and a competent leader. In his teens, Richard had been head boy of Bishop's College in Cape Town, a role that confirmed his confidence in his own abilities – already then, he knew his own mind. He had subsequently performed his national service in the South African Navy. As a result, he liked to compare the role of headmaster to being captain of a ship: he saw himself as captain and the teachers as the crew, there to do his bidding. Absorbed and energetic on the job, he was also forceful in achieving his vision for St Peter's. Richard was responsible for many constructive changes and additions to the school.

He introduced weekly boarding and had two boarding houses built with a dining hall facility between them, where hot lunches were served to day scholars. These resourceful developments help to double the number of learners during his tenure as headmaster: he made St Peter's the largest independent preparatory school in the country.

He was also very brave in taking on the apartheid establishment when he admitted black pupils to the school, making St Peter's one of the first schools to do so. On the eve of the arrival of the new black pupils Richard received a phone call from FW de Klerk, at that time a member of parliament, and serving as information officer for the National Party in the Transvaal (now Gauteng). De Klerk reminded Richard that what he was doing was against the law, and warned him that, should he continue with his plan, de Klerk would send in the police to physically remove the black children. Not perturbed, Richard Todd told De Klerk to go ahead but warned him that he would make sure the world's media would be there to record and broadcast the removal. De Klerk backed down. That was Richard's style.

Richard Todd's footprint at the school was immense and I was in awe of his capabilities.

*   *   *

Once more, I found myself indebted to Richard Todd for coming into my life and giving me an opportunity to settle after the distressing period our family had spent in the precarious setting of a civil war. I was now ready and looking forward to teaching small boys with Richard as the headmaster.

But I was still apprehensive. What were such fundamental changes in my teaching world in a new country going to reveal?

At St Peter's our young family landed very comfortably away from the anxieties of Rhodesia. Even our journey from Plumtree School to the Beit Bridge border post with South Africa had been in a convoy with interspersed support vehicles manned with machine guns ready to fight off any possible ambush attack. Settling into our new environment, we could now move about and sleep safely and peacefully. We could even buy chocolate and other luxuries that had previously been denied us by punitive trade sanctions in our home country. It all seemed good.

Our first home in Johannesburg was on a smallholding at Fourways on the outskirts of Rivonia. It was a converted barn, cleverly transformed by some Swedish architects into a comfortable four-bedroomed home. The house was surrounded by a five-hectare plot which was used as a small stud farm for *Dorper* breed sheep.

The property was owned by Donald Currie, a wealthy property auctioneer, and the stud farm was a ploy to halt the encroachment of the ever-expanding city of Johannesburg into the surrounding peri-urban areas. He needed to show that the land was economically sound. It was wonderfully peaceful and therapeutic living on his property, with its cool highveld evenings and the entertainment of gambolling lambs racing around the smallholding. Our rental payment was met by Noreen's taking on the responsibility of managing the stud flock, which she did marvellously well, often having to stare-down, and prevent being butted over by, the huge and aggressive ram, Rastus. Her science background, and her readiness to try a new adventure, led the Curries to rely on her more and more. We felt welcomed and drawn into their family.

Much later now, I note with some regret that not long afterwards, our first idyllic haven from war-torn Rhodesia became the site of a massive commercial development known as the Montecasino leisure complex, designed to replicate an ancient Tuscan village. Gone are the open grasslands. But as a special place in Johannesburg's rural–urban fringe at a time when our family was most in need, it fulfilled every assurance that we needed to settle in a foreign country. Regrettably our stay at Fourways was cut short after only nine months. Accommodation became available on the St Peter's school property and we had to leave our smallholding idyll. I was obliged to become the housemaster of Waveney House. We moved into a housemaster's flat looking out onto the school's main playing field. Noreen was then invited to teach little Grade 0 boys in a new and beautifully designed foundation-phase school building. We were happy in our new abode.

*   *   *

St Peter's Preparatory was the school where I started my South African teaching career, and while ever thankful to Richard Todd, I was in awe of his omnipotent leadership. He was very decided and firm in all his dealings. He was a definite taskmaster and checked up on everything. The boys understood the tight discipline that he had brought from his own high school background. Consequently they respected him rather than being fond of him. In fact, those boys who did get on the wrong side of Richard gave him the nickname of Headmonster. It was not only the boys who had this view of Richard. At one time he banned Liquifruit, a popular fruit-juice beverage, at St. Peter's because he viewed it as a display of wealth. It was a petty ruling and it raised the ire of several mothers, who did market research to prove that he was wrong. In the end, he had to retract his ruling.

Richard had built himself up from humble beginnings as the son of a clergyman to become an extremely competent and successful person through his self-driven grit and determination. As a result, he exuded a hubris which was perhaps his self-defence mechanism. In his study at his home, he proudly displayed a framed cartoon that was published in the *Sunday Times* newspaper. It shows him reclining in a deckchair sipping a Liquifruit while angry women are gesticulating all around him. He was proud of this picture because he said that whenever he glanced at it, he was brought back down to earth. He did recognise that his strength of character was also his weakness.

*   *   *

For me, teaching at St Peter's prep school was a revelation. I now recommend that all secondary school teachers should have a stint of primary school teaching so as to shed the arrogance that they tend to carry towards what is considered by them to be a lower step on the ladder. I remember one morning at tea-break in the staff common room, Rex Pennington regaled us with a description of his first classroom encounter at St Peter's. Rex had recently retired from his position as Rector (that is, headmaster) at Michaelhouse private secondary school, where he had been used to all the decorum and deference from the boys that his position had demanded. Richard had offered him a post-retirement teaching position and promised that he would not regret it. The little boys at St Peter's, however, paid no attention to Rex at all when he walked into his first class. He cleared his throat to get their attention, and that made no difference. He told us that he was then reduced to shouting 'shut up' in as stentorian a voice as he could muster. It worked, as it brought the boys to a shocked silence. For the first time in his long career, he then got on with what he called "some real teaching".

Little boys are noisy. A good collective noun for them might be a decibel of schoolboys. They are also extremely eager and excitable, especially on the sports field. At Plumtree School back in Rhodesia I had been the First XI cricket coach. My task was mainly fine-tuning the boys' skills as they sought the higher honour of selection in the Rhodesian Schools team. It had been an exacting and serious task.

At St Peter's I was given the responsibility of coaching the Under-10 team which was an entirely different kettle of fish. I had to teach the very rudiments of the game to little boys whose batting pads reached up to their midriffs. Some of them even decided to wear their pads upside down so as to protect their ankles and insteps. It was a lot of fun. But even here I came across Richard Todd's stamp of authority.

He called me into his office one day to learn something about coaching Under-10 boys. From a high shelf in his office he brought down a large lever arch file crammed with correspondence between himself and Walter MacFarlane, the headmaster of St Stithian's Prep School. In it was a toxic exchange between the two headmasters on the size of cricket balls to be used by Under-10 teams. Each accused the other of cheating, and it seemed to go on and on, page after page. I could not believe what I was being shown. The underlying issue was that most schools used a smaller ball of 4¾ ounces for their U-10 teams. However, Richard considered it to be a lavish expense to have two sizes of cricket balls at the school, so St Peter's boys had to come to terms with using a larger 5½ ounce ball.

Walter MacFarlane called Richard Todd a cheat because St Stithian's boys could not hit the larger and heavier ball forcefully enough to reach the boundary. Richard countered the accusation by saying that St Stithian's bowlers had the advantage of being able to spin the smaller ball. The two headmasters would not talk to each other but kept up the poison pen correspondence backwards and forwards for some considerable time.

I put my foot in in it when I suggested that a compromise of one game with small cricket balls for both teams and one game with larger cricket balls might work. I recognised from Richard's scowl that it was time for me to leave his office.

At this time, I got to know Richard as a friend to whom I owed much but I also recognised him firmly as my boss. It was a relationship that continued into my All Saints experience in later years. Then, in 1980, Richard's reputation as a go-getter and an extremely successful headmaster carried all the way to Natal (now KwaZulu-Natal), where the prestigious Hilton College was looking for a new principal. He was invited to take up the reins there, and so he left St Peter's.

*　　*　　*

At about the same time, I was invited – and accepted – a teaching post at Kingswood College in Grahamstown (now Makhanda). We had been comfortable at St Peter's, but Noreen and I disliked what we considered to be misplaced values expressed in the big-city life of Johannesburg's northern suburbs. Big money was the driving force in the lives of those around us. However, money was in short supply in the Burton household. The severe emigration restrictions made by the Rhodesian government on our departure allowed us a meagre $1 000 per family and because we had towed our caravan, the South African customs confiscated all $1 000 as import duty. I had had to phone Richard from Messina (now Musina) to ask for a salary advance, as we did not have sufficient money to buy petrol to reach Johannesburg. Once there, we found that life in the city was expensive. We could barely meet each month's expenses so when Andrew asked why we didn't have a Porsche like his friend's father or a room with an electric train for him, it strengthened our resolve to raise our children away from the city.

Thus, when the opportunity arose, we moved to Grahamstown, where both Noreen and I were to teach at Kingswood College, and our children were enrolled in its junior school department. In some ways Grahamstown was a sort of homecoming, as it was where Noreen and I had first met, as undergraduates at Rhodes University. The town layout is also somewhat similar to Umtali (now Mutare) in Rhodesia, the town where I had gone to school and where we had both started our teaching careers after Oxford, and before moving to Plumtree.

It is also amusing to note that the road that passes through the Kingswood school campus is Burton Street, which added to our feeling of homecoming.

chapter 7
Visionary

"In order to carry out a positive action, we must develop here a positive vision."

— Dalai Lama

I N MANY WAYS Richard Todd was a polymath who relied on the mastery of his various experiences to drive his ambitions. Perhaps his one big weakness was his resultant self-assuredness. He could confidently tell others what to do, but found it difficult to listen to and accept the views of others, especially when they conflicted with his own. He liked to make the big decisions on his own and baulked at consultation. As a result, he did not endear himself to Hilton College's Board of Governors.

Richard Todd the visionary, founder and director of All Saints College

One of the first actions that he took after assuming his position as the head of Hilton College was to order that all the willow trees surrounding the first eleven cricket field be felled because they drew up too much water, in his opinion. This led to a huge outcry from the Hilton community as the ambience of the field was ruined in one fell swoop. For generations families had picnicked under the shade of the willows while watching the match underway. Richard had taken this action without consulting anyone. Perhaps it was a calculated step of his to show that he was now the boss.

So, as a new headmaster, again without the board's permission, he invited Franklin Sonn to be the guest speaker at the school's end-of-year prize-giving ceremony. This was a step too far for the conservative staff and community. As an anti-apartheid activist, Franklin Sonn (Rector of the then Cape Peninsula Technikon) was for many at Hilton far too controversial a figure to address this bastion of private white educational opportunity, designed for the well-heeled colonial community.

Franklin Sonn was the first "black" person to address the school. He didn't mince his words as he painted a picture of what needed to be done in preparation for a new post-apartheid South African society. Richard Todd seemed to have deliberately introduced contention to the proceedings, perhaps aiming to stir things up. The parents and governors were furious about a gesture they considered extremely controversial and directed their anger straight at their new headmaster.

With the support of the Anglo-American Chairman's Fund and Barloworld, Richard Todd introduced a scholarship programme that was to provide full funding for 150 black learners to attend Hilton College in their senior years. When the Hilton community heard about this action, again without consultation, they were enraged. Alumni members of the powerful Hilton College Old Boys' Association virtually owned the school. They wanted to hang onto their own school experiences and predictably were incensed to perceive any wind of change. A rallying cry went out and there was a mass meeting to which large numbers came, many from considerable distances. With conservative indignation, they resolved that this was not going to happen at Hilton.

The predictable outcome from this gathering was a resolution that Richard Todd should be dismissed. He was too controversial. The board of governors was given an ultimatum and Richard Todd resigned soon afterwards in 1983.

*   *   *

He withdrew from society altogether so as to reflect and agonise. Although he was naturally dejected at how things had turned out at Hilton College, he did not abandon his dream of building a non-racial school that would offer world-class education as well as the prospect of entry for talented black children into South Africa's finest universities. Such a prospect was denied to those educated in apartheid's Bantu Education system, described as "gutter education" by the masses.

After a year of solitude, agonising and deliberating, Richard Todd rose phoenix-like from his primitive beach cottage at Kasouga where he had hatched an exciting plan to achieve his dream. With renewed energy he now wanted to make his dream a reality. He was encouraged by those with whom he first shared his vision and who were prepared to give financial backing as well as other support.

His admiration for Franklin Sonn had grown to the extent that he now invited him from Cape Town to be the first to interrogate his vision on the site where it was to unfold. Richard Todd was a man with something to prove. There was no space for listening to any cautionary guidance that might come his way. He was a man embarking on his own special mission with missionary zeal. He had found a window of opportunity that would meet a pressing national need. He had licked his wounds. His retreat at Kasouga had given him his moment of revelation.

In his year of reflective solitude Richard researched and drew up his plans, mainly from developments in the United Kingdom. However, he needed to be sensitised to the very different South African milieu. Enabling this was a role for Franklin Sonn to play – otherwise his whole vision might just be a big misfit. It obviously worked extremely well in the politically peaceful and neutral environment of England, but South Africa's youth declared their educational environment to be fraught with political menace. "*Liberation before education*" held sway. Would Franklin be able to get Richard to comprehend this and come to terms with the ominous signs? Regrettably, as it turned out at the end of the day, he would not.

It was obvious to Franklin that Richard was relying on importing a tried and tested English private school system into South Africa. Richard had undertaken a thorough investigative visit to the United Kingdom in June 1985 where he had discovered the successful "sixth form college" movement in England, which offered places to talented boys and girls from comprehensive and other state schools for their final two A-level years of schooling. The nearest African example that he could find was the Kamuzu Academy, a private boarding school in Malawi, founded in 1981. It was named after the late Hastings Kamuzu Banda, the former President of Malawi. He visited this school, described by its proponents as the Eton of Africa. Rooted in his own schooling at Bishops Diocesan College in Cape Town, with its very strong English roots and conducted on the principles of the English Church, Richard had strong anglophile leanings. His own father was an Anglican cleric.

From his early planning, one could surmise that his vision involved anglicising those who would enter his school – so as to meet expectations of the captains of South African business and industry. And in fact, his wealthy old-school-tie connections did help him raise the necessary capital and backing. Clearly, his research indicated that his scheme would have considerable appeal to the corporate world in South Africa and particularly to international companies seeking well-qualified black employees with leadership potential for the future.

Richard Todd's vision for South African education (based on the British precedent) was of a number of independent or private schools to be founded in racially neutral areas of the country. They would be co-educational and would provide places for both day scholars and boarders in the final two years of schooling. A significant percentage would be staying on for a post-matriculation or bridging year. The scholars were to be chosen, on the basis of their academic record and leadership potential, from schools where their promise might not otherwise be realised. The schools were to be non-racial, although it was anticipated that the majority of learners would be from the locality and predominant ethnic group in the area of each school.

Richard recognised that by reducing the education intervention to only two effective years of teaching at the end of the secondary schooling phase, he could make it work over a short period. It seems as if everything had to be on fast track as a means to prove himself and triumph over the snubbing and humiliation he had experienced in his exodus from Hilton College. He felt that a scheme of this nature would be able to come on stream very quickly. The first school could be operational by 1986, with its first matriculants at the end of 1987, just two years later.

While his schools were intended to be fee-paying, it was expected that scholarships and bursaries would provide for a large number of the scholars according to their needs and ability. Poverty in their home circumstances was not to prevent any identified students from attending.

Richard Todd's vision received the enthusiastic support of a number of well-known educationists, with whom it was discussed, in both the private and government sectors. An important aspect was that the schools would be located in politically neutral areas, so that non-racialism could be achieved.

His plan was to cheat, rather than oppose, apartheid. The system of Bantustans, or homelands, was not recognised by the world outside South Africa but was firmly enforced by the Nationalist Government. Each homeland had been given a measure of independence, so students at schools placed in the homelands were not tied to the racially segregated matriculation examination structures enforced in South Africa. Instead, they were free to enter the Joint Matriculation Board's examinations. He explained that this would be an important politically neutral stance.

State education for the majority of young black South Africans was a key issue for the future of South Africa. It had been a root cause of township unrest and rioting. Demographic and economic predictions meant that it would not be possible in the foreseeable future to provide an education for all South Africans comparable with what was provided only for white South African students. Richard Todd had gone on record proclaiming that a country's most important asset is its young people, and the most valuable of these, clearly, would be the most capable.

Alternatively, he conjectured, the most dangerous people anywhere in the world are young people of real ability who are frustrated and made to feel cornered.

* * *

Just three years after we had left St Peter's Preparatory School, Richard Todd linked up with the Burton family again by inviting us for a weekend visit from Grahamstown to his beach shack in nearby coastal Kasouga. Here Richard shared his exciting plans of developing a non-racial college in the then Ciskei. Once more he invited Noreen and me to be on his staff – this time in an inspiring and pioneering initiative. His appeal and enthusiasm were infectious. In January the following year we left secure and very comfortable teaching posts at Kingswood College and moved onto the All Saints Senior College campus to begin teaching at this ground-breaking institution.

For us, the opportunity of teaching young students from disadvantaged backgrounds, who had thereby been deprived of decent earlier education opportunities, offered much more meaning and purpose than continuing to teach at a private school for privileged children. However, it was a blind step of faith, for we had no idea of the huge variety of issues that would come with such a move. I recall thinking that it must have felt a bit like this when early missionaries left the comfort of home to live in the wild, in a land and with people completely unknown to them, because they felt that they had something important to offer.

* * *

It is January 1985. Mid-morning. Richard Todd stands with his back to the large circular water reservoir at the top corner of the 167 hectare campus. It is a warm summer's day with a clear and tall African sky filled with cotton wool cumulus clouds. He looks out over the rolling brown Ciskei grassland with the Yellow Wood river slowly meandering below, and the pale blue Amatola (now Amathole) mountains forming a distant backdrop – a panorama of beauty and peace.

Just two years after the bitter pill of rejection that he has faced at Hilton College, he closes his eyes and visualises his dream coming into reality.

Standing next to him and taking in the wide and open vista spread out before him is another visionary, Franklin Sonn, invited by Richard to walk the virgin veld with him, and to give advice and guidance. As Franklin listens to Richard's vision of a non-racial senior college, he soon recognises the missing cog in the planning – the aspirations and circumstances of the disadvantaged youth

The peaceful All Saints rural campus with rolling hills in the foreground backed by the Amatola range of mountains on the horizon

of South Africa at this particular time are not being sufficiently considered or addressed within the vision. As Richard outlines his plan, Franklin can recognise its noble intentions but asks himself if it is possibly a pipe dream. Does Richard really understand the dynamics of a time when the youth are taking on the mantle of "the Struggle" against apartheid to the extent that the battle cry is one of educational sacrifice?

The sinister side of this is that for those who ignore the call there are threats in the extreme. It is a time of "one in, all in", and many – when fingered as sell-outs – have lost their lives in the horrific torture of "necklacing", the practice of summary execution carried out by forcing a petrol-filled rubber tyre around the victim's neck and setting it ablaze.

The youth are caught up in this tragic political drama. An attempt to distance them from it, by inviting them away from the struggle to what might be considered an elitist educational opportunity, is something to be considered deeply. Is there a level of naivety in Richard Todd's intended educational proposal that might create unrest and even anarchy amongst the students on the campus to which they will be invited? Some are to be drawn from South Africa's most violent townships, such as Alexandra and Soweto in Johannesburg. Metaphorically, these townships are on fire. Can potential new students ignore the threat of being branded as sell-outs; or might they attempt to justify their situation by insurrection in the name of the struggle at such a school? Does Richard really believe that he can lure deeply suspicious young black people away from the hurt that they are enduring to a peaceful setting, in order to meet the capitalistic aims of commerce and industry, by offering the prize of personal success? These are fundamental questions that should not be brushed aside in Richard's haste to open the doors.

As it is, he is focusing all his energy on convincing the providers (the funders, the trustees and the teachers), while perhaps neglecting the aspirations of the receivers (the students and their communities). This omission might even cause breakdowns with each new intake of students. In the short-term turnaround of a two-year curriculum, the mammoth task of justifying the existence of the institution in the face of deeply suspicious new intakes would need to be addressed every year. It could even suggest the premise that students who are already at the school have been brainwashed and are not to be listened to.

From another viewpoint, Richard Todd has managed to find a very much needed window of opportunity to address a national predicament, by devising a formula to address the needs of business and industry for the future. In return for a two-year financial commitment comes a unique opportunity for business to invest in the future and to provide funding for this vision. There is no doubt that his dream is honourable and deserving of success; but he takes it for granted that the beneficiaries will unquestioningly and gratefully accept his generous offer.

*   *   *

In 1988 Richard received the prestigious national Allied Visionary of the Year award in a glitzy banquet at the Carlton Hotel in Johannesburg's central business district. It was a big occasion for him and it marked a nationally recognised success reasonably soon after his fall from grace at Hilton. His second senior college, St Luke's, established in the premises of the former Kyalami Ranch Motel, had become operational, and he had launched an umbrella structure, the Leadership, Education and Advancement Foundation (LEAF) to drive his vision further. Richard invited Noreen and me to the award ceremony together with the principal of St Luke's, Grant Nupen, and his wife Rose. Right at the start of his address, he paid tribute to Grant and me when he stated:

"Without men of the quality and calibre of the principals of our two colleges, Mike Burton and Grant Nupen, what has been termed my vision would be no more than just another day-dream."

I told him that I deeply admired his ability to rise above the ordinary teacher's structured world, which is so secure with its school bells and timetables. For most in the teaching world, it is just too easy to settle into a mundane existence detached from the issues of the outside world. In his words to the audience:

"In a kaleidoscope of experiences, after a privileged liberal arts education and after twenty-five years serving in some of our country's top private schools, I had increasingly sensed in myself not so much a disillusionment as a desire to get my hands right onto the real education problems of our country. I could not see achievable answers but I knew that they were there for the finding. I wrestled with myself and my conscience, with those about me, and with the systems of established education and their comforts. I agonised endlessly as to what I should do and how I could do it and then I was landed, quite literally, on the beach at a little Eastern Cape place called Kasouga. In a little shack without electricity, without running water, and me without any coherent plan as to what the next steps were. I got sand between my toes. I walked and swam and read and studied and thought, and thought and thought."

Richard goes on:

"We plan to do much, much more than this. We plan to develop more senior colleges, and hope to lead Government to do the same. The system is highly cost effective. And we plan to continue to involve ourselves as broadly as possible in every worthwhile education initiative in our land."

All Saints, thus, was born out of this vision for which Richard justly received public acclaim. The conveyor belt was starting to move into top gear and, true to Richard's timetable, the school welcomed 300 students at the start of 1988, up from the initial enrolment of 78 just two years before. It was the remarkable accomplishment of a man equipped with astonishing drive and energy.

part three

THE MISSION

chapter 8
Dawn

"And suddenly you know… It's time to start something new and trust the magic of beginnings."

— Anonymous

I T IS SUNDAY 5 January 1986. Our family, ready for a new adventure, arrives somewhat disconcertingly at a place that looks like images I have seen of the devastated no-man's-land between the trenches of World War I. At the suggestion of Steve, the site manager, whom I locate in his makeshift container office, I tow my caravan with considerable misgiving along the bumpy, rutted track around the buildings in order to park on a flat bit of grassland around the back.

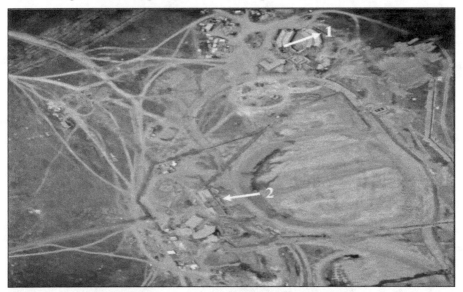

An aerial view of the construction a short while before the students arrive. It shows the many footpaths criss-crossing the land (the college was built on a much used inter-village rural "highway") and identifies where we sited our caravan outside the residence (1) and the location of the administration block (2)

Steve tells me where we can access water and a site toilet, and then gets back to his task of co-ordinating the frenzy of building activity. It has been a worrying surprise to find the place so far from readiness. Roaring engines from earth-moving vehicles are adding to the chaos. It is hot and there is no shade. There is dust everywhere. As evening approaches, I walk up to the top corner of the 167 hectare property where I find a large circular water reservoir.

I sit down on the plinth of the reservoir and survey the rolling brown countryside below. It is hard to imagine what it must have been like before the construction's devastation. I start thinking, How is it that I am sitting here? What scenes are going to be played out on these grounds? What lies before me? I need to take it all in, and spend a while thinking back in time to gather my thoughts around what has led me to this place. Am I having second thoughts?

For the first few days after we arrive, the place continues to be in constructive turmoil. Massive bulldozers are roaring and tearing up the land throughout the day.

As dusk approaches on the second day after our arrival and the engines switch off, workers are collected and taken away, and a peaceful calmness settles. It is time at last for me to take an inspection stroll around the place and breathe more deeply in my new abode. I see a number of local men walking towards me, so I stand still and wait to see if they are just walking through the land, but they are looking at me and it is soon apparent that they are aiming to meet up with me. They are a deputation of community leaders from the four surrounding villages. Meaningful conversation is challenging as I have no knowledge of their isiXhosa language and their English is very stilted. It is difficult to pick up any detail, but I gather that the gist of what they are sharing with much finger pointing is that they are trying to tell me that this is their communal grazing land for cattle shared by four nearby villages – eBhalasi, Zinyoka, Nkqonkqweni and Ethembeni.

We spend the rest of the late afternoon deliberating as best we can on what is happening on their traditionally shared countryside. They shake their heads and there is a noticeable mood of dissent. They have not been brought into the picture and are not aware of why the bulldozers are ripping up and damaging the land like this. It is their Nguni cattle preserve. They have arrived with sullen faces, clearly not happy with what they see happening. No one has sought their counsel or permission to invade the space that they collectively understand as belonging to their communities. I think they are asking me:

"Who has decided to tear up our land?
What alternative grazing land is now available to us?
What compensation is due to us?
Why have we not been informed or consulted?"
I cannot provide any answers.

I have noticed on my walking around the property a number of footpaths criss-crossing the landscape. This reinforces their dissatisfaction because not only is this communal land for their cattle to graze, but the plethora of pathways indicates that it is a well-used rural highway for inter-village visiting and even for collecting water from the Yellow Woods river on the lower boundary.

I perceive that they are airing vexing questions and yet I am simply not in any position to answer any of their grievances to their satisfaction as I do not know the answers. We parley for some considerable time. When they eventually leave, it seems that they are reasonably content with my answers for the time being. I have tried to explain that a special school is to rise up from all this destruction and that children from around the country as well as their own local children will stand a chance to benefit.

The group walks off and I am sure that I have not fully convinced them. I really have no authority to represent the All Saints development in our conversation, I just happen to have been on site when the deputation walked onto the campus seeking answers. Clearly to them I am part of the cause of what is happening and should be able to answer them. There are no other staff members on the campus this afternoon with whom they can share their concerns. The headmaster, David Kirkwood, lives off campus in King William's Town (now Qonce). I have only just met him for the first time this morning. I make a mental note that I must share this encounter with David and Richard when I next see them.

*   *   *

In mid-1985, well before teachers and students were to arrive at All Saints, David Kirkwood was appointed as the first headmaster. He had had a significant and colourful career leading up to this appointment.

David was educated in Scotland at Edinburgh and Glasgow universities. At seventeen he represented Scotland in the high jump and also played cricket, rugby, tennis, badminton and table tennis. For him, golf was a favourite relaxation. He had taught in secondary schools in Scotland, Ethiopia and Turkey, and in Iran he had been the founding headmaster of Kiaat International schools, which offered schooling from kindergarten up to the sixth form. He had been there at the time of the Iranian revolution, but left when schools were nationalised under Ayatollah Khomeini. David had been drawn to All Saints while fulfilling the position of headmaster at Machabeng International Secondary School (an International Baccalaureate school) in Lesotho. International schools tend to cater mainly for students whose parents are not nationals and who work for international businesses and organisations and foreign embassies. Many local students attend these schools to learn the language of the international school and to obtain qualifications for employment or higher education in a foreign country. Because David had previously successfully headed International Schools in the Middle East where learners wrote the International Baccalaureate, he was eminently suited to fit into Richard Todd's vision for a sixth form college as founding principal, competent to guide the first steps of All Saints Senior College.

David Kirkwood, the first principal of the All Saints College

From the time of his arrival in December, David Kirkwood had been locked in planning sessions with Richard Todd. His first task would be to appoint and prepare an inaugural skeleton staff at the start of the new year and to meet the first cohort of students. The college's physical space was clearly unprepared, but this was not to be an obstacle to the four-day induction of the new staff.

*   *   *

Our induction starts in what is to become the principal's office in the skeleton administration block. Banging, clanging and shouting from workers on site constantly interrupts our discussions. Early on the first day of our induction a construction worker's boot smashes through the ceiling directly above us and we dive into evasive action to avoid the body that might come crashing down on top of us. Fortunately, nobody follows and falls through. Instead, a battered boot with its bright yellow sock moves back tentatively through the hole that it has made above us.

Instruction for such a trailblazing adventure is intense and thorough. David outlines operational issues to us while Richard enthuses over what is still on the drawing board. We are promised everything that can open and close. It all sounds very exciting and we cannot wait to get things going. However, it does seem that very little is in place for us to start and that is disconcerting.

Richard explains that the underlying premise of his vision is to meet the future management needs of post-apartheid South Africa by offering this opportunity of an excellent education in the final two years of secondary education. His view is that scholars with proven academic records in the government schooling system might get by with mediocre teaching and learning up to their final years of secondary schooling, but in order to gain entry and cope successfully with tertiary learning a step up with excellent provision is necessary. Our task is clear, we must provide first-class tuition and support. It is a heavy responsibility as we are made aware that everything, the whole future viability of the venture, depends on a good start and continued academic success. As a school our results must show excellence.

Richard Todd reads us a published article in which he has recently been featured in *The Financial Mail*. It outlines his philosophy under the title "Going for the Black Cream". The unfortunate heading will later have repercussions for us all. He did not create the headline, but he initiated the metaphor by referring to his Hilton experience and being quoted in the article as saying:

"...educating the cream, 'the rich and the thick'...did not provide any answers."

We pioneer teachers, drawn from comfortable institutions ourselves, do not question Richard's rationale as we are caught up in the enthusiasm of the teaching opportunities and challenges of providing the best education we can muster from our collective experiences. It is a dream held universally by all dedicated teachers, to be extended by eager and bright learners and to meet a real personal and national need.

Consequently we sense no alarm bells as he continues to explain that outside the classroom the college needs to offer experiences that will equip young black managers to enter the executive realm with confidence. For this he outlines facilities that are due to be introduced as part of the college's offerings. The most staggering of these is a golf course to be designed by Gary Player, South Africa's legendary golfer, and an Olympic-sized swimming pool. Other steep learning-curve sports such as squash and tennis are also on the drawing board. All these plans are very grandiose and alluring and intended to impress us. As it turns out none of them ever happen on the promised scale. What does eventually materialise is two squash courts, two tennis courts and a ten-metre pool, but no golf course. Funders draw the line at perceived extravagances and overstated features. Much remains a wish list.

The pioneer skeleton staff sitting and listening are Quentin Hogge (English Language), Des Cross (Biology), John Bartlett (Mathematics), Noreen Burton (Physical Science) and me (Geography). David Kirkwood is going to teach Mathematics. Ben Tengimfene joins us later to teach isiXhosa. Over a period of four days, we are fully briefed on Richard Todd's vision. We soak it all in. The outcome is that each of us feels that we have been invited to join an exciting and life-changing adventure. We are buoyed by the privilege.

The pioneer staff at All Saints in 1986. From left to right: Quentin Hogge, Ben Tengimfene, Mike Burton, Noreen Burton, John Bartlett, Des Cross

None of us have any real understanding of the background and aspirations of the students who are going to come to this place. Unknowingly we are in for a shocking confrontation with that other side of apartheid. The model of education that we are invited to establish sounds so normal for us since we are drawn from the same camp as Richard and David in terms of our own education and teaching experiences. We are to develop a Bishops, a Hilton or even a Kingswood school, but with black students instead of white students.

The apartheid machine has drawn a very clear line that we will need to cross if we are to understand and gain the confidence of the students. This line is a precarious tightrope on which South Africa's education offering separates its people and prevents either side from connecting. We will soon need to realise that All Saints College is an unwitting crucible to bring the two sides together. On this campus a microcosm of the new South Africa is to be played out, and the most important lesson that we will be forced to learn is that crossing that line is necessary and comes with pain. Our new students arriving out of the smouldering township schooling will not be grateful 'yes sir, no sir' compliant students.

However, we do have some concerns and we try to get answers. The first concern we raise is our unease over future funding prospects and consequently the overall sustainability of the project. We need some reassurance as we have each left a comfortable teaching career behind us to join what is starting to look a bit unstable. During the induction we are told that the initial seed funding to complete building the infrastructure has come from the Anglo-American Chairman's Fund, but once the construction is completed it is the responsibility of the director, Richard Todd, to acquire the necessary funding support to cover the running costs of a boarding institution. This he has to do on an annual basis, and his successful start-up modus operandi has been to secure individual student sponsorships from the corporate world, mainly through his old-school-tie connections.

To us this is a big concern. There is no endowment or capital base to provide us with some form of backup reassurance. We quickly recognise that, year by year, our continued existence will depend upon a one-man fundraising effort which looks very risky. He has no support team in place. The whole continuance of the project rests on the energy and efforts of one man. What if he cannot continue through illness or some other mishap? We cannot be satisfied with the long-term future of his explanations.

We therefore ask David, our headmaster, if we can share our concern with the Chairman of the Board of Trustees, Mr Ronnie Napier, who is a prominent lawyer in Johannesburg. David Kirkwood supports our request and recommends that we follow this course. Richard Todd hears of our intention. We receive a terse response from him ordering that the correct channel to any Trust member is to be through himself as the director. He will not allow us to discuss any matters directly with Ronnie Napier. This unwillingness to allow any open and transparent relationship marks the beginning of a wariness by us. Our mood becomes unnecessarily tense and uneasy. We feel that we have been told off and yet it is clear to us that the whole operation is standing on dicey financial grounds which possibly may became precarious and lead to the demise of the college and loss of our employment.

By supporting the staff's request, David Kirkwood has also shown his hand and unwittingly painted himself into a corner with Richard Todd. His concern, like ours, is summarily dismissed in the refusal. This does not bode well for the future. We are confused as to where our loyalties should lie when the principal and the director give us opposing messages and appear to be butting heads. Strict limits are set and we have been put firmly in our place.

Our second anxiety is perhaps the more pressing. We are sitting in the shell of a half-finished building, and we consider it impossible to accept students in less than a month's time when the place is so far from being ready. The promised teacher accommodation on the property is not nearly ready. Some of us are boarded in rooms in a temporary arrangement at the Amatola Sun Hotel three kilometres away. The Burton family is having to caravan on the All Saints property, which feels more like being in the bundu as it is so rustic. All this is very inconvenient and unanticipated.

With the construction continuing, Richard Todd suggests a plan of cordoning off school spaces so as to separate them from the ongoing building site activity, since they are going to have to operate in tandem. We consider this to be fraught with problems and it does not pacify our uneasiness. He replies that the wheels are already turning and that it is now impossible to halt the arrival of students before the due date. The best has to be made of the difficult situation. The more pessimistic among us start to take mental note of the broken promises that drew us to this place. Instead of turning smoothly in the grand scheme, the wheels are starting to grind and falter, leaving us nervous and not altogether confident that things will improve. We do not see what has been promised and lessons have not yet even started.

chapter 9

Commencement

"You never change your life until you step out of your comfort zone;
change begins at the end of your comfort zone."

— Roy T Bennett

D-DAY IN JANUARY 1986 finally arrives. Eighty-five students trickle onto the grounds throughout the day. The passage from their various homes to All Saints in the Ciskei Bantustan has presented many diverse hardships. Some have had to be collected by us from nearby Blaney railway station and some have walked onto the campus carrying their belongings in a suitcase.

About five kilometres beyond All Saints on the Komga road is a Ciskeian border post. Although the outside world does not recognise such boundaries, politically imposed by the apartheid government, the security forces take their border-guarding responsibilities very seriously. A short time before any of us had arrived at All Saints, some nuns from the King William's Town convent had unwittingly driven past the post without stopping. The border patrol had opened fire with automatic weapons on their car and killed one of them.

Pioneer student Zukiswa Jafta brings a story of her journey from Umtata (now Mthatha) in the neighbouring Transkei homeland. We have been made aware that hostilities are on the rise between Transkei and Ciskei. She explains that she could not come to us with her mother in a car with an XA (Umtata) number plate so they had to find another road that goes through a nearby village and around the border post. However, they were discovered and stopped by the police. Because their identity documents showed that they were Transkeian, they were not allowed to proceed. They eventually phoned a friend who had a car with Ciskei number plates and they managed to sneak through on another road. Of follow-up interest, Dr Zukiswa Jafta was later to become a celebrated oncologist and has research papers published.

As the students arrive, they are all looking wide-eyed and clearly disconcerted at the scene greeting them. To reach the estate, they have travelled up a deeply rutted gravel road and, topping the rise, they look down onto a chaotic scene of building construction. There are some hastily hand-drawn signs directing them to the far corner of the property, which is not easy to get to over the broken ground. Their destination is a residence which is not even remotely close to being ready for their arrival. The floors of roughened-up concrete are not prepared and there are large puddles of water covering most of the entrance hall. There is no electricity. There is no organised reception room. As the residence warden, I am not yet living in my residence quarters and am still living with my family in our caravan a short distance away.

All this is very bewildering to them and not easy for us.

*   *   *

When the students walk onto the campus during the day they cannot hide a general reaction of disappointed surprise as they have been promised university-type accommodation. They had also anticipated that everything would be organised and equipped. But it is immediately apparent that everything is neither organised nor equipped. What they see looks more like the Zimbabwe ruins with its bare outer walls, and little interior completion. Despondent, they have to mill around for most of the first day, many holding suitcases with their belongings, waiting for the construction workers to vacate the buildings. Meanwhile the newly appointed staff of five teachers walks amongst the new arrivals and greets them. We are trying to make them feel comfortable and promote understanding of the situation. It is difficult and most embarrassing.

The residence in a state of unreadiness when the first students arrived to take up occupation

We strive to explain as best we can that everyone is a victim of the unreadiness. We have to be patient and make weak jokes like *"Rome wasn't built in a day"*.

As the late afternoon approaches, the construction workers start moving off. We teachers with our families are now rolling up our sleeves and trying to put some order into the proceedings. I must now allocate rooms by matching the architects' plans with a list of anticipated newcomers (given to me at the eleventh hour). As the students arrive and identify themselves, I need to hold back from informing them which are their rooms because the challenge is that no numbers have been labelled on doors. I have only been given a sketch map of the layout, so to find any room we are going to have to pace and count. We eventually shepherd all the students into the foyer and I explain what we are going to do before it gets dark. I need to help students to find their rooms with boys to be directed into the one wing of the residence and girls into the other wing. If the place had been properly prepared there should have been two completed residences ready – separate from each other, one for the boys and one for the girls. But only one residence is now on offer and it is evidently not ready. Beds are in place but still there is no bedding available. This is a nightmare. The crisis that we had feared at our staff induction is happening and, with the reactions on the students' faces, we are made to feel really uncomfortable.

In the late afternooon, there is an unexpected crunching sound of large vehicles rolling up outside the main door of the residence. When we investigate, it turns out that the trucks parked there – mercifully – have bales filled with bedding and linen. They have arrived only just in time. It will soon be dark. This will make preparations without electricity that much more difficult. I exhale hugely with relief that the laden trucks have arrived, because I cannot imagine telling the students that their first night will be spent on mattresses with nothing to cover them or pillows on which to lay their heads. To add to the pioneer students' bewilderment there is no dining room or kitchen and here they are, hungry and thirsty. Some of them have not eaten all day. Very few know each other and, as a result, there is an individual submissive acceptance of the situation as we do our best to explain things to them. In hardly a romantic candlelit setting they sit around on construction boxes and drums and are fed with fast foods just brought from nearby King William's Town by David Kirkwood. He uses the opportunity to introduce himself as their principal. He also explains as best he can why they find themselves in the foyer of a building which is so far from completion. The students are amused at his rich Scottish accent and several wry smiles between them reveal that this is something new to them. It goes some way to easing our discomfort.

Much is to be done in a very short while, so while the students eat, drink and connect with each other in the gloom, the staff feverishly start unpacking bales and sorting items into piles by candlelight in a small side room in the dry far corner of the foyer. They make bundles for the students including sheets, pillows, duvets and duvet covers as well as soap and towels. When they finish their *ad hoc* meals, the students are asked to stand in two queues, one for boys and one for girls, to collect their bedding. They are naturally very subdued and accommodating.

Then a boy comes up to me to complain that I have allocated him a room in the girls' wing.

"Oh. That must be a mistake. Let me check. What is your name?"

"I am Happy Ntshangase."

Not discerning the sombre mood around me I try to make light of the situation.

"Well, you should be really happy!"

He scowls. This has not gone down well. It is a time to be sensitive and not to joke at anyone's personal expense. We are still all testing each other out.

Eventually all the students have their bedlinen and a lit candle, and are guided off to their rooms. It has been a nerve-wracking first day. At least the ablution blocks are ready. There are working showers in place, but no hot water. Fortunately, it is a warm evening so there are soon sounds of splashing and even boisterous noise upstairs as some students prank about in the shower room under the cold water, giving them a chance to release pent-up emotions.

*   *   *

The next morning arrives and the sun shines brightly. After another fast-food breakfast, eaten in styrofoam containers and with plastic utensils, the students are asked to lock their rooms and vacate the residence to allow the construction company to continue its work. Throughout the morning teachers and students traipse around the perimeter of the property in small groups and spend time conversing and generally getting to know each other. Small clumps of teachers and students can be seen dotted around the estate sharing stories, conversing and discussing what this place is all about, while staying out of the way of the construction work.

The mood, while not yet jovial, has lifted and there are smiles as each shares their background and expectations. It is a time for connecting and getting to know each other out in the open. Thankfully the weather is kind, although there are no shady trees to shelter under. As teachers, we spread the message that we are in the same boat, and about to embark on an exciting educational adventure. We try to push aside doubts about the readiness of the place and promote that we are collectively building something special.

Not too long afterwards, classrooms, lecture rooms and a canteen, although still not completed, are made available for use. Out of this unpreparedness something special is starting to happen – a sense of shared ownership is beginning to grow amongst both staff and students. We have pulled through the first few days together. Through the frenzy of construction activity around us I have seen the college buildings taking shape.

I wonder how it would have been if we had all arrived to find everything in spotless readiness, with all that opens and closes in place. Perhaps a sense of entitlement would have prevailed instead of a feeling of "Let's all get stuck in together and make this thing work. Let's do it because it's ours". The unfinished campus is helping us to shape a unique kind of bonding from the grass roots of this venture. We have to accept the rough conditions because we are all experiencing the same distress and discomfort. We soon begin to recognise that we are sharing the same goal. We can be developers in the dawn experience of building up this place in our troubled land.

One telling response stated by a student was:

"I have a whole room to myself. I have never had this."

This was picked up by others who were used to sharing home accommodation with many in one room. Some are nervous at having a room to themselves. Several students pair up and by moving furniture around, they designate one room as their shared study and the other as their sleeping room.

As it is turning out Richard Todd was right in insisting that we make a start. Perhaps this is a better option than holding back and delaying the opening with the hope of readiness first and comfort for all. As teachers we had been fearful that the students would reject what was being offered based on our own background experience. Yet the students appear to be taking it in their stride.

This is a first fundamental lesson learned by me and the teaching staff: we had little understanding of the backgrounds of our new students. For a number of them, from deprived rural and township home situations, what is being offered here is luxury.

From the outset teachers and students have so much to learn from each other. In so many ways this will play itself out in our days together and especially when misunderstandings and confrontations arise. Perhaps the obstacles are offering all the All Saints stakeholders a rite of passage, an initiation to toughen and teach us all that cooperation is the best way forward. We are discovering that we are able to work together despite not knowing each other and to face any possible future difficulties.

We all know we are in a challenging time and place. There is a political emergency in South Africa, and we are in the bitterly disputed Ciskeian homeland. Looming over us is the question of "how safe are we?"

Pioneer student Zukiswa Jafta notes many years later about our start:

"Politically I must say life was contained within the school. We knew exactly what was going on through the radio. But it never bothered us or changed or disturbed school attendance at the time. School continued, classes continued and all our teachers were within."

The country is burning all around our unfinished but politically peaceful All Saints campus and external threats are still uppermost in the minds of many students. By May of our first year, David Kirkwood reports that the number of students has dropped to seventy-seven. Three have been unable to leave Alexandra township in Johannesburg, two have been called back to Port Elizabeth (now Gqeberha) because of threats against their families; and three have withdrawn because of academic pressure and difficulty.

How long can the All Saints ship sail in supposedly calm waters and pursue its peaceful mission, as its founding director has planned? This is 1986. There is a national state of emergency in South Africa. The call in the seething townships is forcibly *"liberation before education"* and at All Saints we are flying in the face of this with our offering of *"education with liberation"*. Perhaps our stance is unrealistic. We will have to survive the questions that will be asked.

Through 1986, the All Saints project is an exciting adventure shared by a small band of pioneer teachers and students. We are not yet affected by off-campus turmoil. Then in October my life is abruptly turned upside down. I am totally unprepared for the major change that unexpectedly faces me.

chapter 10

Appointment

"Difficulties break some men but make others."

— Nelson Mandela

SOMEHOW AS 1986 proceeds, the year that a national state of emergency is declared, the political dramas that engulf South Africa remain off our stage, hidden in the wings. At All Saints, schooling is still on the centre stage.

But at the top level of the school's management, a new in-house drama is unfolding. Enmity between the director and the principal is becoming increasingly noticeable. It is escalating to an extent that the two men are visibly antagonistic towards each other. There is much treading on toes, and angry raised voices are regularly heard in the corridor. It seems that Richard Todd does not trust David Kirkwood to get on and manage the school in the way that he expects. David has his own views, stands up for himself and is not prepared to be dictated to in managing the start of the school. Although Richard lives in King William's Town, which is only ten minutes away by car, his daunting, unrelenting presence fills the principal's office daily. He won't let go. Clearly, the two of them are not having a collaborative relationship and their conspicuous confrontations are exposing a widening gap between them.

Eventually the flash point comes at the end of September, when David Kirkwood disappears from the campus without notifying anyone. He is away for two whole weeks before any of us know where or why he has gone. During this time, Richard Todd asks me to stand in as an acting manager in David's absence. The other staff members accept this emergency measure without question. I settle into the task by making sure that I record all the things that I must deal with because I now carry a load of responsibility and am accountable for any developments in David's absence. It is very disconcerting, because none of us is sure of what is happening. I feel confident that I can carry out the task if it is to be a short-term one. However, days pass by without any news and

I become progressively more and more anxious. We all become increasingly worried about David's disappearance and even consider contacting the South African Police Service Missing Persons Bureau. However, this poses difficulties because technically we are not in South Africa but in Ciskei, which is under a different jurisdiction, and there is no equivalent service offered in the bantustan.

We eventually learn that David is in Lesotho, having left in a blazing temper after a hostile bout with Richard Todd. He has chosen to spend a cooling-off week playing golf with a colleague from Machabeng School. He has simply gone AWOL. We don't really know what issues between him and Richard Todd led to this. Nor do we want to. Sadly, we never see David again. This upsets us because in the short time that we have been together we have all developed real friendships with him, and there is hurt that he has walked out on us without even saying goodbye. Some of us worry that we might be the cause of his troubles; although he probably senses that sharing his side of the story with us would be the dishonourable thing to do.

*   *   *

Hard on the heels of David's golfing breakaway, on Tuesday 14 October 1986 I am summoned to a meeting of the Board of Trustees and am asked to wear a suit for the occasion. This is unusual. I am instructed not to inform anyone of being called to the meeting, not even my wife Noreen. It all seems unnecessarily clandestine. I don't like this turn of events one bit and am filled with trepidation. What is going on? Might the events that are happening lead to a meltdown which will put me and my family at risk – and in search of new employment? All of us on the teaching staff have been very supportive of David Kirkwood's leadership. We feel frustrated that we have been kept largely in the dark and second-guessing what has led him to disappear.

The meeting of the Board of Trustees is at Richard Todd's home in King William's Town. I am made to wait for an hour in the lounge before I am called in. During this time Richard's wife Judith has kindly given me a welcome cup of tea and has sat chatting with me.

We know each other well, having together produced a musical on the stage of St Peter's Preparatory School, but I can't help feeling that she is trying to put me at ease before something adverse is unfolded. I have no inkling of what is about to be revealed. At last, I am called into the meeting, suit and all. After a brief welcome from Ronnie Napier, the chairman, I am informed that the Trust has decided to fire David Kirkwood, under cover of a pretext of his having to return to Scotland where he has an ailing mother.

Then the bombshell is dropped. With a lot of smiles and congratulations all around the table, I am told that I will be taking over the responsibility of principalship with immediate effect. So many jumbled thoughts race through my head in those brief seconds. Am I being offered a poisoned chalice? I really want to say 'no thank you' but I am not even given the chance to respond. The meeting moves on. Instead, I am asked to stay on for the rest of the meeting in an *ex officio* capacity. It seems to be taken for granted that I am accepting what I'm told. I am not even given the chance to consider a response or to confer with my wife and family nor with colleagues on the staff. It all seems too hasty for comfort. I am plunged into a very uncomfortable and awkward situation. It dawns on me that I am being given a higher position without due procedure (which should have been through advertisement and application followed by interviews and finally selection). Most of all I haven't even applied for the post. There are bound to be questions asked. I feel that I am being hung out to dry.

The urgency in the Board of Trustees' circumvention of the impasse between David Kirkwood and Richard Todd becomes apparent immediately after my sudden and what I consider inappropriate elevation to the office of principal. The next item on the meeting's agenda is the principal's report. Suddenly, just thirty seconds after my appointment is announced, this becomes my responsibility. I am asked to give an impromptu report which will be recorded in the meeting's minutes. I feel rushed and again a reluctant pawn in someone else's game of chess.

Somehow, I put together an unprepared oral report covering the short time that I have held the reins in David's absence. Afterwards, Richard Todd informs the meeting that a school assembly will be called at the college on the following morning when he will explain the status quo to the staff and students. Next the chairman says:

"Richard will soon be moving to Cape Town to focus on his quest of opening further new colleges."

This is good news – if David Kirkwood's experience is anything to go by. I am now suddenly and without warning being trusted with the full and ominous responsibility of growing and managing All Saints College. I am also being given a free hand to lead without any further debilitating daily interference from the director who has been so intrusive in David Kirkwood's efforts. There is of course an unspoken presumption that I am ready and willing to toe Richard Todd's line of forceful management. It is expected that I will do what I am told to do.

That is the last matter on the meeting's agenda which then closes and Richard takes me aside and out into his garden. He tells me that he wants to offer some words of guidance. The only words that I remember are:

"Mike, you will find the post of principal to be the loneliest job in the world."

I stiffen because I am feeling uncomfortable anyway and suspect that I am being used to meet his expectations and not mine. I sense that I am back teaching at St Peter's with Richard as my headmaster and I have an unnerving feeling of being patronised. It makes me resolve to prove him wrong. I resolve that if I have to take up the All Saints headmaster's baton, I will go the way that my conscience takes me and not the way I am told to by Richard Todd.

My immediate concern now is how all this is going to go down at the school tomorrow. Everyone on the staff will surely see through the fabrication around David Kirkwood's departure. He has been popular with the staff, and the students are mesmerised by his thick Scottish Highlands brogue. He has been a well-liked and charismatic pioneer principal. I know in my heart that I would far rather listen to David's counsel than Richard's. We all seemed to have had fun with David.

After a short while of collecting my thoughts, I drive the seven kilometres back to the college from the Todd home in King William's Town, determined not to pre-empt anything but to take things as they come. Once back on the school campus I sit in my car for a while, going through in my mind what has just taken place and what I should be doing next. Becoming the principal is not a responsibility that I have sought. Surely no staff member has been oblivious to the animosity between Richard and David that is the real cause of David's departure. But how will they react when the news is broken that I am to replace David? Others on the staff might have liked to apply. Students will be puzzled and may question this sudden change.

I am now the principal of All Saints and have made my first report to the Trust. Here I am back at All Saints in an apprehensive mood. A concern uppermost in my mind is how to break the news to Noreen and our children. They know that we had come to All Saints from our comfortable and enjoyable time at Kingswood College because I had not wanted to take on the mantle of headmastership in a private school, for various reasons important to me. They had accepted this, despite the disruption that it had brought them. My initial exit plan from Kingswood had been to enter a career of teacher training and I had prepared for this by registering for a master's degree in education at Rhodes University. I had not yet graduated when Richard Todd extended an invitation to join his All Saints venture and an alternative future presented itself.

Now I would have to share the news that I was taking on the role that I had earlier shunned while at Kingswood. I am all of a sudden the *de facto* headmaster of All Saints. When I walk into my home, I break the news to Noreen in as matter of fact way as I can. Andrew and Simon are away in Grahamstown, boarding at Kingswood College, and Debbie is too small to understand. It has been so sudden and unexpected. Noreen's response and mine are perhaps best described as one of reluctant acceptance and bewilderment.

Noreen listens to me offloading my concerns. I even go down the path of suggesting that it might appear to others that I have engineered a coup d'état, since they know that my connection with Richard goes back a long way. Of course I am concerned with how others – staff and students – might react to my sudden and dramatic appointment.

What will this really mean and how will our lives change from today?

chapter 11

Principal

"Difficulties break some men but make others."

— Nelson Mandela

E ARLY IN THE MORNING an assembly of staff and students is called. It is the start of my first day as the college's principal, and Noreen and I are the only ones on the campus who know this is so. Students and staff traipse up to the arts block and we all sit and wait on the cold cement tiers in the yet-to-be-completed lecture room. There is a sense that something important is going to be shared since the director has called the meeting and will be addressing us.

When we are all in place Richard Todd comes in through the side entrance and strides to the podium in front. He waits briefly for the hush to soften, faces us, clears his throat and cuts straight to the chase and announces:

"Your principal, Mr David Kirkwood, has flown back to Scotland to attend to his ailing mother. He has left us and he is not coming back."

There is an audible gasp of dismay. Richard's attempts to explain the cause of David Kirkwood's departure as the consequence of a family crisis sound hollow and do not fool everyone in the gathering, especially not the staff, who have witnessed the bickering and the deterioration of his relationship with the principal. Then he blithely goes on to say that:

"The Board of Trustees is pleased to announce that Mr Michael Burton will replace Mr David Kirkwood with immediate effect."

Understandably, this news is greeted somewhat coolly. I later learn that many students suspect that during my period as acting principal while David Kirkwood was away, I had used the opportunity to plan and connive with Richard Todd to white-ant David and have him removed. It is going to take some time for this perception that I have orchestrated a coup d'état to fade. The rumour is driven by the view that since I have known Richard Todd for some time beforehand, I have somehow manoeuvred things so that I can prise David from his position.

This does not make it easier for me to start, under such a cloud. It is bad enough to have to step up to the task; but to do so under circumstances that are viewed suspiciously by some, strengthens a resolve that has been growing in me in the past few hours to prove myself capable. There is no backing down now so I must think and act positively. Yet I feel as though I am being forced to stand exposed way up on the top of the highest diving board and needing to jump into the deep end of a murky pool.

Perhaps I unnecessarily feel that the unexpected and bizarre nature of my appointment has somewhat isolated me from the students and my colleagues. It takes a long time for this feeling to go away. It adds an emotionally harrowing dimension to my first year as principal in what is already a pioneering situation fraught with challenges both on campus and all around us.

After the shock of the announcements explaining David Kirkwood's departure and my on-the-spot succession, Richard Todd continues with another dramatic message. It takes us all by surprise. He reveals to the already astonished audience:

"Thirty students are presently on their way from Johannesburg in two buses to join us at All Saints. They are part of a group of gifted pupils selected by Mr Stan Edkins, a businessman who runs a school for the gifted in Soweto. They have been attending his Saturday classes and they will be preparing for their DET matric exams in November away from political disruption in their Sowetan township schools. You must please all treat them as welcome guests at All Saints."

I am then directed publicly by Richard to organise immediate accommodation and bedding for the visiting students as well as meals in the dining hall for all the guests. The thirty students are to be accompanied by four adult escorts. These chaperones apparently are not teachers or people with any school authority. Who are they? Are we expected to accept this thing that is already happening and has been decided before we who are affected hear about it? Does it leave us with no option but just to accept the situation?

Richard Todd then announces that he will arrange for beds, bedding and other furniture for the accompanying chaperones to be brought in. He asks for the keys to the vacant staff home on the campus and for me to arrange for him to have the college's bakkie for Saturday morning. I am also to coordinate a timetable for our staff so that we can offer extra teaching for the new student visitors.

What are we going to do? Richard Todd has gone ahead and offered the college as a venue for these Sowetan students to write their examinations in the Ciskei. He has put a Christian slant to his message when he shares the news of his decision with us, that we at All Saints should open our doors for our brothers and sisters who otherwise will not be able to write their final examinations and so matriculate. Yet, is he overlooking the fact that the comrades in the townships are controlling examination boycotts?

He then walks out of the hushed assembly and drives away from the campus in his car. In his authoritarian manner he has, without any consultation, painted all of us into a corner. I am to jump to attention and carry out his orders and students are to comply without question. We all feel bulldozed.

Moreover, what about the staff being expected to take on the burden of extra lessons? This is another example of being taken for granted. Why should we, without any prior knowledge or consideration, respond positively to such a directive? At present we are still only a staff of six people, already busy enough in our demanding teaching programmes, including guiding six students through Unisa post-matric courses.

Soon after Richard Todd's departure from his special assembly, I am approached by members of the Students Representative Council. They look concerned and indicate that they are very worried about what Mr Todd has announced. I invite them into my office to hear them explain and they tell me that the Soweto group will create a very difficult situation for our Johannesburg-based students. Many of them had not told their friends and comrades where they were going when they left home. There are potentially huge personal risks in being found to be studying at a private school in a homeland while ongoing strikes and boycotts prevent others from studying where they live. In the political heat of the time, there is no way of forcing the student body to accept any decisions made by the authorities. They have been compromised with all the attendant dangers. They ask to speak to Mr Todd and to explain their predicament.

I consider their request to be understandable and reasonable, so I phone Richard at his home in King William's Town and attempt to explain the situation on their behalf. His response is abrupt and dismissive:

"You are the principal and this is the kind of situation that you have been appointed to handle. Tell them that I am too busy and just because there is a problem at the workplace, one does not immediately take it to Oppenheimer at the top. You must deal with it. You are the principal. It's time for you to show your leadership!"

He is obviously peeved at my apparent incompetence to handle what is to him a small matter of procedure. He ends our conversation by putting down the phone on me. I report his response and the bit about Oppenheimer faithfully to the group in my office, but they are far from satisfied. The response of Darius Simelane again makes a lot of sense to me:

"Mr Burton, you did not cause the problem. If Oppenheimer causes the problem, then Oppenheimer must answer to it himself."

I cannot find fault with this logic as I agree fully with it, and so not without trepidation I phone Richard Todd's number again. This time his domestic servant answers the phone and says that Mr Todd is not there. He has gone out to play golf. I tell the SRC delegation about this. So much for his being too busy.

James Mlawu, the SRC chairman, then asks:

"Please Mr Burton will you take a delegation to meet Mr Todd at the golf course?"

I hesitate, but I can see no other sensible course to take, and urgent action is needed. Again, I agree to their request. (Is this a case of the tail wagging the dog? Is there some other sort of control that I should take?)

Soon I am in my car driving the student delegation to the golf club. I know I am stepping onto a landmine, because in Richard Todd's book a leader should tell people what to do and not be a pliable listener to follow their bidding. Lead and don't be led. But I am not prepared to talk on the students' behalf. I really have no understanding of what it must be like to be in their shoes. I must allow them to explain their concern themselves in full.

The King William's Town white community was by and large a very conservative one, relatively indifferent to and, in some quarters, perhaps even supportive of apartheid regulations. The golf course is designated for 'whites only'. So, I have to warn the student delegation that we have compromised Mr Todd as he is clearly not too busy to see them; and since they have found him out like this, they should not expect cooperation from him. There are also hidden dangers in walking into this whites-only recreational domain. I feel very uneasy, at risk of his predictable wrath and whatever else might arise at the golf course clubhouse.

This is the morning of my first day as the principal and I have not yet even had a chance to sit at my desk and plan anything. All I have achieved in my new position is to lead for a few minutes in a shortened staff meeting, whilst the SRC waited for me, trying to connect and make a few promises. And here I am on the run at the bidding of students. I question myself over and over – am I showing weakness or strength by acceding to the students' requests? Actually, in my mind, they are more like demands. This is looking like a possible crisis. Perhaps a storm in a teacup, but am I up to handling it?

The question that crosses my mind is, how am I to facilitate a win–win situation when the one side is so intransigent and the other so insistent? I decide that I am simply going to go with the flow whilst trying to make sense of my responsibilities. I feel that I can only go with my instinct, but I am not confident.

And so, I find myself driving a small delegation of black students to an ostensibly white enclave and wondering where it will all lead. It even crosses my mind that perhaps it might mean my exit from the helm at All Saints even faster than David Kirkwood's. We arrive at the golf course parking area. As we climb out of our vehicle, I am sensitive to hostile stares towards our group from a number of white golf club members who are gathered at the doorway to the entrance foyer. So, I whisper to the student delegation that we will walk around the side of the clubhouse and they can wait on the veranda overlooking the first fairway where a few chairs are placed. There are no members in view so they nervously sit down on the edge of the seats while I approach Richard Todd who, with his son, is on the practice putting green below us. I walk with trepidation up to them and speak as firmly as I can:

"Richard, because I know what your reaction will be, and yet I have still come here with a student delegation, I am now imploring you to come and listen to them."

To my obvious and visible relief, he reluctantly agrees, but not without an exasperated sigh. A club member calls down from a balcony above as we walk together towards the clubhouse:

"A bit of a problem with some of your students, Richard?"

"Oh, nothing much that I won't sort out in a few minutes!"

I feel demeaned. Have I bungled matters so much in his eyes that he feels that he can solve the situation in a few minutes? He will show me how, whilst here I am making heavy weather of it and taking unnecessary time trying to unravel the threads. I decide to wait in the car-park as he sits with the delegation on that clubhouse veranda. It is a long two-hour wait. What possibly could be extending the few minutes that Richard said that he needed? Finally, the students come out to my car as Richard returns to the putting green.

"So, tell me guys, what took so long? What was the outcome of your talking with Mr Todd?"

"Mr Todd is going to come to the college this evening and he has agreed to meet with the whole student body to decide on a way forward."

Well so much for the few minutes to resolve the matter. More importantly for me, it seems that my move to bring the students to the golf course and my insistence that Richard listen to them to settle the issue has been justified, albeit temporarily. I hope that his negative perception of my way of handling things will be lessened now that he has bothered to face and account for the Pandora's box that he has unwittingly opened.

When I later think about this incident, which happens in the first few hours of my term as the principal, I can see that it is very significant. The way I have listened, empathised and then acted upon the students' grievance will go a long way in forging a workable relationship with them in the days to come. My early impression, soon to be reinforced, is that if I want to succeed as principal at this institution, I will need to take real cognisance of the students' concerns and opinions about what happens both on and off the campus, and only then take action.

As much as we as teachers insist on student compliance in the classrooms of All Saints, so the students have demonstrated to me with this early encounter that we teachers are compelled to listen to, become conversant with, and take a stand on the issues of the day that blaze outside the campus and that deeply affect them.

Although the incident has been a small and localised predicament, it is hugely significant in my mind at this embryonic stage of my leadership. It is still my first day in the hot seat. I am realising that I need to work together with the staff and students and not act from a position of detached superiority and telling people what to do. I am learning that listening is so much more important than telling. Anyway, Richard Todd's expectation of an authoritarian 'tell-them-what-to-do' boss approach is just not in my nature.

All the headmasters of my experience had been strong-willed bosses who issued commands. It was for this reason that I had shunned opportunities to take up such a position earlier in my career. The headmasters I knew, including Richard Todd, were captains of their ships and their mission was to stamp their footprint to be able to say *"this is my school, I am in charge"*. Their imprint on the school was all-important to them, as well as to leave some sort of legacy – which was usually a building or a field named after them. But this was not for me. I felt that my role was to work with and help to build people up, and thus together we could build the school. This was a significant point of departure for me.

*   *   *

That evening, Richard Todd meets with the staff and students. We all settle down in the foyer of the residence to listen and share. The atmosphere is electric. He starts by explaining more fully why he decided to invite the Soweto group to All Saints College. He is still convinced that it is the right thing to do and says so.

Then the students have a chance to air their views. They are not happy. They tell him that some of them are now under extreme threat if it becomes known that, in coming to All Saints, they have put their personal interest in furthering their education ahead of the struggle's maxim of liberation before education. It is possible that they might be recognised and exposed as sell-outs. This is the time of the gruesome punishment of necklacing, the shocking and horrifically painful death meted out to perceived sell-outs.

Murmurings show that emotions are starting to rise in the meeting and the mood is turning ugly. The students are more and more outspoken and demand to know why Richard Todd has, without any thought of how it would affect them, gone ahead and unilaterally made such a decision that could seriously threaten them. One after another speaks out and they don't hold back. I and the staff remain passive as it is not directly our issue and we only need to know how it will pan out. Privately, my sympathy is with the students. By keeping quiet I am choosing not to be drawn away from my view that Richard Todd is acting without due sensitivity. However, after a while it is clear that he is visibly shaken. He has seriously misunderstood the severity of the situation and has shown his ignorance of the real issues that confront the students with whom he is dealing. They will not deferentially accept the position in which he has unwittingly put them.

After a while Richard recommends a supper break. He concedes that he has unintentionally made a grave error of judgment, but the buses are on their way and cannot be stopped. He tells us that during the break we must think positively and come back with solutions. We have aired the problem sufficiently. He needs a respite before the temperature of the meeting reaches boiling point. After we disperse, he does some phoning from the office and then he returns to the staff who are waiting outside on the field. He is looking much more relaxed. He tells the small gathering of staff members that we are not to worry any further as he thinks that he has found the solution to the situation. He seems pleased with himself, but he does not enlighten us any further. We are to just wait patiently while he plays out his game. Is the director really going to be able to show us how to resolve the impasse?

When the meeting resumes with the students, there is a noticeable restlessness and we are all on the edge of our seats. Of course, there are not enough seats so we are in bunches all around the foyer some standing and others perched on a low wall and several even sitting on the floor. Richard starts by appealing to all to focus our collective thoughts on how best to solve the predicament positively. He says that we have discussed and clarified the situation sufficiently and now it is time to make decisions on how to solve the problem. He emphasises that we must move from negative thinking to positive thinking. Then he asks for ideas from the students. There are very few forthcoming – short of setting up some sort of road block and sending the visitors back home.

He listens for a while to what students have to say and it is clear to me that he is edging to share something significant with us. After a short while his face lights up and enthusiastically, he announces the solution:

"We no longer need to worry. The problem has been halved as only one bus, and not two, is coming."

He stops and waits for a positive reaction. But instead, there is a horrified silence, then a deluge of muttering followed by raised voices. Eventually one student calls out:

"What has happened to the other bus?"
Others follow:
"Did the comrades in the township stop it?"
"Why is it not coming?"

Richard cannot answer. Far from resolving the crisis, he now realises that he has unwittingly enlarged it. Why is there only one bus coming? He is not able to respond, so he fabricates that he is required urgently at his home. He turns on his heels and walks out of the entrance and we remain, as does the messy situation that has been placed before us. Together we will have to find a way out of it.

We talk on and our consensus view is that trying to stop the bus will lead to questions being asked and this might be bad for us. Rather let us divert the bus to another venue, perhaps in King William's Town. We set about urgently finding alternative accommodation in King William's Town.

As the bus passengers do not know exactly where All Saints College is, the planned rendezvous on their arrival is the Catholic church in King William's Town. Soon after our meeting closes, I drive a small delegation of students into town and we go first to the Catholic church where we are received with understanding and offered help with accommodation. The Soweto guests will write their examinations in the church hall. With the help of Judith Todd, All Saints staff members would pull up our sleeves and coordinate, invigilate, and undertake all the administrative responsibilities associated with a formal national examination. The Soweto guests are to be kept away from us and are warned not to visit the campus.

Mercifully the outcome was that none of the All Saints students were compromised or threatened. It was a harrowing experience that thankfully had a positive outcome. In fact, in 1987 several of the Soweto guests applied for places at the college and a number of them were accepted.

The tightrope between education or no education had been tested without mishap.

*   *   *

What I realise from my first days as the principal of All Saints is that a situation can become volatile with just a small spark of insensitivity or ignorance. I remind myself that I did not apply to be the principal and so I have not prepared a blueprint in my mind of how I am going to run the school. I have no aspirations of applying my stamp of authority and making this "my" school, to fit any pretensions of vision or legacy. Richard Todd is the visionary and power behind All Saints College, but I have to face the fact that he is a teller and not a listener. It will be very difficult to confide in him. I have the distinct feeling that whatever I come up with will be brushed aside. Richard Todd has a strong personality and I can see that our paths are already starting to deviate.

From all these early happenings, I have learned that the best way to solve a problem is to draw others in and share ideas and not try to shoulder the responsibility alone. So I reconsider Richard's warning statement:

"*...you will find the post of principal to be the loneliest job in the world.*"

Maybe not.

chapter 12
Preparation

"By failing to prepare, you are preparing to fail."

— Benjamin Franklin

OCTOBER 1986. Now that I am in the hot seat, it strikes me forcibly that I now have only two months to put everything in order for the coming year. The first thing that I want to do is engage the staff and to capture a mission statement as clearly as we can. We must start together from a firm understanding of our base in a creed to which we can refer back. We spend two full afternoons workshopping this and it is recorded in a charter. It takes note of the foundation stone's dedication to provide an excellent education for those who may lead and serve in southern Africa. To the glory of God.

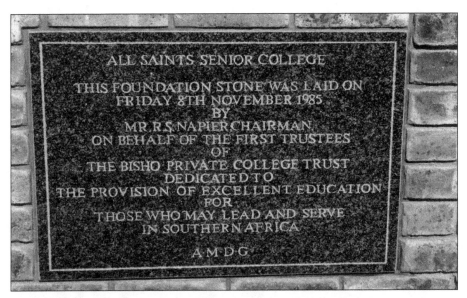

The foundation stone promoting excellent education for those who may lead and serve in southern Africa

This is our task and our co-constructed charter reads:

"*RECOGNISING the injustices of our country's past, and especially the fact that generations of citizens have been deprived of the opportunity to achieve their potential through education;*

RECOGNISING also our responsibility to free ourselves and our society by fulfilling our duty to teach and to learn and to serve;

WE THE TRUSTEES, THE TEACHERS, PARENTS, STUDENTS AND WORKERS OF ALL SAINTS SENIOR COLLEGE HEREBY AFFIRM OUR COMMITMENT:

- *to serve the peoples of our country irrespective of race, ethnicity, sex or religion;*
- *to create and sustain a climate in which effective teaching and learning can occur, and in which students can therefore strive to achieve their academic potential;*
- *to strive to achieve a sense of common nationhood, and a recognition of the fraternity of nations;*
- *to respect the cultural and linguistic diversity of our country, and to promote tolerance, understanding and an appreciation of the dignity and value of one's fellow human beings;*
- *to promote an awareness of the need to respect and properly manage our environment and to properly manage the natural resources of our country for future generations;*
- *to respect freedom of speech and assembly;*
- *to develop consultative models of leadership and administration;*
- *to respect due process of established systems of discipline, and to presume the innocence of alleged offenders until proved guilty;*
- *to respect freedom of thought, conscience and religion, and to encourage the deepening of spirituality in personal and community life.*"

I feel bolstered by this first step because it has brought the staff together better than before. We have co-created our mission and are ready to move forward as a cohesive and cooperative group bound by sharing the process. It is the first step of instilling a democratic approach to managing our school.

* * *

In the two months ahead of me, I now have a lot on my plate in putting systems and people in place in time for the start of our second year. I need to appoint ten more teachers and three administrative staff for the coming year, as well as ten maintenance staff from the surrounding villages. These I can do from my office although I only have one part-time secretary to help me. But to find a hundred and fifty new students an outside agency has to be approached. I connect with the MaST organisation in Johannesburg straightaway. In another moment of synchronicity I find that Derek Jooste, formerly a fellow teacher at St Peter's, is just the right go-to person at MaST. Between the two of us we devise an application test. Our aim is to find potential and not absorbed learning. Our test focuses on thinking, understanding and problem-solving by using words, numbers and patterns. MaST advertises and administers the tests which are forwarded to me and I invite a small team of teachers to help me to choose and send out acceptance invitations.

*   *   *

One big regret for me at this time is that I need to step out of the classroom. Through 1986 I had been enjoying the teaching challenge and the freedom to implement my own methods. Geography can be an outdoors subject and I had been able to involve the classes in a lot of fieldwork. One outcome of this was that we entered a small team project in a Science Expo in Grahamstown. As a result of our exhibit we were invited to publish an article which we titled *The structure of the seaside* by Titus Modingwane, Milton Ntwana, Khanyisa Qangule, and Floyd Sixolo. It was published in *The Naturalist* in November 1986:

"*This article is about the geography of a piece of coastline at Cove Rock. It is the work of four Std 9 students at All Saints College, Bisho, and was exhibited at the GEC Science Expo in Grahamstown. The students were awarded gold certificates – an outstanding achievement – especially as Geography was a subject that none of the students had tackled before this year, and that for two of them, the field excursion was their first visit to the sea.*"

Suddenly, teaching seaside geography has to be put off centre stage as I face a tsunami of tasks that come with occupying the hot seat. I am now the key reference person for the continued construction of the college since the director has already moved to Cape Town. This means accountability to the trustees and sponsors. It entails attending on-site meetings with architects, quantity surveyors, the construction foreman, engineers and a host of sub-contractors very early in the morning every day. It is then necessary to relay the outcomes of these dawn meetings to the estate manager, the director and the trustees before settling into managing the day's college matters. With all the construction-speak I feel very much a fish out of water and yet supposedly I am standing in the shoes of the client. Therefore I am responsible for accepting and questioning all the construction decisions made at these meetings. It's a crash course in pipeline gradients, the planting of grass, removing the plague of "Peelton weed" from the fields and loads of building jargon.

Before Richard Todd had set off to Cape Town, I had asked permission to move out of the residence and into the headmaster's house at the top of the campus to find a bit of tranquillity away from the responsibility of being the warden of the residence. He had denied my request, saying that it would be too disruptive for the students to have a new warden in the residence in the same year, so I have to continue with my duties as the residence supervisor. I do not accept his logic but feel I must ride with it. Perhaps I should not have asked permission and waited for him to leave, and then just moved. Too late now.

One urgent assignment that I face is drawing up the college's budget for 1987. It is to be a zero-based budget. Such a task on this scale is new to me but the Trust wants it to be presented at the end of the 1986 trustees' meeting. The budget must take in all the financial considerations of an increased staff and student intake, and increased catering, transportation, salaries and running costs. Once drawn up, any departures during the course of the year will need to be accounted for and I have been told that I may not use underspent portions of the budget to compensate for overspent portions as the year progresses. It is important to get it right from the start, and my special challenge is that I have no prior experience. At the same time, I have no bursar to help me nor any access to a financial institution for guidance. I am expected to "just do it" – and do it urgently and do it correctly.

Another high priority is the food issue, which has been a major area of concern through this first year. Catering for the college has been done by a dubious individual private contractor. It has been a disastrous experience. Lennie is a rough-looking individual, who is an uncommunicative person at the best of times. He drives in from East London every day loaded up with eggs, second-rate processed meat and other low-value victuals. He arrives with a firearm strapped to his waist, which he claims is for protection whilst in transit in the early morning dark. His presence, while we all sit on low benches at trestle tables in a basement room to eat, gives us the heebie-jeebies. Early every morning, Lennie arrives on the campus with a few staff to prepare breakfast of deep-fried eggs served with greasy trimmings and lots of white bread. Almost every day it is the same predictable fare. Lunch very seldom varies from "flat meat", coleslaw and salads.

The dining room and kitchen complex are not yet completed so, to be fair to him, it is not easy for Lennie with his primitive equipment. He has a few gas burners lined up against the back wall and the washing up facilities are very suspect. He cooks in front of us in conditions that would not pass any health inspection. Our meals are being eaten in what is a very large rough cement floored garage. Our trestle tables are rickety and our benches rough and ready. No windows and a wide-open garage door complete the scene of the facility for meals that staff and students share. In winter we have shivered and in summer we have perspired.

Jayshree Pather, a young Indian pioneer student, reports in an interview:

"Worst thing? The food. As a person of Indian origin food is very important for me. In the first year there wasn't a dining hall. We did our eating in the basement of the admin block, played table tennis there... The caterer used to come from East London every day, bring breakfast, lunch and dinner. He was just another crazy character. But Munovar Gaffoor and I, both because of our backgrounds, had food issues. I grew up not eating beef and pork and she had to eat Halaal food, and there was no provision for that. So, in the first year, I'm not kidding, we ate pilchards for breakfast, lunch and dinner. Except when there was lamb. I would have it and she wouldn't because it wasn't Halaal. Very occasionally when it was fish it was fine, and there was chicken. Otherwise, I've eaten pilchards in every combination you could think of and that was really hard! That was Len's idea of catering. He couldn't be bothered to do anything for us, so he just brought pilchards".

I am promised that at the start of the new year, a proper catering complex will be available. For All Saints to be peaceful and effective, it is imperative that the students are fed good, nutritious and plentiful food. I therefore straight away set about jettisoning Lennie's agreement and negotiating a contract with a reputable catering company. I choose Fedics. One positive outcome of this is that it makes budgeting easy for me, as Fedics do it all.

It works well and Jayshree Pather then reports:

"Then, in the second year, we had a contract with Fedics and the guy from Fedics came. He was observing. We would all stand in the queues waiting to get our food and the two of us would go and get our pilchards. Then this guy came and said: "Is there a reason why you're eating these pilchards?" And we explained this was our diet. In the second year it was much better. Fedics went out of their way to cater for us and that was very sweet."

Within my first two weeks as the principal, one really unpleasant task rears its head above the wave of concerns flooding me. I know I have to dismiss the estate manager. Japie is a close personal friend of Richard Todd. His appointment was made at the golf club. After he had retired from his office job, he wept on Richard's shoulder about his misfortune of feeling lost and without a job. He had recently lost his wife and was clearly very depressed. Richard, always the good Samaritan, offered Japie employment as estate manager at All Saints. But it soon is obvious to all that he simply neither has the drive nor the skills required to establish and then manage the infrastructure of a campus which is one hundred and sixty-seven hectares in size and needs a lot of energy to maintain. Energy Japie does not have.

Because of his inability to cope he was spending much of each day in the secretary's office, sitting on a side table and swinging his feet, staring at her and making her feel very uncomfortable, to the extent that she complains to me. He is harassing her so I have to give him notice. Sadly, he then goes into a downward spiral and seeks solace in alcohol – which further impairs his ability to cope with anything.

Then I hear that Japie is telling all in his King William's Town circle that he is being unfairly sacked. His reaction to his dismissal is unfortunate as King William's Town citizens are already unhappy with the All Saints College project and dub us "the communists on the hill". So he has many sympathetic ears in that community, and this does not make our lives at All Saints any easier. People in the town who know who I am shun me whenever I have to go into town. I am surprised that Richard Todd takes my dismissal of Japie without comment. It is probably because he has seen that the appointment was a mistake in the first place, and has been hindering important maintenance and development at the college.

* * *

Somehow, by the end of December, I manage to complete what has been really urgent and to some extent overcome the crises of expectations that had faced me in October. It had meant no holiday break to refresh myself for the new year. However, I emerge stronger for the hands-on experience in all aspects of All Saints' early development and future modus operandi. This first-hand trial by fire means that I have had to examine thoroughly, and become involved in, all aspects of a running a residential college.

When I have a chance to reflect, I am reminded of the Chinese character *ji* (挤), which means "crisis". It was used as a trope by President John Kennedy in his motivational speeches in the 1960s. Simply translated, *ji* is presented as being composed of two strokes, respectively signifying danger and opportunity. Crisis, therefore, does not just mean despair, it also means opportunity. It can have both negative and positive characteristics.

I had needed to seize the opportunity afforded to me to establish myself. But soon I had found out that I could not go it alone. Since I had never had to steer a school before, I had always been a passenger in an established system. I needed support and guidance to navigate All Saints successfully through the very choppy waters surrounding the venture.

chapter 13

Democracy

"Co-curricular activities are those activities that are undertaken side by side with curricular activities. They supplement curricular activities and prepare students in the 'Art of Living and Working Together'."

— Anonymous

THE QUALITY OF RESIDENTIAL SCHOOLING is determined by how its days are filled. At All Saints, teachers and learners live on the same property. To succeed academically we need to allow students to participate in all that we do, through a variety of interventions that draw us all together. I recognise that it is important to promote a balanced environment where everyone can enjoy life and grow together. We must work hard and have enjoyable things to fill our days outside lesson times. It is my responsibility to make sure that all the necessary systems are in place and I am going to do this by engaging everyone in the planning process.

First, I will embrace the things introduced by David Kirkwood and Richard Todd that are working well. These include the handbook as a guide, and the tutor-group system. So far, I have noted, days are largely empty after lessons are done, and I need to expand enjoyable activities beyond the classroom. I set about inviting staff and students to get involved in finding extra-curricular activities for the afternoons and evenings. Next, I look at our rural surrounds with its several villages. I recognise that we need to connect and interact by offering our premises to neighbouring teachers and learners or suffer the disapproval of being considered an ivory tower.

This is my three-part plan: to adopt the things that have been effective, introduce more activities, and make sure that we interact with our neighbours. The process to establish these three initiatives will be an emergent one where staff and students have a chance to contribute rather than being imposed upon unilaterally from my office.

*   *   *

During the year of preparation in 1985 David Kirkwood had introduced the idea of a handbook for All Saints. He had produced a comprehensive tome with all the school rules in it in time for the induction of the new staff. Richard Todd, however, was very much opposed to setting rules and had wanted a school with no rules at all. So from the start we were getting conflicting messages. Richard had motivated his view by claiming that rules are only there to be broken, and that students who are given opportunity and trust would behave appropriately at all times. This would show the world that it is possible for a school to operate without rules. The implementation of school rules is normally the bane of every school's existence as people became divided once punishments are given. The principal is usually the fall guy as parents and students clash with authority. However, when David had introduced the concept of no rules to the first cohort of students, they rejected the idea. They demanded a rule book. They wanted to know what the limits were. Theory and practice do not always follow the same path.

Now that I am the principal, I feel that it is a very good idea to apply the college handbook concept. It will be a much-needed guide for how things should work at the college. However, David Kirkwood's method has two shortcomings: it is prescriptive and it is imposed from above. This is the outcome of a results-driven approach. I decide to adopt his initiative of a handbook but to follow the lead recommended by Franklin Sonn. This is to consider a process-driven approach. So I introduce the concept of a negotiated college handbook. A word that might describe this process is ownership. I ask myself, "*Who owns the school modus operandi and rules?*" To get complete and full buy-in from all at the college, I need to ensure that everyone participates in the process of constructing the handbook. In this way everyone, staff, students, parents – and even relevant community members and structures – can share ownership of the college's way of doing things and its rules.

Several positive outcomes from this approach become apparent straight away. Two in particular make our way of doing things at All Saints unique. They concern two fundamental issues, i.e. expulsion from school and school rules. When I am invited to address a national headmasters' conference of traditional state boys' schools, I challenge the gathering with two questions:

"*Can a parent or pupil change a school rule on their first day at your school?*" and

"*Do pupils at your school ever expel themselves without parental criticism or student rebellion?*"

My claim is that both of these might happen with us because of the shared democratic processes of negotiation at All Saints. They are questions of accountability and ownership of a process. If the process is inclusive, then the outcomes are inclusive. People abide by consensus if they have been involved with the process. If the practice has been imposed, then there is room for disobedience, confrontation and reserving the right to be critical.

To answer the first question about changing school rules, I explain that at All Saints we have an all-inclusive meeting of teachers, parents and students at the beginning of each year and everyone is obliged to attend and participate. At the start, these beginning-of-the-year meetings drag on and on, taking up most of the first day. However, patience is essential if we are to get it right. Everyone has to be satisfied that their opinions have been aired and respected. We work through the previous year's handbook item by item and any participant can question an item. If the question leads to a consensus decision that an amendment is necessary, the change is made. That amendment can be promoted by a newly arrived student, parent or any member in the meeting. Provided that the house accepts the change, a parent or pupil has changed a school rule on their first day at our school.

The answer to the second question, about expulsion, illustrates the effectiveness of the process of negotiation. I present the example of how a major area of beginning-of-year debate is annually about the residences. One is for boys and one for girls. The debate goes something like this:

MB: *"Last year, at the risk of expulsion, boys were not allowed in the girls' residence and vice versa, unless the residence is on fire or at the risk of other such disaster. What are we going to do this year?"*

Boy student: *"But surely we can go into the foyer/common room to socialise? There is nowhere else."*

Parent of a boy: *"I agree, if we trust our children, they will behave properly."*

Parent of a girl: *"Our daughter is just 15 and some of the boys are older than 20 years. Our daughter needs protection, so I say 'no'."*

This issue is at centre stage of our early debates. This year it is called the electricity rule. We all agree after much discussion that no boy should go into the girls' residence. If one does the guilty party must leave school without argument or resistance. Introducing this rule is not accepted, without much debate

"How can you punish someone by taking away their education for a social misdemeanour?"

However, the overwhelming response is that the seriousness of the offence must be met with a very serious punishment.

After the decision that expulsion without argument is taken by consensus, one mid-term evening, with the electricity rule in place, Peter King, the warden of the Girls' Residence, accosts two boys who have ignored the rule and are trespassing inside the residence after dark. This is then reported to me to deal with. I say that I will confront the two boys the following morning in the dining hall. I find the miscreants at breakfast and say:

"Guys, we have a problem."

"Yes sir, we know. We have packed our bags and have made our preparations to leave after breakfast."

They leave the campus quietly without song and dance and there are no reactions or reprisals from other students. The reason is that everyone knows that a rule has been made and now broken by individuals who are accountable to us all because they have been part owners in the process along with everyone else.

This outcome is particularly significant and momentous because at this time students around the country are crying out in collective protection *'One in, all in'.* Expulsion is a very hot issue around which students and parents rally. Yet here at All Saints expulsion has been self-inflicted and without supportive resistance. There is no confrontation between "the masses" and "the authorities" and there is no parental resistance as the students have left of their own accord. There is no division. The headmaster does not have to face wrath from any quarter.

We are riding the crest of a wave as the various measures we are implementing are tested. We are increasingly looked upon as a model. Leading a school democratically has such profound implications that I am invited to address the Natal Teacher's Society on how democracy happens at All Saints. It is captured in their journal *Mentor.* At the same time a paper is presented by Sharon Caldwell at an International Democratic Education Conference in the United States of America as *A Case Study in Student Democracy in South Africa: All Saints Senior College.*

* * *

Often discipline is used as the yardstick by which to measure and compare schools. All Saints stresses self-discipline, discipline by personal influence, persuasion and gentle pressure. All procedures that relate to discipline in the college are set out in a disciplinary code in the handbook, which has to be accepted by the student body in a consensus debate. This code is ratified by the Parents' Committee and then by the Border Education Co-ordination Committee, which is regarded as the ultimate relevant body facilitating acceptable decisions relating to discipline. I learn later that our *Discipline Code* as laid out in our handbook is being adopted by many schools in our region and is promoted by the Border Education Co-ordination Committee.

Putting it together is a painstaking but rigorous process. In the end a discipline committee consisting of student SRC members and teachers investigates all reports of indiscipline and makes recommendations to me for the final decision. We all feel that my role comes in only at the end of the process. One of the important lessons I learn is put very clearly to me in a discipline negotiating session by student Josiah Moshatane when he says:

"You must find and treat the cause and not the symptoms of misbehavior. When students throw food against the walls in the dining room, look for the cause and do not only react to the food throwing."

He is teaching me that too often we try to solve a predicament at its surface. A school principal's natural reaction to a grievance list is either to dismiss it out of hand or to attempt to answer each point with clinical logic. But often this does not solve the problem, because there is something malignant at a deeper level. There must be sensitivity in seeking solutions to problems and a recognition that views expressed are held by individuals or groups and, as such, should be respected and not dismissed with slick answers. Thorough and often painful counselling is required before the real problem surfaces.

*   *   *

At our induction, from their overseas experiences, Richard Todd and David Kirkwood had introduced the concept of a tutor-group system for All Saints College to the new staff. It was carefully explained. It was felt that the idea, imported from the United Kingdom's sixth-form colleges, would suit our senior college approach. Each teacher was to be responsible as a tutor to a group of students of different ages and classes. The idea is that tutors would take a special pastoral interest in the learning and social progress of each student in the group. It had worked very well in 1986 and I decide to continue with the system.

Our tutor-group practice offers the all-important vehicle for mentoring. In its simplest form, mentoring is a relationship in which a more experienced or more knowledgeable person helps to guide a less experienced or less knowledgeable person. An important bonding for teacher-to-student and student-to-student relationships at All Saints is afforded by our tutor-group system.

Each teacher at All Saints is tutor to a group of about fourteen students. Time is set aside in the teaching day for each tutor group to meet in a convenient and relaxed venue to discuss matters and to distribute any notices for the day. The general health of the college community depends largely on the effectiveness and morale of each of its tutor groups. The tutor needs to be guide, philosopher and friend to the students in the group. As a counsellor, the tutor gets to know each student so that when any problem arises, whether academic or personal, it is an easy and natural thing for students to turn to their tutor to seek a solution.

Tutor groups do more than just meet daily. The unit is often involved in fun or recreational activities, such as hiking and overnight camping in the nearby Amatola mountains or along the Wild Coast beach trails. We even hold entertainment in the form of tutor group concerts, or playing inter-tutor group fun soccer or volley ball involving boys and girls in the course of each term.

The outcome of implementing this system at All Saints can be summarised in just two words: ownership and understanding. Ownership is affirmed by debating and participating in all aspects of school life with a view to every teacher and student recognising the privilege and responsibility of accountability and ownership. Understanding is pursued by striving to keep everything together through cooperation rather than confrontation. It takes away the us-and-them mindset often found at schools where the authorities are seen as the students' enemies who are out of touch with student aspirations.

An adjunct to the tutor-group structure of All Saints is the college's assembly style. Students participate as much as the principal or any teacher. Confidence in public speaking becomes clearly evident and we all learn from each other in friendly and sometimes serious addresses.

At our informal assembly one student announcement that has us all in fits of laughter comes about when a student makes a report of the previous week-end's back-pack hike on the Amatola mountain hiking trail. He thanks his tutor for the opportunity and for the experience and recounts that all has gone well except for the Fattis and Monis (a well-known South African brand name generally pronounced "fatties and moanies").

On my hike into the mountains with my tutor group I am surprised to discover how vulnerable many of these streetwise township youths feel when walking and sleeping in the wilds of the Amatola forests. There are whisperings of mountain lions, ambushing pythons and stalking leopards. The wilderness of Africa is clearly not part of the life of many of these young city types. Some are nervous and quite fearful.

Perhaps the most valuable feature of the tutor group is that it gives students a sense of belonging. It is a family away from home. Hiking has an added advantage beyond the physical rigours. It nurtures informal and friendly communication. Friendships are bonded and many alumni count their hiking experiences as highlights of their stay at All Saints.

* * *

In 1987 we introduce so many activities that I am proud to see a kaleidoscope of opportunities filling everyone's time. Lots of them originated as suggestions from tutor-group discussions. Clubs and societies are active mainly in the evenings and a variety of sports fill the afternoons. There are fifteen clubs and societies and fourteen types of sport.

One of our teachers, Craig Andrew, had introduced an interest in the Duke of Edinburgh Award Scheme, later to be known as the President's Award Scheme. James Mlawu is our first student to receive a Gold Award at a national level.

When Craig leaves us to become the national director of the scheme, Noreen embraces the initiative and introduces an in-house equivalent, which she calls the Leaf Award Scheme, as an incentive to students to develop themselves. The aims of the scheme are:

- *To encourage students to participate and extend themselves.*
- *To develop a healthy body, mind and spirit.*
- *To develop leadership skills.*

Three levels of achievement are Green – easily attainable by all; Silver – more demanding and requiring more commitment; and Gold – very demanding, and those who achieve this level have their names written on an honours board for permanent display in the foyer. They also receive a gold badge to wear on the award T-shirt.

* * *

An important aspect of our way of doing things is to recognise and actively promote the college as part of the surrounding community both politically and educationally. Consequently, I recommend the phrase "community interaction" rather than the usual phrase of "community outreach". I feel that a certain arrogance is implied in the term outreach as it infers that we have something that you do not have and we are here to help you. In other words, we are reaching out because we can. Outreach suggests that we are on a higher level whereas interaction levels the playing fields. For me, interaction says I have something for you and you have something for me. The result is a mutual respect between the parties as opposed to a superiority-and-inferiority vibe.

Under Peter King's leadership as our director of development, All Saints College begins to offer a number of initiatives to surrounding schools. A popular programme on offer is holiday special tuition described as a schools' partnership that is being coordinated by the college. Over thirty-five surrounding schools eagerly participate in the specially constructed courses and it is not only students who are invited but also local teachers from the surrounding schools.

Peter King also devises and coordinates a very successful Rural Science Enrichment Programme (RSEP), which incorporates a hundred surrounding senior schools. For this we have to seek funding outside our school budget. For several years we receive very generous financial support from a German church foundation EZE (Evangelische Zentralstelle für Entwicklungshilfe) that utilises German taxpayers' money for its social responsibility programme of support to developing countries.

Analysis of year-on-year science results of the schools involved show marked improvement. Based on the data captured, our belief is that the RSEP is playing a crucial catalytic role in our region by giving momentum to the campaign to restore a culture of excellence and a work ethic in all our schools.

Another educational community interaction programme that we coordinate from our campus is the Primary Science Project (PSP). The PSP, a national non-governmental organisation (NGO), has its headquarters in Johannesburg. Our partnership is funded substantially by the Genesis Foundation based in the United States of America. The initiative focuses on upskilling teachers in science teaching and is coordinated by Raj Kurup on our staff.

At a different level, All Saints hosts the Masimanyane sewing project, which is housed in a specially painted downstairs room in the basement of the science block. In addition to providing accommodation for this project, the college successfully seeks funds from overseas to support it. The focus of the programme is on empowering rural women. We recognise and state that women are

Rural Xhosa women from surrounding villages developing entrepreneurial skills at All Saints College as part of the college's community interaction

amongst the most disadvantaged members of our society owing to numerous factors. The primary goal of this project is to teach women basic sewing skills. On completion of a one-month course each trainee aims to have the ability to understand a commercial pattern, lay a pattern correctly, pin and cut the fabric, sew a complete garment, maintain a sewing machine in good order and to have the ability to pay attention to quality and detail with reference to manufacturing garments. The outcome is an empowerment of rural women through improved self-esteem, equipping each trainee with the necessary tools to return to her community and confidently share the skills that she has learned, and enabling trainees to manufacture clothing more economically for their families and friends, and motivating them to have confidence in their abilities to contribute to small business employment.

All our service staff, the cleaners, kitchen and ground staff, live in nearby villages. On a daily basis, the estate manager collects them for work and then transports them home in the evening. In this way the All Saints family extends itself into these villages. When, for example, the Ciskeian security forces disrupt the people of Nkqonkqweni and Peelton by forcing a resettlement programme, many seek refuge at our College. Eventually I and some All Saints staff, working with the Border Council of Churches, saw to the successful return to their traditional homes of those who had been displaced.

chapter 14
Schooling

"Education is not an affair of 'telling' and 'being told', but an active and constructive process."

— John Dewey

I N 1987 we managed to stay a step ahead of the political turmoil of the time and to fulfil our brief to produce academic excellence. How did we do it? This question was asked of me one day, much later, by Smuts Ngonyama as he and I met in the baggage collection area of King Phalo Airport (East London):

"Mike, how is it that your students at All Saints do so well in their examinations when they are so politicised?"

I replied:

"Well Smuts, we have a story to tell, but I wonder if anyone really wants to listen?"

Where do I start to answer Smuts Ngonyama's question? It is a loaded question because it insinuates that we should not enjoy success in the classroom in view of the political pressures of the time. The short answer is that it is vital to get the academic focus right from the start. I suppose that "start" happened as early as my baptism of fire into the principal's hot seat.

When David Kirkwood leaves under a cloud, I am supposed to pick up the reins and move on as if nothing untoward has happened and build up a winning school. Then in rapid succession a number of incidents occur on campus. They lay the foundations for me on how I am to deal with and embrace the storms to be unleashed by the government-imposed state-of-emergency regulations and the ensuing countrywide defiance campaign, whilst at the same time nurturing a pioneering model schooling endeavour.

We find it difficult to understand our role as teachers in terms of the anti-apartheid struggle: we have been instructed by the director that our mission is "education with liberation", but without the freedom to venture beyond our classroom subjects. The formula I set for myself as the principal is to listen first to our students and then perhaps seek counsel if the issue appears to be too complex for an immediate response. What I do is always a response to the situation that presents itself rather than my second-guessing or trying to be proactive. As a result, I am always on the back foot, trying to unravel what has happened in front of me. Perhaps this is what is needed of me rather than a confident know-it-all, front-foot approach that may have been expected from some quarters. I had soon recognised that showing indifference to the anti-apartheid struggle by retaining a distance and staying neutral is fraught with traps and definitely not the path to travel. The passage from the Bible's book of Revelation 3:15–16 where indifference was reviled comes to my mind:

"I know your works: you are neither cold nor hot. Would that you were either cold or hot! So, because you are lukewarm, and neither hot nor cold, I will spit you out of my mouth."

Since October 1986, I have been thrown in at the deep end of the emerging All Saints Senior College. I find that the expectations from the Trust, the teachers, the students and the surrounding communities are quite different and at times beyond reach of each other. Expectations include keeping up with the continuing construction of the campus, budgeting and equipping the school for an influx of new people – teachers, students and estate management staff – as All Saints expands into its second year. A complex pattern of competing responsibilities faces me. How am I to meet all the expectations without experience or support? I have to dig deep.

Richard Todd has explained in his vision that education is a key issue for the future of South Africa. Fury at "gutter education" is a root cause of township rioting. Demographic and economic predictions show that it will not be possible in the foreseeable future to provide an education for all in the country comparable with that provided for white South Africans. A country's most important asset is its young people, and the most valuable of these are the most capable. He claims that the most dangerous people anywhere are young people of real ability who are frustrated and feel cornered.

The entire future of the All Saints College venture is based on the premise that academic success can be achieved with excellent teaching in a stimulating environment for otherwise deprived but capable students within their last two years of high school. The underlying pressure to achieve this vision comes from the sponsors and the Board of Trustees; it is a vision they embrace and advertise. Now we at All Saints have to produce the outcome they seek.

In order to attain this goal, teaching at All Saints College has to find its own means to achieve effective learning. We have recognised early in the college's experience that ownership of the schooling process needs to be shared by both students and teachers.

All Saints Senior College stands or falls by its academic results in the final senior certificate (matriculation) examinations, which will then lead into further success at tertiary level. Staff member Peter King writes:

"The extraordinary success of All Saints throughout its relatively short institutional life was due in no small measure to the many men and women who, believing in the vision of a different tomorrow, committed their energies and a fair part of their lives to make the dark night shorter and the dawn brighter.

All Saints would not have been the place it was without the contribution of every person, young and not so young, who collectively made the institution into the unique place of learning and liberation that it was.

The teachers and other staff, many of whom left their suburban comfort-zones, careers and insular communities to make a difference, who greeted the future before it arrived, and whose determination and persistence to make it work regularly bore testimony to a conscience and commitment beyond duty."

We soon find that a major obstacle to achieving academic excellence is to get our students onto the same starting line. The time span that we have to reach a successful finish is just two years and the students come from such diverse learning backgrounds, some of them way behind others. Our founder has overlooked that we have to gather widely dissimilar education experiences into one basket before we can make a meaningful impact – without leaving some behind or frustrating others. The assumption is that if they had shown promise in Standard 8, we can step forward from there. There is soon consensus amongst the teaching staff that we have to start almost from scratch, particularly in subjects such as mathematics, because the building blocks need to be secure before we can set out for academic success in the final Standard 10 examination. Time is short. We remove the concept of standards and, in its place, we devise two one-year courses for each subject which we labelled M1 and M2 for Matric 1 and Matric 2.

To achieve what we all seek, we have to increase the number of contact hours by insisting on afternoon and Saturday classes. We also introduce a two-hour teacher-controlled homework time for every evening. Because such measures have never been experienced before by our students, they are initially resistant but soon knuckle down when they recognise that we are serious in offering a path to academic success and opportunity.

"All Saints was quite different. The concept of going to class on Saturday! Saturdays you must relax... The big difference was a lot more responsibility; like more critical thinking, so much more space for creativity." (Jayshree Pather)

"Saturday school in the beginning was not very popular. But then you just had the feeling that it was first about education and then the social things were secondary. The first thing was education; that came across very strongly." (Tracey Naledi)

Back row (left to right): Annemarie Cross (Nursing), Belinda Harry (Bursar), John O'Connor (Biology) Noreen Burton (Biology), Shani Grové (Counselling), Anne Thompson (Afrikaans), Sindisile Maclean (Student Liaison), May Swana (isiXhosa)
Middle row: Margot Sennet (Career Guidance), Angela Solomon (Counselling), Cathy Bunn (Mathematics), Penny Hogge (English) Luvuyo Gqili (Mathematics), Hugh McCormack (Technical Drawing), Joan Schmidt (College Secretary), Sheila (Dabs) Haya (House Mother), Priscilla Murugan (History)
Front row: Raj Kurup (Physical Science), Peter King (English), Desmond Cross (Biology), Andrew Stevens (Mathematics), Mike Burton (Principal and Geography), Quentin Hogge (English), Mike Thompson (Physical Science), Elroy Jacobs (Afrikaans), Ivor Pitt (Geography)

I make it clear that at All Saints Senior College we are to offer a two-year matriculation course. In the first year all students can make sure of the building blocks. Those who have already attempted the full course will be in a position to help those who are new to the content material.

For the M1 year we abandon the Standard 9 national syllabus. Instead, each subject teacher has to formulate a first preparation year. This needs careful explanation to the students, some of whom have already been in Standard 10 and will find it demeaning if we insist on calling the first year the Standard 9 year. Being recognised as a repeater is unnecessarily humiliating. Some see going over content again as a backward step, but teachers see it as necessary even if some students have been in Standard 10 before.

We adopt the slogan at the time of *"each one, teach one"*. This gives the older students a boost as they recognise its political significance and assume the role of unofficial tutors. The origin of this call in South Africa comes from the fact that many of the political prisoners on Robben Island, held during apartheid, were illiterate. The inmates used the term, *"each one, teach one"* as a battle cry to ensure everyone in the movement was educated.

In all subjects I insist that the teaching focus should be on questioning, thinking, understanding and problem solving. At the end of the M1 year, all our students should be able to interrogate their subjects in a manner totally new to almost all of them. The majority had come from chalk-and-talk teaching where rote learning of content material without necessarily understanding it was the order of the day. At all times the focus is on attaining excellence in the classroom.

The words of some students who come across an entirely new approach to their learning from what they had experienced in DET rural and township schools are enlightening. They describe the big difference between their previous schooling which uses words like regurgitation of notes and spoon-feeding, writing notes to be read at home.

"The teaching was outcomes based. We came from an environment where we were led by the teacher, now you had to lead yourself." (Zukiswa Jafta)

The new experiences that students find enlightening at All Saints are challenges to think and stretch the imagination. They remark that the teaching is more engaging, dedicated and really capable. Challenge and debate in class is invigorating. A responsibility and onus on the student to study and understand, and the space to learn at their own pace are appreciated. Questions in class are new and are engaging and informative.

"When you raise an issue as a student you can also engage with other students in the class. That is also encouraged. We develop in confidence and we are not shy to voice our opinions. We push ourselves a lot more." (Tenjiwe Qona)

Students feel that the subject matter stretches them and that is quite different from their previous school experiences.

*   *   *

The first books-down student strike at the college comes about because of a misunderstanding of an announcement I make in a morning assembly when I say:

"At All Saints College we teach you how to learn, not only what to learn."

The students are incensed. They believe that this is an insult to their capability. They imagine that I am suggesting they do not know how to learn. The chairman of the Students' Representative Council leads the strike and explains that they take exception to my racist arrogance. It is pleasing to receive a letter several years later from the same person while he is pursuing a successful university career. The letter is an admission that it was because All Saints College staff taught students how to learn – by viewing things critically, solving problems and answering questions, rather than by merely accumulating content knowledge – that he and others are succeeding at university.

The key to our teaching strategy at All Saints College is to set problems for students in all subjects for them to solve. This moves them away from the chalk-and-talk teaching method that encourages rote learning and instead promotes the beginnings of academic discussion and debate.

Regularly, students are seen using their study periods between formal lessons to sit around the campus and engage each other in questioning the lessons they have just received. This is a healthy way to learn. Problem solving is exciting and leads to a much better understanding of the subject matter.

This is not only new for them, but is set at a higher level than they anticipate. Some suspect a deliberate attempt by staff to discredit them, since they have experienced marks in the 80%–90% range in their township and rural schools and yet now are only achieving 40%–50% at All Saints.

For the principal and staff, learning while teaching is a key experience. Students learn from the teachers and teachers learn just as much from the students. It is a two-way encounter. The outcome is that our education path takes us through the specific circumstances of our students and into their world.

In a horribly troubled national educational landscape, All Saints College students achieved arguably the best matriculation results attained in any English second language institution in the country. Over a ten-year period, All Saints College achieved an overall pass rate of 98,5% in the senior certificate examinations of the Joint Matriculation Board and its successor, the Independent Examinations Board, and a 92% university entrance level pass. The students achieved academic excellence way beyond our initial predictions and expectations. Significantly, three leading universities drop their "Swedish points" entrance requirements for All Saints students as our alumni soon prove to be an unprecedented success at tertiary institutions.

In the Swedish points system, used in major universities in South Africa to rank final senior certificate grades, a given number of points are allocated to each grading level. University faculties that require a mathematical foundation, for example commerce, load the points for mathematics grades. In order to gain entry a student's mathematics results are thereby given prominence and a minimum overall total of points in that subject is required.

Because the throughput of All Saints students at tertiary institutions was nearly 100%, these universities confidently invited our students to follow their courses of preference without reference to their matriculation points.

The proof of academic success is mostly found in numbers. Our record at All Saints stood proud.

An article in the Anglo-American publication *Optima* of that period lamented the state of education as reflected in the matriculation results of schools under the Department of Education and Training (DET). The article focused on the all-important mathematics results in the Johannesburg township schools of Soweto and Alexandria. As reported, a total of 1 441 students had written senior certificate mathematics. Of these, only 41 (2,8%) had passed and only 14 (0,9%) achieved a university level pass. This dismal result for mathematics somewhat supports former President Hendrik Verwoerd's infamous statement:

"There is no place for the Bantu in the European community above the level of certain forms of labour. What is the use of teaching the Bantu child mathematics when he cannot use it in practice?"

All Saints Senior College proves the opposite. Andrew Stevens, in charge of mathematics, devises an M1 year which goes right back to the basics in a course we label "Accelerated Mathematics". A key in this one-year course is that students help each other to understand even the earliest primary school concepts so that when they reach the final secondary school year they can cope. They more than cope. They excel. Our students race through lower grade work, and with greater understanding. It is an exciting project and it pays off.

In the same year that the *Optima* publication decries the state of affairs in mathematics in Bantu education, All Saints College enters one hundred students in the Joint Matriculation Board's (JMB) senior certificate examination (which is a step up on the DET examination available to rural and township schools). All one hundred of our students pass and ten achieve distinctions. Anele Mpepo, aged fifteen, is one who achieves a distinction. She goes on to study at the University of the Witwatersrand (Wits),and in her first year is the top student in the Statistics class. She had come from a humble township background. She and the whole All Saints class must have made Hendrik Verwoerd turn in his grave.

Each year about 100 students wrote the Senior Certificate so we can claim that we helped around 985 students to achieve a matriculation pass and 920 to continue with tertiary studies: a proud record, and one that fully justifies our existence as well as our methods of teaching and learning.

The record is all the more remarkable when one considers the workings of the ogive curve on mark attainment in national examinations. The ogive curve is an accepted way of manipulating the raw score marks of an examination so as to maintain a standard from year to year. In simple terms, if an examination is easy in the one year and too many distinctions are recorded, then the ogive curve pulls marks down and vice versa; if the examination is much more difficult then marks are raised.

The All Saints College students mainly speak English as a second language, and this puts them at a language disadvantage with the mainly white students who write the JMB examination from privileged private schools. Afrikaans-speaking schools have their examination papers set in their home language and they answer in their home language but that is not yet so for the black languages. This is a very controversial issue. However, whichever way one looks at it, an examination is a ranking of candidates and consequently our students are at a disadvantage in competition with English first-language candidates. Yet our overall record stands proud throughout.

chapter 15
Tragedies

"Sometimes painful things can teach us lessons that we didn't think we needed to know."

— Anonymous

Students are safe when they are on the campus, but not once they leave our premises, when they become vulnerable. In order to promote physical fitness without the facility of a gymnasium, I devise a jogging challenge, which is called the Four Corners Challenge. A pole is placed at each of the four corners of our property to mark touch points. Competitors can run in any direction but they have to touch each pole and start and finish at the same point.

The ground is uneven with *vlei* (marshy) areas at the bottom of the campus. There is a rocky line along one boundary and the difference between the highest point and the lowest point means some challenging toil. It isn't an easy run. I introduce a grading system for boys and girls and certificates are awarded. The event becomes very popular and every day students are to be seen loping around our property's boundaries.

S'bongile Nabo, a fifteen-year-old first-year student, goes outside our gates in the afternoon after classes and starts jogging with a friend, Nosisa Ngezi, on the side of the road. At about five-thirty in the afternoon I am working in my office when I am hurriedly called by Andrew Stevens to the main road on the corner of our property. Something alarming is happening there. A crowd is gathering around a minibus taxi and S'bongile is lying lifeless at the side of the road. She has been hit by the taxi and she lies crumpled and motionless. Her jogging friend is lying stunned and barely conscious further away in the grass.

A very angry group has gathered, possibly passengers from the taxi. Andrew questions and tries to control the crowd while I lift S'bongile off the roadside and carry her to my Mitsubishi Star Wagon to take her to the nearby Bisho hospital. Despite a faint hope, I fear that I can see that there is no life left in her. The anger of the crowd is directed at the taxi driver who lost control of his vehicle while trying to pass another taxi. The front taxi started to turn to the right without signalling, forcing him off the road and he could not prevent crashing into the two girls. The crowd gives every indication that they are going to lynch him but with my heart in my mouth I leave the scene just hoping that S'bongile can be revived. Andrew is left to care for Nosisa who is semi-conscious but alive, and he drives her off to the hospital in King William's Town.

S'bongile Nabo who lost her young life when a minibus taxi drove into her outside college gates

The Bisho hospital verdict is what I feared most. We have lost S'bongile in tragic circumstances. Back at the college from the hospital, I phone some of her nearby relatives who come to my office within minutes. They advise me that it is best that they take the news to S'bongile's parents and her brother, who is a student at the college. A hush descends on All Saints. Everyone is devastated that one of us, so vibrant this morning, is no longer alive this afternoon.

Later, a group of teachers and I visit S'bongile's parents at their home in Alice (now eDikeni) and we read a Bible passage and pray together with the family. At the funeral service held at the University of Fort Hare, our All Saints College choir sings and I give an address to a huge gathering. It is a very depressing occasion.

One very telling moment is shared with Nosisa Ngezi, her jogging partner, when she is recovering in hospital. She has been lucky to have survived the full force of a direct impact because she was on the outside of S'bongile, but she was nevertheless injured as she rolled off into the bush. Nosisa remarks when her tutor, Raj Kurup, and I visit her:

"But you really care!"

This simple statement speaks volumes about our relationships at All Saints College. Nosisa goes on to explain that the consensus student perception is that the staff do not really have the interests of the students at heart. Students think that our commitment is to the college and not to the them as people with their own particular needs. The damage that apartheid has done to the people of this country means that suspicion is very deeply entrenched and we must recognise the fact that every year the teaching staff will go through a period of scrutiny and distrust.

*   *   *

Kedibone Maepa comes to All Saints from Soweto aged sixteen. She is a special girl with such a wonderfully free and infectious spirit that she is liked by everyone. I have looked forward to her appearance at the college as she has already stamped her mark as a confident young leader even before her arrival on the campus. The occasion where she did this was at the beginning of the year at a special meeting in Soweto.

Kedibone Mayepa who was a victim of a serial killer soon after leaving All Saints College

At the start of each year, I travelled to Johannesburg because many of our students came from there. The intention of such visits was to meet new students and their families before the first term started. I had recognised that taking time to interface with families beforehand is important and I accepted that they would otherwise find it very difficult to come to Bisho in the Ciskei. We all needed to develop an early sense of mutual trust and connection. The venue was a church hall in Soweto and I would make a presentation about our college and then answer questions that followed. I also used the opportunity to distribute our handbook and invite comments concerning its contents as I led them through it. In this way, all would have a chance to suggest changes and to embrace our way of doing things.

When I arrive at the large hall, I am ushered onto the stage, which is furnished with a table and a few chairs and invited to sit down. Everyone else in the room is seated as an audience below. A pastor in the hall opens proceedings with a prayer and this is followed by a hymn, sung with beautiful harmonies. Then I am left alone on stage to make a start. I call for someone to come up and join me so as to chair the meeting's proceedings. No one volunteers and there is an eerie silence as I wait. So, I call for a parent to step up but still no one moves. After a few embarrassing moments, suddenly a hand goes up and this smiling young girl calls out clearly:

"I will do it!"

It is Kedibone Maepa. She clambers up onto the stage, and sits beside me with an infectious smile. How well she controls the proceedings! She handles the question-and-answer session like a seasoned professional. I learn later that it is a spur-of-the-moment decision on her part – she has never before taken on such a task on a stage, and with adults as the audience. Once she is in charge, she does marvellously well. I just have to conclude the meeting with a few words about how we really look forward to receiving students like her at our college. She shows so much promise.

At All Saints, Kedibone passes her Joint Matriculation Board final examination without distinction but her mark at the college is one of *joie de vivre*. Her presence has been a breath of fresh air at a time when South Africa is in turmoil and even on our campus uncomfortable currents are flowing from time to time.

Two years after graduating from All Saints her life is cruelly ripped away from her. Kedibone is the fifth victim of the notorious serial killer and rapist Lazarus Mazingane. She is just twenty years old. She is raped and strangled. Her body was dumped to be found later near the intersection of Spencer and Main Reef roads at Roodepoort, quite far away from the safety of her home.

I am alerted to the heartbreaking news of Kedibone's death soon after it happens and am so struck by the tragedy that I phone her mother, who invites me to visit them in Soweto. The subdued gathering at the Maepa home welcomes me and I am asked to say a few words to the assembled group of mourners. I start by recalling my first meeting with Kedibone; how she took charge of the situation when others all hung back in the church hall in Soweto just four years earlier. I cannot finish what I want to say as I get uncontrollably choked up, start to sob and cannot say another word.

The tragedy is incomprehensible and beyond my ability to put emotions into words. I feel that I am failing the family but I can see by their reactions that we all need to weep together. That is what we do as Kedibone has been so close to all of our hearts.

*   *   *

A most unpalatable and repulsive event surfaces after our mid-year school holiday when four girls come to my office to report something to me. They look very distressed as they bring a friend along with them. Apparently, they found out that the girl was pregnant just before the holiday. They tell me that they made a pact then and they agreed not to disclose this if the friend gave birth at her home during the holiday and did not return to All Saints afterwards. And yet here she is back again. I must please make a decision because the girl is here.

After long and careful questioning, I discover to my horror that the girl had induced herself and given birth to a child without assistance in her room at the college residence just before going home for the holiday. She put the baby into a plastic packet. Dead or alive? She then went home for a month's holiday with her family who were therefore none the wiser of the happening. At the start of the term the stench in her room is so offensive that no cleaner is prepared to go into the room during the holiday. When the student gets back, she gathers the packet and furtively buries the evidence at the bottom of the property and claims that the smell in her room is from a dead rat. It is so awful that it has permeated the whole residence.

I tell the group that we all now have knowledge of a criminal act and that there is only one course of action before us. We have to go to the police and make a formal report or else we will all be implicated in this tragic affair. The Ciskei Magistrates' Court finds her guilty of disposing of an unwanted child and she is given a suspended jail sentence. As required by the court I remove her from the college by personally escorting her home to her family in Soweto. But when I arrive there, the reception that I receive from the family is unexpectedly antagonistic. Then I realise that they have been unaware of her pregnancy and it is a shock for them to hear from me why I have brought her home. They do not believe me as the girl says openly that I am lying to them. She claims that there is no evidence of what I am saying. However, I have brought with me the official ruling from the Ciskeian magistrate and I show it to them. No argument, they have it in front of them in black and white in an official document. Yet, despite the suspended jail sentence hanging over her, they still seem to claim that she has done nothing wrong and insist that I take her back to school with me. I tell them that unfortunately such a decision is beyond my jurisdiction and I am bound by the ruling of the court to remove her from the college.

There is nothing I can do further so I leave the house with voices angrily hastening my departure.

*   *   *

A series of increasingly nightmarish events unfolded around Simon Lamont, our newly appointed Estate Manager. At his appointment interview he describes himself as a rolling stone who wants to settle down. He has two young sons from his marriage and is due to take custody of them as part of divorce proceedings. He is now engaged to a girl who works at the Amatola Sun just up the road from our college. He wants to settle down from his previous maverick lifestyle and put his life together.

Simon really puts his back into the work on the campus and I am pleased I appointed him after my unfortunate experience with his predecessor, Japie. Under his management, the campus ground staff are soon making a positive difference to the maintenance and look of the college. Then, after a long weekend holiday visit from his sons who are soon to move in to live with him, Simon is to face horrendous news and I am the one who has to inform him. His new fiancée and his two little boys have all been killed in a head-on car crash caused by the blinding smoke from a veld fire. They were on their way home to Natal after spending the weekend visiting him. Simon is devastated. The grief is just too overwhelming for him to absorb.

He leaves the college for a while to attend to the funeral arrangements with his estranged former wife. He leaves his house at the bottom of the grounds on our campus locked but unattended. Soon afterwards I receive a report that a window has been broken at the house. I fear that a break-in burglary will compound Simon's problems to breaking point, so I ask the teaching staff if anyone is prepared to volunteer to house sit and safeguard Simon's possessions while he is away.

A newly appointed bachelor on the staff, Leon Snyman, volunteers and we are all grateful for his offer. Leon does not come to classes the next day. Two of us go down to the house but he is nowhere to be seen. After he has gone AWOL and missed his teaching for two days, we check the house carefully and find that almost all of Simon's liquor has been drunk. Simon is typical of many former Rhdoesians, very proud of his bar with all its collectibles and mementos and a variety of beverages. It is apparent that the alcohol has been consumed by Leon and the place is in a mess with empty bottles strewn all over the lounge area. It is an appalling situation, as he has obviously held a party in Simon's house. He then disappears altogether on a month-long drinking binge. During this time, he invites schoolgirls from nearby Breidbach to join in his binge. As a consequence, I have to handle public telephone calls of concern and complaint that a teacher from All Saints College is taking under-age girls out at all hours of the night.

This is a nightmare, and it is getting worse. We cannot track Leon down and I fear that Simon will find his home devastated on his return. After collecting a few staff members we do the best we can to clean up the house and replace the liquor that was removed and consumed.

A month later, all unshaven and downcast, Leon returns to my office, repentant and pleading for a second chance. This begging is accompanied by members of his family appealing for clemency. It is especially difficult for me to handle as they all put pressure on me to allow Leon to return to his teaching post. It is a miserable situation and I know that my greater responsibility is to the school community. When it looks like I am not going to give way to their appealing, I face the accusation:

"Call yourself a Christian… and you have no compassion for someone in need!"

I know that I must remain steadfast. All respect for Leon has been lost. Everyone at All Saints is aware of what has happened and I cannot give him a second chance. Leon has reached rock bottom and now he has to pick up his life without any help from me. He has to be dismissed summarily.

When I had initially appointed him to the All Saints College staff, I was aware that he was the brightest student at the University of the Western Cape (UWC) in his time. It was therefore no real surprise to find that after his alcoholic walkabout, he proved to have the capacity to pull his life together. He successfully researched for and gained a PhD, became a leader in the Alcoholics Anonymous movement, married and started a family.

Leon later becomes the Chief Education Officer for King William's Town and from this position it is an irony that he becomes the Department of Education's appointee to sit on the All Saints College Board of Trustees. In a roundabout sort of twist of fate, he thereby as a trustee is someone to whom I am accountable. It is then that he comes to me to tell me that I saved his life in not giving in to him when he wept and asked for a second chance in his job. He had needed to reach the lowest point in his addiction before turning his life around. If I had accepted him back, he says, he has no doubt he would have continued with his alcoholic problem.

*   *   *

After the funeral Simon Lamont returned to All Saints, but not for long. The rolling stone was still within him and it had gathered momentum. He needed to get away, to travel without a planned destination, just to escape.

Several years later I received a letter from him all the way from Canada where he said that he was working in a travelling circus. His job was to walk around with a large bucket and spade behind the elephants. Simon then found a travelling partner with whom he bonded. They travelled the world and eventually landed up in Australia. The couple settled happily and have two sons from their marriage.

chapter 16
Safety

"We all need somewhere where we feel safe."

— Emma Thompson

MOST OF THE TIME we feel secure. But it is a time of state-declared emergency in South Africa and anything could happen, as we are beyond the reach of the tentacles of the South African Defence Force. One morning I have just finished teaching a lesson and as I walk through the foyer, I see an unsavoury looking character lounging back in a chair with his forefinger buried up one nostril. I ask him if he is OK, and if I can be of help. With a surly expression he mumbles out that he is feeling sick and he has come to see Mr Tengimfene.

Ben Tengimfene is our Dean of Students and isiXhosa teacher. He has formerly been the Principal of Mzomhle High School in Mdantsane and then Director General of Education in the Ciskei. He is an imposing and well-respected figure in the community and on our staff.

A moment later Ben walks into the foyer. The man's illness suddenly disappears and together with others who have been waiting outside he bursts into action and confronts Ben. While they are leading Ben away, I try to ask the group what is going on and am told that they are security police and to keep my distance or they will take me away too. They have come to arrest Ben and I should stand aside. Ben warns me to keep out of it as there is nothing I can do. He is detained for three weeks and later successfully sues the Government for wrongful arrest.

In the early afternoon on the same day as Ben's arrest, our afternoon classes are suddenly disrupted when a shattering sound of automatic rifle fire breaks out. It is clear that this is happening right on our property.

I locate the flash-point at the lower part of our campus just beyond the residences. Clearly it is my responsibility to investigate. I hurriedly clamber onto my small Suzuki scooter and putter off on bumpy footpaths in the direction of the firing, my trepidation growing with my winding progress. Student spectators gather on the veranda of the administration block looking out at the lower campus and follow my progress. A thought strikes me that I am a bit like the eponymous Don Quixote tilting at windmills. I have no idea what I will find or what I will do when I find it. Could my weaving progress along the grassland pathways towards the rattling gunfire even be the last trip of my life? I have a flashback sensation to my Rhodesian bush war experience when our school was attacked by automatic rifle fire. There is sporadic shooting after the earlier burst of gunfire, so there is still an unknown threat somewhere on our property.

What I find when I reach our boundary fence is an armoured Defence Force casspir vehicle parked below the residences on our property. Nearby, a number of men dressed in civvies are shooting with AK-47 automatic rifles from within our property at targets that have been set up inside our fence line. Is this some form of provocation? I walk up to the nearest of them and ask for the person in charge. I am directed to a small belligerent looking man holding an AK-47. I ask him for his name and make a point of recording with a small battery-operated recorder which I hold up while asking him what he thinks they are doing.

"We are shooting at targets – can't you see?"

"But this is private property. It is a school!"

"Ag, school – this is Ciskei!"

I inform him in what I hope is my most confident voice that I am going to report him to Ciskei's President Lennox Sebe if he is not off our property by the time I get back to my office. I actually have no idea how to contact Sebe, but I make an authoritative about turn on my scooter and ride off hoping that I am not going to be a moving target for them to fire at.

As I ride up towards the admin block, the casspir surreptitiously makes its way off the property along the bottom fence line. The group of semi-military trespassers has packed up the targets and made a beeline for the exit gate. Not seeing this happening behind me, I arrive at my office to tumultuous applause and a hero's welcome from the students – David and Goliath re-enacted.

We never get to the bottom of this invasion of our campus and disregard for our privacy. I am convinced that it is linked to Ben Tengimfene's arrest earlier in the day and that someone is flexing muscles to intimidate us. It is unnerving to think that they moved so easily onto our property and put us at risk.

*   *   *

Then, a short time later during the matriculation examination period, a South African Defence Force helicopter decked in camouflage disrupts proceedings for nearly twenty minutes as it circles noisily over our property and eventually lands fifty metres from our arts block. The occupants who alight are senior Defence Force officers of the apartheid regime in full regalia, displaying uniforms and medals.

Again, it is my responsibility to accost them and to find out what is going on. The exchange is not cordial and I have to warn them off the property. I am more confident in my aggressive approach this time as I do not see any firearms held by the invaders and an attack is not imminent. As a consequence of this provocative display, however, none of us at All Saints ever feel really secure. To us, unannounced intrusions onto our property by military personnel are acts of provocation. There is a sense of foreboding as we are clearly very vulnerable and unprepared to meet any incursion. Why would security personnel in military vehicles come onto our school property?

*   *   *

The apartheid-driven political enigma that surrounds All Saints impacts on us in a number of different ways. We are not living in a normal place in a normal time, even by South-African standards. Our environment is fraught with apprehension. The bizarre geographical and political situation of the time is clearly illustrated with the criss-cross of roads on our borders. The citizens of King William's Town, seven kilometres away from our gates, have voted to remain a part of South Africa embedded within Ciskei and not to be part of the Ciskei state. Every road out of King William's Town in every direction has a border post within five kilometres. The road corridor to East London is a parody of the air corridor that separated East and West Germany during the Cold War era. The road between Zwelitsha and Bisho, both located in Ciskei, crosses at right angles over this road corridor by means of a bridge. This provides an absurdly paradoxical situation which I use as a conundrum to puzzle geography classes.

"How do you map one country crossing over another at right angles by means of a bridge?"

Imagine the insurance and legal confusion if an accident happens on the bridge and a car plummets over the edge from one country into another. I am sure that nowhere else in the world can this anomaly be found.

*   *   *

We know about and are intimidated by the Ciskeian security forces who operate random aggressive road blocks all around us. It is still fresh knowledge about the shooting at the nuns, one of whom was thus murdered, when they unknowingly drove through a road block.

The first time I am personally confronted at a Ciskeian security force road block is during a late afternoon return from Grahamstown with four students in my car. We are returning from a Science Expo and the four have won medals for their investigative marine geomorphology project on the Cove Rocks structure just outside East London. This holds no sway with the armed guards. We have to disembark and the car is searched thoroughly. I am made to stretch my arms across the top of the vehicle and am frisked from top to toe. The political difficulty is that three of our four students come from Soweto in Johannesburg and thus are not isiXhosa speakers. We are in hot water because we seem to fit the stereotypical revolutionary anarchist profile – a white adult with youth from Soweto. It takes some careful explanation in isiXhosa by our only local student, Khanyisa Qangule, to clear the air. After a long and anxious wait, we are eventually allowed to continue on our way with just a few insults hurled at us.

*　　*　　*

On another occasion one of our girls, Nombeko Makwela, receives the tragic news that her brother in Cape Town has died. She naturally wants to go home to mourn with her family as soon as she can. This means a short drive to Blaney station just ten kilometres from All Saints College, and around dusk I collect her to take her to catch the train. Two of her friends ask if they can come with us to offer support and, naturally, I agree.

On the way we come upon the inevitable Defence Force casspir blocking the road. Once again, our car's occupant profile appears to be suspicious to the military road blockers. What is a white guy doing with three young black girls in his car? The road blockers do not accept my explanation and are making ready at gun point to detain me. We are anxious because the train through Blaney does not wait long at the siding and it looks as if Nombeko might miss the connection. Fortunately, Nonthuthuzelo Mkungwana can explain the situation in the vernacular and so they reluctantly let us proceed, but it is clear from their mumblings that they are unsure and disgruntled.

It is not the end of the incident.

The train rumbles into the siding as we arrive and Nombeko catches the train only just in time. Now we have to return by the same route past the casspir road block once more. Again, the reception is confrontational and aggressive, with weapons at the ready. Again I prepare myself to be detained. This time the Ciskeian Defence Force personnel manning the road block become even more obstinate and do not want to let us through.

"What have you done with the other girl?"

Again, I suffer the indignity of having to step out of the driving seat and place my arms over the roof of the car while they frisk me and search the boot and interior of the car. Eventually, after a lot of needless explanation, we are allowed to proceed. The absurdity of the situation is that, even though I point out the silhouette of the All Saints College buildings which are visible from where we are being held up, it takes a long time for them to acknowledge that as our destination.

*   *   *

The premise of apartheid is one of racial difference. Separation of people is based on race with many specious tests such as the infamous pencil and hair test, a method of assessing whether a person has ethnic-textured *hair or not*. In the pencil *test*, a pencil is pushed through the person's *hair*. How easily it can be withdrawn from the hair determines whether the person has qualified as white or black. It is a spurious yardstick, without any scientific proof that it is in any way valid, and yet it is partially responsible for splitting existing communities and families along perceived racial lines.

All Saints College declares itself to be a non-racial, not a multi-racial, institution. The difference is fundamental. An organisation claiming to be multi-racial nevertheless recognises the differences between people according to their race. Non-racialism however denies race as a scientific or social category. Embracing different racial realities is to acknowledge and integrate different South African experiences.

While we espouse non-racialism at All Saints, it is difficult to say whether we are all non-racial in practice. By far the majority of those students who are drawn from disadvantaged communities are black. In fact, white students who apply for places have to be carefully scrutinised before we accept them, as we did not want students who have been turned out of their earlier, usually privileged, educational backgrounds. Why would they want to leave that schooling to join us? Reflecting on the day-to-day relationships around Jaime Knott, one of our very few white male students, fellow student Tando Bonga writes:

Jaime left us because we could not accept him, a very lovely guy I must say, with a beautiful personality. His mother had struggle credentials. But we could not accept him or he was not accepted the way he should have been accepted, the way I accept my

Tswana cousins, my Sotho brothers, and so forth. I guess that was the only real blot that we came across. There was the other lady from England, she was in '91. And they left a black mark at All Saints, that was a black mark on the history of All Saints..."

Jaime's mother records:

"I understand that Jaime was elected onto the SRC at All Saints, but members called him an impimpi *[collaborator] when violence broke out at the school.*

Jaime did not want to be at the school and he felt angry being branded an impimpi. *The students who spoke to me tried to persuade me to change my mind. They said that the school could not be called 'non-racial' if no white students attended it. I suggested the entire SRC should have thought of that beforehand."*

At a LEAF strategic planning meeting, Noreen Burton presents her observation that "non-racial" is taken by our students to mean that while anybody can apply and be accepted by the governing council, only black and selected coloured students are acceptable to the student body. The intimidation and threats of violence against white and Indian students seem to bear this out. She also notes that there are continual accusations against white staff members from certain students who show a belligerent attitude at times when they do not get their own way.

It is inevitable that clashes of culture, political understanding and misunderstanding will lead to conflict, which carries with it insurrection, threats and anarchy. My challenge is to work out how I am going to handle all of them.

part four

THE TIGHTROPE IS SHAKEN

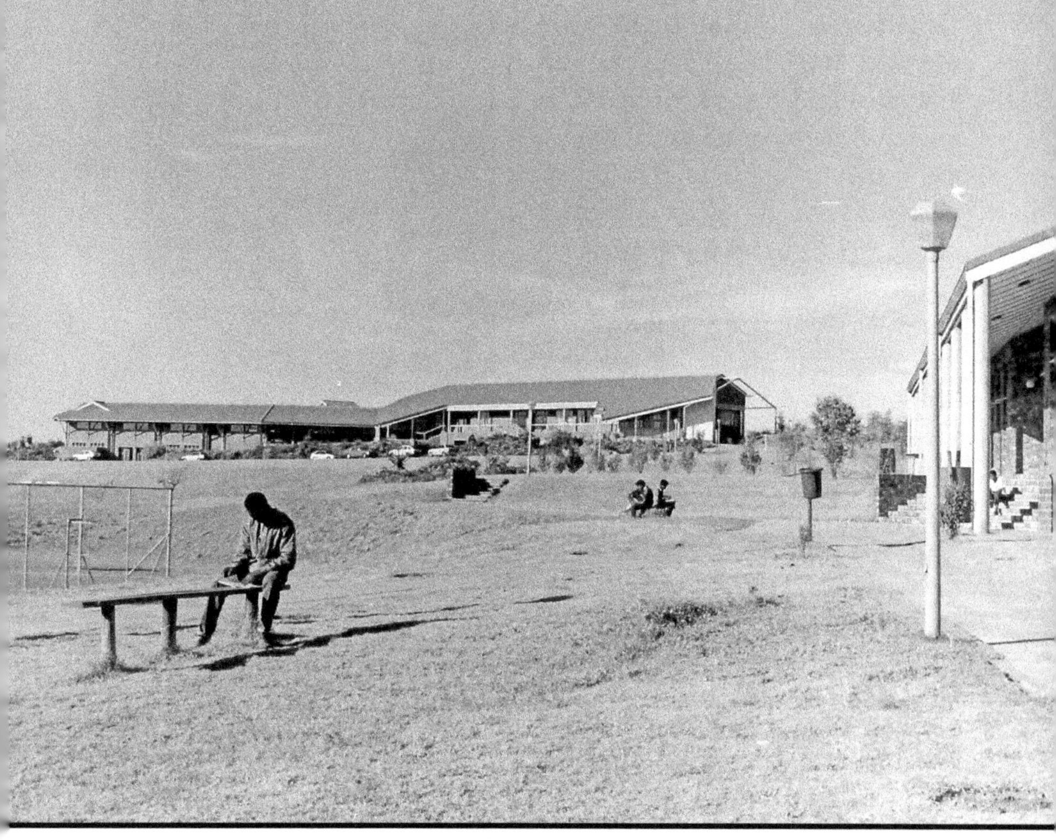

chapter 17
Guidance

"A fool despises good counsel, but a wise man takes it to heart."

— Confucius

I N HANDLING THE CHALLENGES that confront me, I am indebted to people of tremendous stature who help guide me along the precarious journey across the apartheid divide. They are my mentors in every possible positive meaning of this role, helping me to understand and embrace what is on the other side.

Dr Franklin Sonn is chairman of the All Saints Trust at a time when we most need a prominent and influential leader at the helm. He is a man of deep integrity. Franklin is the person who makes the biggest contribution to and impact on me and my attempt to navigate the All Saints journey, as both guide and mentor in the early days of my principalship. As a celebrated educational academic and leading community figure in the Western Cape, he is widely regarded as one of the stalwarts in the fight against apartheid education, and in keeping alive the vision of a democratic future. He is known for his strong organisational abilities as well as for

Dr Franklin Sonn, a Chairman of the All Saints College Trust whose footprint on the development of the college and its people was immeasurable

leading peaceful public protest marches and sharing platforms with, amongst others, Professor Jakes Gerwel and Archbishop Desmond Tutu. He lives and embodies his philosophy of fighting for justice, freedom and equality in the face of serious odds from the apartheid establishment. During the student strikes in the Western Cape, he faces rubber bullets, teargas and detention, not only as a mark of solidarity with the cause of the students but also to protect his staff and students.

Franklin shepherds me from having a naive lack of awareness of the currents of struggle politics towards an understanding of the steps necessary to position the college as an institution with a meaningful anti-apartheid contribution to make. Franklin puts me in touch with prominent leadership figures who play an important part in the liaison between the students and me when the road becomes rocky. He leads me down a focused path and weighs in with his full support at each step I take. This angers Richard Todd, who feels I am straying from *his* path and that I should restrict my leadership and management of All Saints College by staying neutral, and having accountability directly to himself and the Board of Trustees, rather than to leaders in the struggle, the community, or the students and their parents.

The road that I follow rankles with Richard but I feel that it is the only way that I can hold onto the vision and broker the college's successful academic (and struggle) footprint. Richard is angry because he thinks that I am handing the management of his project over to people unknown to him instead of keeping it in-house. He also thinks that I am losing the control that he needs for continued funding for the growth of his vision.

Yet Franklin Sonn is for me the most valued influence during my term as principal of All Saints College. There is no doubt that it is he who holds the tiller that directs my path when the going gets tough and I am in danger of losing direction. Franklin keeps me aware of the political currents that threaten to subvert our educational mission. He would later write:

"What to do with the 'lost generation' was the question that tormented many during those heady years of struggle for a new and better society.

It was a time of sacrifice for a big cause yet the continuous loss of young lives could somehow not go unchallenged. A way had to be found to salvage and nurture our best talent in the townships while keeping their revolutionary zeal alive. Some of us were convinced that when the inevitable freedom comes, educated young people would be needed to lay claim to our victories and help to take our country forward.

It was a very difficult dichotomy but equally compelling. Richard Todd not only spawned the idea of All Saints but he immediately decided to sacrifice his position as principal of the prestigious Hilton College and started assembling a few of us and commenced his hunt for funding.

With the support of a handful of highly respected leaders like Ronnie Napier, the late Mike O'Dowd and Ken Hartshorne as well as the help of the Anglo American Chairman's Fund, the idea became a reality in the old Ciskei, which was the only place where a non-racial school could be established.

A band of outstanding and visionary teachers was found and came to live on the school grounds at Bisho. Michael Burton, a Rhodes Scholar, came highly recommended as the second headmaster of the school. None of us realised what kind of storms would be precipitated by the countervailing forces wanting to participate in the struggle as an end in itself and the desire for education as a means to an end. Similarly, to be understood when political struggle and public demonstrations at times had been included almost as part of the school programme.

The redoubtable hardiness, sensitive heart and deep convictions of Mike led him to find his own unique way of achieving all three objectives and in the main to remain academically excellent.

In some way, I was very privileged to play a part as chair of the school governing council and member of the central committee for LEAF schools in Johannesburg. I truly cherish the memory of the times I had to leave the turmoil on my own campus, the Peninsula Technikon, to travel hurriedly to Bisho to address students and convince them of the correctness of their choice and to assure them that when the prize was finally won, they would be leaders of the new democracy as it happily turned out to be.

Mike Burton's leadership must truly be remembered as one of the markers on the course of doing at times the impossible, viz to teach excellently as well as to struggle with conviction."

Franklin furthermore wrote in one of his publications:

"Someone once said that education is the handmaiden of the political force which wields power at the time. If this is true it stands to reason that those opposed to a particular government in power would tend also to use education to advance their cause. For that reason, education has always been and always will be politicised."

The mid-1980s is a time in South Africa's history when gutter education is actively rejected by young South Africans who are denied so much because of their racial classification. As a non-racial college, All Saints is clearly established in resistance and defiance to apartheid's rules. However, my experience and understanding of politicised education is nil. I am appointed to lead the initiative and I need a guiding influence. Franklin is that guide, a great friend and my inspirational mentor who walks every step with me.

Our initial meeting has an amusing side to it. When I have my very first meeting with him his opening words are:

"Congratulations, I am so glad that you have been appointed because this post does not need an ex-Rhodesian or someone from Oxford University!"

… and my reply?

"Thank you, Franklin. Well actually I am both an ex-Rhodesian and someone from Oxford University."

Apart from the amusing and perhaps embarrassing angles of this first exchange, Franklin's allusion to two stereotypes is valid and insightful because the All Saints initiative is not going to be typical of any of South Africa's leading private schools, most of which have invited Zimbabweans or Britons as principals. All Saints could not be like this or a place that is insensitive to the cries of the majority.

I reflect that perhaps it is for this very reason that Richard Todd's private school association had earmarked me as that kind of headmaster that was being attracted to lead top private schools in South Africa. He could sell my Oxford connection to funders.

Franklin Sonn's assessment of the situation that I will be facing makes a very big impression on me. He says that, as principal of All Saints Senior College, I have a unique opportunity to bring two completely different human paradigms together. The challenge is to bring the best out of each and not succumb to and become a victim of the worst of each. The western, white, European, call-it-what-you-will approach, is a results-orientated approach. In general, for the schooling and the culture of this paradigm, the focus is on the what, or the achievement of results. The boss will say about a proposal:

"We don't have time to go through the whole thing just give me the bottom line and let's make a decision."

The other, the African or black approach, however, is process orientated. The focus is on how an outcome is achieved. The African tradition has the whole community sitting under a tree, working together towards a consensus decision.

Process-orientated decision making may test a westerner's patience to the nth degree because it affords everyone an opportunity to participate. This stretches the time needed to resolve any issue. Its big advantage, however, is that every person owns the decision and everyone is accountable and responsible to see that it works. Buy-in is one hundred percent.

Alternatively, the advantage of results orientated decision making is that it is efficient, but this is outweighed by the responsibility not being shared, and too many then reserve the right to stand on the sidelines and criticise those left with the responsibility of playing the game.

My All Saints story is an account of how I respond to his advice. As both friend and mentor, Franklin helps me find answers to vexing problems and situations, both directly and indirectly, by connecting me with relevant leadership. I am personally transformed by exposure in the resistance environment to situations previously off my radar both on and off the All Saints College campus.

He gives me two of his publications and he writes a personal message in each:

"Mike – a good friend. We need each other as we move together into uncharted seas. Our faith provides us with no guarantees except faith itself." Franklin (18.6.88)

The cover of a publication by Franklin Sonn with a cover picture of him leading a protest march with Archbishop Desmond Tutu and academic Dr Jakes Gerwel together with a personal note to Mike Burton

In line with international icons of struggle such as Mahatma Gandhi and Martin Luther King Jr, Franklin Sonn sets an example of how to seize the moral high ground against the apartheid stranglehold and this becomes extremely important to me. Perhaps Franklin's words, *"It still remains true that many shout for change, but few work for it"*, sum up my All Saints story: I become an activist for change, a cog in the transformation machinery. I am not a shouter but I walk the walk and do not just talk the talk. It is a big step on the tightrope journey. It involves crossing a line, or a point of no return.

A colossus in the education arena of the struggle, Franklin Sonn is eventually rewarded by being asked to be South Africa's first ambassador to the United States of America in Nelson Mandela's democratic government.

I treasure our many telephone conversations and the times I spend at his home while he generously gives his time and counsel to me. To Franklin I owe so much.

*   *   *

In 1988, Franklin Sonn introduces me to Mluleki George. He comes to be my on-site confidant, since Franklin is a thousand kilometres away in Cape Town. These are the days before cell-phone and e-mail communication. Mluleki George becomes the single most influential local sounding board and counsellor for me during my time as principal of All Saints College.

120

At the time he is Director of Human Resources at the nearby Kei Brick Company. Whenever I meet a challenge that is not pedagogical, and that I think is insurmountable, I take leave of the college and drive to his office at Kei Bricks, situated about ten kilometres away and just beyond Zwelitsha township. He always finds time for me and receives me graciously. As I discuss the matter in hand with Mluleki, never once does he give me the impression that I am unnecessarily taking up his time. He considers the situation carefully before weighing in with any advice.

I am really privileged to be able to share my concerns with a man of such political nous and stature. His struggle credentials are out of the top drawer, and include his arrest in 1976 and sentencing to five years imprisonment on Robben Island in 1978 as a political prisoner. Since his release he has taken a leading role in building anti-apartheid structures. He is a founder member of the United Democratic Front (UDF), formed in 1983, and a founder member of the National Sports Congress, formed in 1988 as well as a founder and executive member of the National Olympic Committee of South Africa.

Besides his advice and counsel, Mluleki George grooms me to take on issues of sports unity in the lead-up to the new post-apartheid South Africa. The apartheid regime had long recognised that sport was its Achilles heel, as it gave international exposure and legitimacy to the struggle. Consequently, in the mid-1980s this is dangerous terrain to tread, and I need Mluleki George's astute guidance. He is the president of the Border Rugby Union and is to become the president of the Rugby Union on the Border South African Rugby Board from 1986 to 1991. He is also to become vice president of South African Rugby Football Union (SARFU) from 1993 until 1998.

*   *   *

Lex Mpati's story is remarkable and inspiring: from petrol pump attendant at the old garage in Beaufort Street, then a bartender in Grahamstown, to President of the Supreme Court of Appeal, and Chancellor of Rhodes University. He had started his law degree at Rhodes in 1979 at the age of 30, paying his first year fees from his earnings as a bartender. Admitted as an attorney in February 1989, he worked as an advocate on his own from his chambers in Grahamstown until 1993, when he took up the post of in-house counsel at the Legal Resources Centre and immersed himself in human rights work in the Eastern Cape.

I had known Lex Mpati before coming to All Saints. He had been on the same South African Committee for Higher Education (Sached) committee that I had chaired in Grahamstown during my teaching days at Kingswood College.

Together we had been involved in empowering teachers from the adjoining Rhini township by providing them with an opportunity to matriculate. Most had only a Standard 8 pass.

In 1988 I meet up with Lex Mpati again when he accompanies Mluleki George onto the All Saints College campus at the request of Franklin Sonn. As a trustee of All Saints (1989–1996) Lex also becomes an influencer in my career.

*   *   *

In 1988 I recognise that the students at All Saints who come from the Reef do not respect or want to listen to the local Xhosa leaders, so I ask Vioreti Nkosi who should I visit in Johannesburg if I wish to connect with relevant leadership there, to share our story. I am given the names of Eric Molobi and Murphy Morobe. I meet them both.

At this time, Eric Molobi can be described as small, soft-spoken and an unlikely revolutionary. He listens carefully to my presentation and immediately offers his support whenever I might need it.

Eric had spent much of his youth as a political prisoner on Robben Island. The business he had formerly established was regarded as pioneering because its main aim was the creation of funds for projects that benefitted poor people. It was only when he had called at the local trade union offices that he had discovered it was illegal to employ black people in a skilled capacity. In the eyes of the law, all black people were labourers. As a result of meeting members of the banned ANC in Botswana, an offence under the South African Terrorism Act, he had been detained, tortured by the security police, and sentenced to 11 years on Robben Island.

The then European Commission had set up the Kagiso (peace) Trust to fund the development of black South Africans. Archbishop Desmond Tutu and another prominent anti-apartheid cleric, Beyers Naude, had been appointed trustees in the hope that churchmen would ensure that the money was properly used. Eric Molobi had become the administrator, presiding over the disbursement of hundreds of thousands of pounds.

Eric is passionate about the future of the country's young people and plays a major role in trying to address educational needs. In 1985 he had been instrumental in forming the National Education Crisis Committee (NECC), formed with the aim of addressing school boycotts as well as the breakdown of the culture of learning in Bantu Education schools. The NECC was spearheading the idea of People's Education to create equal opportunities for advancement, to advocate non-discrimination, and to fulfil the social, economic and development needs of South African society.

On a number of occasions, my friendship with Eric helps me to resolve confrontational situations with students that arise from time to time on our campus.

*   *   *

In 1990 it is clear to both Mluleki George and me that we need a resident influencer on the campus, someone who can interface with students so as to subdue any uprisings and misunderstandings, through engagement and debate with the students before their emotions get out of hand.

Mluleki finds just the right person to be this catalyst, Sindisile Maclean. At this time Sindisile is regional secretary of the Border African National Congress (which of course is still banned). I believe he is someone the students will naturally respect and, to a large extent, that proves to be the case when Sindisile takes up accommodation in the residence as our student liaison officer. However, student politics are so complicated at the time. Some students affiliated to the youth wings of the Pan Africa Congress (PAC) known as the Pan African Students Organisation (PASO) and the Azanian Peoples Organisation (AZAPO) known as the Azanian Students Organisation (AZASO) did not recognise Sindisile as their leader. They formed a hostile element within the student body. Nevertheless, on many occasions during his first two years in residence Sindisile is able to help quell flash points on campus before they explode.

We have a wonderful jocular relationship and whenever we greet each other, no matter the time of day, it is with the words "good night". On the serious side of things, he is a supportive right-hand man who helps me to face and overcome a number of dangerous scenarios that regularly flare up between students and me. Since I represent the authority ("oppressor") figure against which they can vent their frustrations and issues, Sindisile's role as a pacifier is invaluable to me.

*   *   *

Smuts Ngonyama is another prominent leader with whom I regularly seek solace. He is working in the offices of the Border Council of Churches in Buffalo Street, King William's Town, just seven kilometres from the All Saints campus. It is a space that is regularly under surveillance by the South African defence forces as they recognise it as a place of potential subversion. Visiting Smuts was therefore stepping into a danger zone. In fact, at times in the years that follow, I receive threatening phone calls in the evenings while at home.

"Hey, Mike. We know you and George and Smuts. We are going to get you."

These are dangerous times and things are becoming heated. Franklin Sonn outlines the serious need of security measures for protecting the principal of the college at a meeting of the Board of Trustees. He points out that the campus is very dark after sunset. He proposes a thorough investigation into providing appropriate safety measures for me and my family as we appear to be very vulnerable living on an open campus and away from the main building complex.

Smuts is a good friend and he too gives wise counsel when it comes to student affairs and in helping me to come to terms with the political currents of this loaded time. Smuts stands by me when our peaceful protest in 1989 is attacked by baton-wielding police. He joins me and the student representatives in the delegation that drives to Dale College to seek peace.

We also walk the same path as sport moves into a phase of unification at the first ever national non-racial schools' sports event at the Bisho stadium in April 1990. We share the podium and together address the gathering of thousands.

Working closely with Franklin Sonn, Mluleki George, Sindisile Maclean, and Smuts Ngonyama is important to me, if I want to nail my colours to the anti-apartheid movement and carry the students along with me in recognising that All Saints Senior College not only claims behind closed doors to be part of the movement, but is stepping out in proclaiming resistance.

Nowhere in my job description does it require me to step into the danger zone. In fact, my doing so draws the wrath of the director, Richard Todd, who unfairly calls me an absentee headmaster more interested in off-campus activities than in keeping a politically neutral stance.

* * *

To gain an understanding of the political unrest I rely tremendously on the wise counsel of Peter King. Peter joins our teaching staff in 1987, almost as a refugee from South Africa. He faces the possibility of arrest in his homeland because, as a conscientious objector, he refuses to be drafted to fight for the South African

Peter King, member of the All Saints College staff and our guide in keeping the staff aware of off campus movements as the struggle against apartheid intensified.

Defence Force (SADF) and thereby possibly find himself in a position where he is under orders to kill the very people with whom he is directly working.

After graduating from Rhodes University and teaching English in Uitenhage (now Kariega), he had joined the lay ministry in the Anglican Church there, working mainly in the nearby Langa Township. He had had direct experience of the dynamics within the struggle, particularly when in 1985 tensions between the African population in the Uitenhage township and the apartheid government reached boiling point. From 15 March police patrols were no longer issued with tear gas, rubber bullets and bird shot. Instead they were given heavy ammunition to disperse crowds. On 21 March a crowd of protesters had been marching in peaceful protest, resisting police orders to disperse. When the crowd had failed to follow their orders, the police opened fire on them and the shooting left 35 people dead and 27 wounded. Later the Kannemeyer Commission had reported that the majority had been shot in the back. Langa Township was one of the most volatile of places in South Africa at this time.

Peter has joined the All Saints College staff directly from this turbulent and raging background. Clearly, he has much that he can share about the anti-apartheid movement with the rest of us on the staff, who have come from privileged and protected backgrounds.

Peter stands by me at All Saints when I find myself in situations where there is potentially considerable personal danger on and off the campus. On one occasion during this time he is even fired upon and arrested by Ciskeian defence force members when, for humanitarian reasons, he had entered nearby Nkqonkqweni village. It had come to his notice that, in the course of the forced removals from that village, a woman had lost her little daughter and was distraught with anxiety. Peter collects fellow staff member Raj Kurup and sets off in our school kombi to find the missing child.

He is no firebrand, but a sincerely dedicated teacher who sees the need to understand and embrace the background of our students' deeper sentiments. Peter's commitment to non-racialism is not mere tokenism. He plays his favourite sport, cricket, in the ostensibly black cricket league in our district. He is the only white person to do so.

Although I at times lean heavily on Peter's advice, I sense that others on the staff are envious and perhaps even resentful of the fact that he brings to the table what they cannot – direct understanding of what is happening in the anti-apartheid struggle. Most importantly to me, Peter is able to discern what is central and what is peripheral in our dealings with students, in terms of their involvements outside the classroom.

Peter King is ideally placed to take on the responsibility of community interaction. He accepts the portfolio of Dean of Development to expand this important connection. From this position he contributes towards our college being recognised, as one commentator put it, as:

"a shining beacon for our disadvantaged schools in our region."

We could not be accused of being an ivory tower or an opportunity for a selected few. Programmes such as holiday schools for teachers and learners in surrounding schools become the norm and go a long way towards our school being considered by many as their school too. Peter even secures overseas funding for these courses so that they do not impact upon our college's running costs and budget, or on the limited financial resources of those who attend.

*   *   *

John O'Connor, a person of considerable talent and insight, joins the staff at All Saints in 1992 from nearby Breidbach Secondary School. His two pillars of strength are his passion for teaching and his recognition of the importance of sport in providing a platform to promote a peaceful transition from racial segregation to a unified non-racial society.

John is a deep thinker who brings a very necessary and timely perspective to the staff. It is the perspective of someone living on the other side of apartheid. He brings me into a world that I did not know existed when I had originally accepted Richard Todd's invitation to join the All Saints staff.

John O'Connor, member of the All Saints College staff and our guide in keeping the staff aware of off campus sporting developments and keeping the college in the fold of the unity movement

John is just exactly the person we need to help the All Saints staff to recognise that our educating and being educated goes beyond our subject teaching in the classroom. I enjoyed the path that he, I and others took in setting up the very first sporting unity movement at school level in South Africa.

In 1996, when the demise of All Saints College within LEAF is imminent, I offer John an opportunity to be Dean of Students at the college. One day he comes to me for advice about his career path. Should he remain in education or should he follow the opportunities presented in sport? I have to reply that I am not going to help him choose, as he will be the one to live with the outcome. John chooses sport, and his career blossoms to the extent that he soon becomes president of the United Schools Sports Association of South Africa (USSASA) and director of the national youth-focused AIDS awareness campaign, loveLife. Combining his experience and passion for sport and education, John went on to build up a group of companies that are today recognised by clients in several industries as a leading national vocational institute, using sport to empower and educate people.

*   *   *

I was extremely fortunate to have the wise counsel of these people of stature, and to be able to count each of them as a friend. There is no way that we would have managed on our own as just the principal and the teaching staff without the backing of these leaders who supported us.

chapter 18
Affiliation

"Sport has the power to change the world. It has the power to inspire.
It has the power to inspire people in a way that little else does.
It speaks to youth in a language they understand.
Sport can create hope where there was once despair.
It is more powerful than government in breaking down racial barriers."

— Nelson Mandela

IN 1987 the student numbers at All Saints swell by another 149 new M1s. This means that the first pioneer students who have experienced a year of building trust and a working understanding between themselves and the teaching staff now find themselves outnumbered by nearly two to one.

The new students are suspicious, feeling that there must be something sinister beneath the calm façade of All Saints College. Here is what seems to them to be an uneasy peacefulness while all around, in townships and the rural areas from where they have recently come, the country is on fire. The national state of emergency, declared the year before, is deepening in intensity and is being met by a determined resistance that is described by the National Party government as a "total onslaught". As a consequence, arrests and detentions increase dramatically, including thousands of youths of the same age as our students. Many of the All Saints College students have witnessed and even been victims of clandestine operations that include the widespread intimidation, kidnapping, torture, poisoning and murder of opponents of apartheid. On the other side, there are necklacings of *impimpis* (sell-outs).

A student conspiracy theory holds that All Saints College has perhaps been established as a subtle tool in the total strategy plan of the president of the apartheid government, PW Botha. It is understandable that such fear will lurk in some of their troubled young minds. Starting in 1987 and flaring up in the years that follow, there are rumours that lead to violent reactions and resistance in the form of student insurrection and insurgency on our campus. I have usually been the focus of the animosity because of my position as head of our institution. As a consequence, I have to handle outrage that is often pitched at a very offensive and very personal level.

The first serious showdown between All Saints students and those whom they term "the authorities" happens in May 1988. The issue is the role of sport in the anti-apartheid struggle.

At the time, sport is identified as a platform for what is initially known as the boycott movement. Since the 1970s, its demonstrations have disrupted sporting tours involving South Africa. This means that much-publicised anti-apartheid protesting as well as boycotts of events overseas and within the country are making headlines. It is naive to think that All Saints College can stay out of the on-going sport mêlée. At our induction at the start of 1986, the initial position that Richard Todd as director had instructed the new staff to follow was essentially apolitical. We were ordered to stay out of sport controversies. His understanding of non-racial sport, which he set for us to follow, was that we should promote playing matches against whoever wished to play against us, regardless of race. Friendly openness was to be our official stance. However, this wasn't a stance of the students' making, nor did it fit with what was happening on the wider politico-sporting front.

Richard Todd's sport philosophy for All Saints is summed up in the initial campus infrastructure – two squash courts, two all-weather tennis courts and the promise of a golf course to be designed by Gary Player. These are described to us as fast-learning-curve sports, intended to help the students manage the transition from their township backgrounds to the corporate world's management environment. We are told that the task of the teachers is to promote these sports and encourage student participation as a means of equipping them for future executive status.

*   *   *

Our first friendly inter-school rugby match under this neutral sports policy draws much excitement on our campus. It is a match against a 5th rugby team from Dale College in King William's Town. It is played on a small rough-and-ready field on our campus with makeshift rugby posts made from extended poles tied to our soccer goal posts.

Early in the game the All Saints wing collects the ball and streaks down the touchline all the way to the try line, gathering speed and ending in a spectacular triumphant dive to score our first try. Lots of fist-pumping accompanied by screaming from all the girl spectators! The Dale College boys stand still, open mouthed, and let him sprint unhindered into his dramatic try-scoring dive. The reason the Dale team is dumbfounded is that our wing scores his try at the wrong end of the field and behind our own try line. It is rugby's equivalent of an own goal.

Oh dear, we have some learning to do! The Dale team will no doubt enjoy telling this amusing story of the first try scored by All Saints College when they return home. After initial embarrassment, the situation is met with loud back-slapping laughter by all the players and spectators, the match resumes and is enjoyed by all. Our students need to learn the difference between the rules for soccer and rugby. The referee is very accommodating and, in the end, nobody has kept a tally of the score, so no one knows who wins. This is good in the sense that our first inter-school rugby sortie is a great success from the viewpoint of the enjoyment of players and spectators.

Our only off-campus soccer football visit is to Phandulwazi Agricultural High School where there is no embarrassment as the whole team is well versed in the rules of the game. This time a score is kept and our team can boast a comprehensive win.

It seems that Richard Todd's approach to sporting fixtures is working but there is no structured organisation for matches so our students are frustrated by the paucity of fixtures. Things are about to change dramatically.

The All Saints College 1st XI proudly wearing their blue soccer kit in the college's first inter-school fixture which they won

*   *   *

The catalytic issue that transforms the All Saints sporting platform happens at a sporting tournament held at the Malcolm Sebe Teacher Training College in nearby Zwelitsha township, where our students are embarrassed while participating in some informal inter-school sports. They are challenged to describe the All Saints College stance with regard to sport. The national boycott is the subject of a meeting held in the hall of the training college after the sporting events are played out. We have no stance that they can uphold if All Saints is to be counted as being genuinely anti-apartheid in sport. Our distressed students return to All Saints and thoroughly debate what to do. Although I and some interested staff have been watching the sporting events at the training college in support of our players, we are unaware of the strong current that is rapidly gaining momentum.

The next day I am vigorously questioned by student representatives, and confronted with a request to affiliate the college to the South African Council on Sport (SACOS). On the night of Friday 6 May 1988, the boys hold a meeting in their residence to discuss the matter of sport affiliation. The next morning after breakfast, the rest of the students are prevented from coming to classes and instead they all gather in the dining hall.

When I go down there to investigate what is happening, I am told that the students are sharing their grievances with other students who were not involved with the Malcolm Sebe College fracas. They will elect a delegation to come to brief me.

As our Dean of Students, Ta Ben Tengimfene advises me to challenge the students, demand that they return to classes by 11h00 and tell them we will deal with the issues after classes. This autocratic approach, supported by the rest of the staff, fails. The students in the dining hall will not listen to me at all so I am forced to leave them with my tail between my legs.

Still thinking that I must be proactive, I return to the dining hall later in the morning when no students appear to be coming up towards the teaching block. In the hall the meeting is continuing excitedly in isiXhosa so I ask one of the catering staff standing on the side of the hall near the entrance if she will go up to the staff room to call other staff to come down and help me. She is told by a nearby student:

"If we burn Mr Burton, we will burn you."

So no one comes to my assistance and I leave in as dignified a way as I can. Once again, I have been summarily dismissed from the discussion. This is an early experience of how not to go about things. I am being perceived as an intruder and an aggressor because I appear to be promoting a confrontational stance.

The impasse continues for three days and teaching comes to a halt. There are meetings, confrontations, delegations and speeches. The students' prevailing idea is that the college should affiliate to SACOS, which is seen to be the sports body that is most effectively opposing apartheid sport on the world stage.

Eventually, a delegation of six students comes to meet with me and two members of staff. They once again present the students' position and demand that All Saints College applies for affiliation to SACOS. I question the delegation's bona fides and ask for a secret ballot to see if the majority of students do, in fact, support such a move. This is rejected outright and is perceived as attempting to impose a system which has never before been used by the students in their student body meetings. They believe in consensus democracy. To them I have no right to question their methods. The more I appear to be going out on a limb, the further I am moving away from achieving anything of a resolution.

It is a long time before I understand what they mean by consensus democracy and an even longer time before I accept it. I am sceptical. I feel that a few can hold the rest to ransom as it seems to me that fear and intimidation can rule the day. I eventually understand when a student explains to me that if a vote is taken and the vote goes 51% in favour with 49% against, then while logic would say that the 51% carry the motion, they look at it the other way around. Their point is:

"We lose 49% of our comrades and how can we keep them with us? Unity is everything."

This is struggle democracy and it succinctly reflects what I label as the politics of the oppressed. It is important to the student body that they should not lose their cohesiveness and thereby their power base. They cannot be divided. I am learning this the hard way.

I learn again that the Richard Todd approach of asserting one's authority, recommended this time by Ben Tengimfene, is a disaster. Ben is supposed to advise and ease our "white authority" relationship with the black students. Perhaps I should have insisted that he talk to them instead of sending me. After all, he is our Dean of Students. The students are only practising a democratic right to question a perturbing issue. This is something I should have recognised and respected. I have gone about it quite the wrong way by making things divisive and confrontational.

Through this period of anxiety, which lasts a full three days, I further learn that I am missing an important opportunity. I am displaying an indifference, and in the students' eyes, a contempt for their grievances and their way of doing things. What I should be doing is patiently waiting and then attempting a collaborative resolution together with the students rather than showing a somewhat hostile, antagonistic and oppositional attitude up front. I am unwittingly positioning myself as an enemy to their cause, a position from which I will find it difficult to extricate myself. I have just waded in and those who have pushed me – my staff – can then sit back and reserve the right to be critical of the outcome. The students are way ahead of me and the teaching staff in understanding the issues with which they are grappling. It's taking a while for me to realise that we should be working together to resolve such issues and not confronting each other.

Time to make a mental note: that if I want to succeed in conflict resolution, my strategy must be to try to gain a win–win solution and not to alienate the student body from the outset – which can then only lead to a win–lose outcome. I need to practise Franklin Sonn's advice on getting the process right. This time round I fail dismally. I have to admit that my understanding of the SACOS philosophy is a negative one. Their slogan in my mind is reactionary:

"No normal sport in an abnormal society."

Therefore I take up a position of hiding behind the Board of Trustees and saying to the delegation that I do not have the authority to grant permission to affiliate the college. I am just an employee of the Trust and not the owner of the institution. It will have to be a Board decision. I doubt that the Board will accept their demand because it can possibly have a negative impact on the funding support for the college.

In the end, I say that the student body can affiliate but the college as an institution will need to remain neutral. That doesn't work. The issue is resolved eventually because I choose to learn from my initial tactless slip-up. However, it takes much longer than it needed to have done, and it has aroused a lot of angst for which I am unintentionally responsible.

*   *   *

It is time for me to take counsel and possibly see how to handle such matters in the future. I decide to phone Franklin Sonn, who is in Johannesburg, and ask his advice. He reassures me that through his connection with Ebrahim Patel there will be a means of help for me to resolve our impasse. I do not know who Ebrahim Patel is and why he should be an important player who might help me to resolve our college stand-off. Franklin phones me early on the Sunday evening to inform me that he has contacted Mluleki George and Lex Mpati and has asked them to come onto the campus to talk to the students at 04h00 the next morning. At this time, I do not know Mluleki George but I do know Lex Mpati from my Grahamstown teaching days.

I accept their credentials on Franklin Sonn's advice and urgently call an ad hoc meeting of teachers to report what Franklin has suggested. This will be the first time we are opening our college to the outside struggle community. I feel uneasy and there are puzzled looks from the staff, all of whom hail from establishment schools. I emphasise that we must trust the chairman of our Board of Trustees. Our collective experience does not equip us to deal with this situation. I am clearly a fish out of water. However, if help comes from outside, and it is help that the students will listen to, then surely this is the only way to find a win–win solution to our confrontation.

When I go to bed, I find it difficult to fall asleep with so many things churning in my head, not least of which is my own role of responsibility. Are the staff behind me or are they beginning to become twitchy? At least I feel comfortable that Richard Todd will accept the way we are now going about things because I am following the recommendations of our Trust chairman, Franklin Sonn. I set my alarm for 03h30 so that I can be awake when the emissaries arrive on campus. I am not going to join in, as I must show confidence that they know exactly what they are doing. They do not need to show that they have my permission. The alarm wakes me, I shuffle through to the kitchen, make a mug of coffee and wait in the dark, staring out at the residence from my study window. At exactly four o' clock I see a car's headlights piercing the darkness and then settling outside the boys' residence. Not long afterwards a downstairs light blinks on inside, which indicates that the boys have collected and are being addressed in their residence foyer. I do not venture down there but choose to wait it out for some sort of report back.

Later in the morning I am informed that a delegation of sports representatives will come back in the evening and that we are all invited to attend the gathering in the arts lecture theatre. We attend in the evening, and the corporate college meeting for students and staff together is addressed by stalwarts from sporting structures of the liberation struggle. They are Lex Mpati, Mluleki George, Greg Fredericks, John Bennet and Zola Dunywa. I glean from this encounter that a new sporting structure is in the offing and its stance will be a more accepting one than the hardline SACOS position with regard to sports teams playing against each other. The new philosophy is to be one of transformation through sport, rather than no sport until transformation.

Armed with this understanding I phone and explain the proceedings to Richard Todd. He agrees that we give the students a written mandate without conditions to affiliate All Saints Senior College with the Border Senior Schools Sports Union (BSSSU) which is the school sporting structure under the SACOS umbrella. This is a big turnaround for Richard, and I am pleased that he agrees. It seems that he and Franklin have conferred on the issue of aligning, as opposed to adopting a position of neutrality.

The understanding of the role of sport at All Saints, which Richard had imposed on us has been rudely challenged by the abrupt wild-cat student resistance strike. This trial by fire also moves me into a new understanding of the situation. I enter a fast learning curve on the importance of sport as a resistance strategy and then later, and more importantly, as a unifying force.

The BSSSU is essentially a teacher-run structure for teacher participation. Our students gain credentials to attend the BSSSU AGM on behalf of All Saints College. I am curious to know how things might turn out, so I ask the student delegation if I might join them as an observer and I offer to drive them to Breidbach in the college's kombi. The teaching staff is aware that I am going to observe and they are supportive of my move. Now that they are armed with written approval from the director, the students accept my request without any qualms. At least now, All Saints College has one teacher representative. I drive to the annual general meeting of the BSSSU together with our students and prepare myself to listen and learn by sitting at the back of the school hall in the nearby township of Breidbach.

*   *   *

We all sign the attendance register at the entrance to the school hall. The hall is full and I sit alone at the back and away from our All Saints student representatives. At the outset I am not comfortable, for when I look around I feel that I do not fit into this gathering. I am the only white person there and I feel that I am something of an intruder. It is my first time of being in such a gathering, albeit as an observer. It is an Annual General Meeting of an organisation that I have previously shunned.

The first item on the agenda is the appointment of an election officer to carry out the election procedure for choosing the committee for the following year. To my alarm and disbelief someone in the body of the meeting calls out:

"I propose the name of Mr Mike Burton."

I am totally taken aback and naturally object, saying that I am merely an observer at the meeting. My protest is overruled and holds no sway. My credentials for attendance had been accepted when I signed the attendance register. Therefore, as a bona fide member of the meeting, I have to step up when asked to do so by the assembly. So I hesitantly walk up to the podium and look out at the sea of unfamiliar faces, wondering just how I am going to conduct the election. Do they use a secret ballot or a show of hands? I take up the microphone and ask the gathering. Someone calls out that it is a show of hands. I'm sure that the All Saints student delegation sitting near the front is bemused that I, who initially opposed affiliation with SACOS, am now guiding the very meeting of the organisation to which I had resisted their connecting.

First up on the election agenda is the position of President. Greg Fredericks is nominated but he declines to stand once more. No other name is proposed. I am in a quandary as I am amongst strangers in more ways than one and yet I have the mandate to guide decisions on their behalf. Fortunately, Greg Fredericks acquiesces under pressure from the members around him and he accepts the nomination. Whew!

Next up on the election agenda is the position of vice-president. From the floor someone calls out:

"I propose the name of Mr Mike Burton!"

Again, I object, but my reasoning of merely intending to be an observer once more falls on deaf ears. Things are getting out of hand. Again, my protesting is overruled. I learn then and there that objecting in this sort of meeting is known as howling. Howling is not permitted. My learning curve is progressing uncomfortably in leaps and bounds. I have little time to reflect that a short while ago I intended merely accompanying our delegation and watching from the back of the hall. Yet, now I am at the forefront of proceedings. I am voted in, unopposed, as the vice-chairman of the BSSSU and am now part of a committee of a structure that I really know so little about. Why have they voted me in? Am I being led or primed for something that I don't yet understand? However, if the delegates have had sufficient confidence in elevating me to their committee, I feel that I must show that I am up to it. The script is new to me and I have lots to learn. How it will impact on my, until then, sheltered principalship I have yet to find out.

At the end of the AGM, I meet the other elected members of the new committee. Greg Fredericks is very friendly and makes me feel welcome. After we have agreed on a date and venue for our first meeting, I leave the hall and collect up the All Saints delegation to drive back to the college. My passengers are unusually silent. Their driver and principal has just been unanimously elected vice-president of the BSSSU, the official student anti-apartheid sport organisation flying the SACOS flag. Clearly, they are in some sort of shock at this turn around. For me it means I am drawn into participating in activities off the campus. It is not of my intended doing. I did not seek membership of an active anti-apartheid sporting body. Twenty-four hours ahead of the meeting I was angrily accused by the student body at All Saints for being reactionary and resistant. Yet here I am, democratically elected to the executive of the regional anti-apartheid schools sports movement and being cast as an activist in the anti-apartheid struggle outside our campus. No wonder they appear to be in shock. What will they tell the others when we get back to the college?

Despite his earlier acquiescence to the call for affiliation, my election to the executive committee does not sit well with Richard Todd. He believes that I have deliberately manoeuvred myself into this position to gain popularity with the students. Yet it was he, not I, who gave the students the green light to proceed with affiliation.

A pattern starts here which is to replicate itself as I try to embrace democracy in all its guises. I have been unwittingly jockeyed into a position where the establishment could tag me as an objector working against apartheid. It comes with its nasty side as suspicious minds now try to undermine me.

My profile and stance are becoming very public. As I step out on the tightrope, I wonder what lies around the next corner?

chapter 19
Resistance

"You're going to go through tough times – that's life. But I say, 'nothing happens to you, it happens for you.' See the positive in negative events."

— Joel Osteen

As it happens, conspiracy theories and grievances are now to lead to a number of harrowing events that bring a great deal of tension onto the campus and a complete halt to our schooling.

On 21 February 1989 the male students hold an unscheduled meeting in their residence about their grievances (which they pronounce "grieviences"). This is the first time I receive complaints in writing and it is also the first time that I hear of complaints being called grievances. I am immediately on my guard because to me a grievance is a much stronger word than complaint. It has a definite air of confrontation, used mostly by workers and trade unions.

It is also the first time that there is a clearly expressed undercurrent of political unease from the students about the leadership structure and sincerity of intention at All Saints College. The grievances come in the form of ten demands. This is also something new to us. Demands, not requests, shouts provocation to us. The students indicate that they feel uncomfortable with the college's image in anti-apartheid engagements despite our recently resolved sporting stance and its transformation. They want more and are demanding a change to our structure to meet their struggle aspirations.

Their demands are radical. We as staff are taken aback when we are faced with a protest couched in such confrontational words. We recognise that while we might be able to engage the students positively on a number of the issues, their requirement that people's leaders, community leaders and anti-apartheid structures such as the NECC take control, none of these bodies are funding the college and we don't have the authority to meet such demands. We are managing the school and are not in a position to set or change policy.

In summary, the students are indicating that they do not see All Saints or our umbrella body LEAF as being part of the liberation struggle. They believe that capitalist money and support is directing us, which of course is the fact of the matter. They do not recognise the college's claim of non-racialism because the student body is mainly black while the teachers are mainly white. To them, this is a microcosm of the wider South Africa, with oppressor and oppressed communities.

In our classrooms many students are clearly taking strain with workloads never before experienced. They express this as a grievance, claiming that the academic structure of the college produces more stress than success, even to the extent of deliberately aiming to suppress students' performances to meet apartheid's needs. Because they are used to attaining marks of over 80% at their previous government (DET) schools, they have to find an excuse or reason to explain why they are now awarded marks in the 40–50% range at All Saints. The explanation obvious to them is that it must be a deliberate plot to suppress them and to dent their self-confidence. The fact of the matter is that they are used to lower-order learning, involving rote learning of content. At All Saints they are confronted with higher-order teaching and assessment, involving understanding, explaining, critical analysis and interpretation.

The students are angry and rebellious. Our immediate reaction is to question why they are so hostile. After all they are accommodated, fed and taught at the expense of sponsors. I ask myself, how can they possibly now have grievances?

We don't understand that they feel uncomfortable at being given all that our college provides while their comrades are suffering back at home. Theirs is a feeling of guilt and of obligation to resist in one form or another. Their brothers and sisters are all fighting, and they must be seen to be fighting something too.

I recognise that there is no easy solution to such an unexpected confrontation. I remind myself that Franklin Sonn has earlier explained to me that to be a successful head at a non-racial institution such as All Saints College, I must handle such situations by recognising two very different approaches. I must somehow to broker a win–win solution using the positive methods of both. My own western, or "European" strategy in conflict resolution is results orientated, an approach that looks to find a solution in as efficient a way as possible. The African approach, however, is more focused on process than results, with the premise being that a fitting result will happen if the process is inclusive, exhaustive and appropriate.

But how am I going to do this? Josiah Moshatane, a concerned student, has told me in confidence that when students mobilise, I should look for the deeper, often hidden cause. I should not act in a knee-jerk response to the symptoms which are immediate, more easily visible on the surface and therefore easier to address. Slick answers are not going to help.

My first step therefore is to attempt to establish how valid the grievances are. Is there a deeper cause? Peter King, the residence warden who reported the meeting to me, suggests it is led by a rabble-rouser who has an agenda of his own, and that the grievances are in many cases irrelevant. What to think? Student structures such as the Students' Representative Council are bypassed by the dissidents, the girls are left out; and so the student movement appears to lack real legitimacy. The rabble-rouser is sparking something that is then gaining support and momentum. Soon the girls are also involved.

Josiah Moshatane's advice is to look for some deeper cause – he explains his counsel of not dismissing matters out of hand as 'elastoplasting' – and to allow the process to lead the way in solving the issue. I need to think about how to do this.

The next day I call a college meeting for students and staff to show some sort of respect for the students' stance. In a carefully worded response on behalf of the staff, I painstakingly address all the grievances that have been listed along with responses that we have workshopped as a staff. We do not offer any remedies or judgements, but I am obliged to add a few grievances listed by staff against student behaviour, including engaging in a wildcat strike, as well as bypassing our conflict resolution structures and processes. My key message to all is to think carefully about the mission of All Saints College. Its mission is to offer an educational opportunity at a time in the country's history when education is in turmoil. I ask if this opportunity should be jeopardised by confrontation.

The logic of the address seems to suffice, because lessons continue for another two weeks, but then on 15 March a group which calls itself "the concerned group" stirs things up once more. Emotions are energised again. I and the staff are disconcerted with a déjà vu feeling of "here we go again". The real underlying cause for student unrest is starting to emerge. It is 1989, the year in which the national Mass Democratic Movement (MDM) identifies a defiance campaign against the oppressive apartheid regime. It is apparent that the students of All Saints feel guilty for enjoying a peaceful educational experience away from the township heat where their brothers and sisters come under the loud resistance call to boycott. Our students feel a need to be seen as part of the struggle's defiance campaign. All Saints College is vulnerable because it can be construed as a microcosm of the wider apartheid South Africa.

Many of our students' grievances might appear trivial to us on the face of it, but we cannot claim distance and immunity from the wider context of the deeply emotional currents of the struggle. The student manifesto says:

"…we stand by our fellow colleagues who have shown great courage to identify and defy some oppressive factors of the functional system of this school."

Is this political-speak meaningless or is there real meaning behind words like "oppressive" and "functional system"? The reference to courage implies a perception of danger. To the teaching staff this would be laughable if the situation were not so serious, and most of the students' grievances are seen by the majority of the staff as inconsequential claptrap.

I sense that the way forward to achieve a win–win outcome is to interrogate openly our claim of non-racialism as well as the validity of the college and LEAF as part of the liberation struggle. I believe that the students' suspicion about our authenticity is the root cause of the trouble. We need to discuss this issue openly at a reconciliation meeting.

It is clear that the trust between staff and students is being severely bruised. It is both threatening and personal. A confrontational gap is openly evident. The angry students demand an early end to the term to allow for a cooling-off period. We agree. In a widely distributed letter I invite parents, students and community structures to All Saints College at the beginnning of the second term to start a period of discussion, clarification and reconstruction.

Before we are overwhelmed, now is the time for our staff to be sensitised to the political environment surrounding us and which is seeping onto our college campus. We need to be comfortable with where we should be placed in the middle of the tightrope balance, with the aspirations of LEAF and its director Richard Todd, together with the funders and trustees, on the one side; and the expectations of the students, their parents and communities, together with the defiance campaign on the other. It is pie-in-the-sky to think we can pretend it has nothing to do with us, and remain untouched by events all around us because our students live their lives off campus.

As a staff we cannot enjoy the luxury of claiming to be just teachers on a college campus with our connection to our students being limited to classroom and curriculum only. All Saints and LEAF advertise themselves as being opposed to apartheid, but it is a discreet opposition and not sufficiently obvious to appease the students. And yet there is the ever-present danger of becoming too noticeable to the security forces, who are trying to keep a lid on any inkling of unrest. It is difficult for us to be expected to teach normally when the black students who come washed-up, battered and bruised from outside onto our calm and sheltered campus, and the wild political and social ocean rages and its winds howl around us.

Our students are accusing us of indifference. We are not sufficiently active as agents of the resistance. In fact, to many of them we are even perceived to be opponents of the struggle. Richard Todd had asked us to focus on classroom activities, but that was in 1986 and this is now 1989. All in the country are being called to resist apartheid actively. Schools are identified, together with beaches and hospitals, by the Mass Democratic Movement as being terrain where this resistance should be evident. We are a school community, but we are divided in our understanding of what we should be doing.

On our staff, Peter King is the most knowledgeable and conversant on struggle developments. He follows the movement meticulously and builds a daily newspaper article archive for our teachers to educate themselves. Not all are drawn to it as they hang on to their comfort zone and don't want to go there. For me, Peter plays a big part in my political sensitisation. It is clear to me that we need to become more noticeably involved.

Meanwhile we surprise the students by making immediate arrangements for transport to return them home the next day. On the day of their departure, I walk down to the boys' residence and ask to talk to the chairman of the SRC, David Mokhetsu. He and I talk in his room for nearly two hours as I try to uncover the deeper cause of the student unrest and protest. I am still searching for the underlying grounds of the student dissatisfaction. What or who is putting them up to this resistance?

One of the students in the insurrection is seen on the last day of schooling walking around in white overalls with a logo "BLACK MAN YOU ARE ON YOUR OWN" emblazoned on his back. There are two schools of thought displayed by staff members in discussion about this overt display. The first is that it is a racially provocative statement against us. The second is the one I lean towards. Steve Biko, the leader of black consciousness in South Africa, coined the phrase. It promotes the idea that the down-trodden must no longer act as victims but should regain some pride and recognition that black people are not inferior. When interviewed on the meaning of his statement, Biko had replied:

"A black man should be more independent and depend on himself for his freedom and not to take it for granted that someone would lead him to it. The blacks are tired of standing at the touchlines to witness a game that they should be playing. They want to do things for themselves and all by themselves."

We never get to question our student in overalls on what motivates his paraded statement, but perhaps it is not as provocative and confrontational as some might think.

*   *   *

While the students are away, the staff and I workshop the situation and conclude that there are four currents flowing. Under Peter King's guidance we identify the first concern as doubt in the student body about the anti-apartheid character of the college. Does the umbrella body LEAF go beyond a theoretical support of the non-racial democratic movement in opposition to apartheid, and can it identify how it acts? Is it connected to the legitimate structures in the struggle such as the United Democratic Front (UDF) or the Congress of South African Trade Unions (COSATU)? This is justifiable questioning and Richard Todd's neutral stance is not going to resolve the situation. In fact, we feel that Richard should be taking the responsibility of responding on all of our behalf since the issues are clearly questioning LEAF's *bona fides* rather than our college's, but he refuses to assist and he leaves us to deal with it.

Secondly, there is deep suspicion concerning the sponsorship, as well as the implied capitalist expectations and possible manipulation of student futures. Capitalism is seen by the students to be in collusion with apartheid. Capitalists want good, civilised and passive blacks who will fit into the capitalist system, thus emasculating black resistance against apartheid and promoting a continuance of the status quo. Is All Saints a stage where this is happening, and is this the college's hidden agenda? Again, a very reasonable question under the circumstances.

Thirdly, the academic pressures at All Saints are beyond their earlier experiences of township schooling where rote learning reigns. Many students are feeling the heat of possible failure. In addition, they find no education at All Saints College to be relevant to the struggle.

The fourth issue is the perception that some staff members appear to them to show racist tendencies. None are named. The students question why such staff can be employed by an organisation that proclaims itself an agent of the struggle against apartheid through education. They question the staff's lack of deep loyalty to the cause of resistance. This too is a legitimate line of questioning as the majority of the staff are following Richard Todd's politically neutral formula. The students see this approach as hollow.

All in all, they feel that they are uncovering a devious plot: a conspiracy theory is growing. The college staff claims to oppose apartheid, but this is not obvious to the students and they perceive the reality to be different. In their minds the participants of LEAF, the teachers and the sponsors are colluding to manipulate the minds of young black leadership so as to maintain the existing state of affairs of South Africa's apartheid regime.

The students from Soweto, who are more politically astute, galvanise support from their parents at home and form a crisis committee back home to investigate what they believe they have uncovered.

*   *   *

Early into the holiday, with the staff taking a break, I am contacted telephonically by a Mr Malinga, who describes himself as the chairman of the Soweto Parents Crisis Committee. He informs me that a committee of parents wishes to accompany the students back to All Saints at the start of the next term to help resolve our impasse.

I think about it and, on a whim, I respond by suggesting that I can forestall all this by coming to Soweto and meeting all parents during the holiday before the next term starts. He agrees. I feel that issues can be addressed directly with all parents at once in this way, and I can be seen and heard by the parents face to face. It is a daring offer. I have volunteered to face the music alone and yet the discord in this situation is not of my making. What they are actually questioning is the bona fides of Richard Todd's vision.

I call the few remaining staff on the campus and talk the matter through with them. We feel that it would be a big risk to ask Richard to address the parents as he has made it clear to us that he needs to hold on to the expectations of the corporate world and not the movement against apartheid. His key responsibility is to ensure continued financial support. We cannot see how he will help this situation.

The staff members present are told that I have offered to go to Soweto and I invite any of them to join me. However, it is felt that it is best for me to represent the college on my own, as long as I emphasise that we only manage the school, and cannot address some of the demands as they are beyond our jurisdiction as employees. So I fly to Johannesburg alone and full of foreboding. How will things pan out? I am walking right into the lion's den at a time when very few white people venture into the closely guarded townships of South Africa. Noreen is very apprehensive. She says that she fears that there is even a possibility of me not coming out of Soweto alive and nobody will know how I disappear. It is not a far-fetched thought because, apart from the antagonism of the students and perhaps their parents there, the gun-toting SADF is patrolling and could quite easily remove me from the scene.

A man who identifies himself as Mr Malinga collects me at the Johannesburg airport and drives me into the heart of Soweto. During the journey, I am subjected to a barbed and hostile tirade clearly aimed at making me feel uneasy. He is surreptitiously spelling out that he sees me as a white oppressor and is openly implying that I do not have any empathy with the lot of the black community. This confirms my premonition that I am in for a very rough time at the organised meeting, to be held at the hall of the Young Women's Christian Association (YWCA) in central Soweto.

We drive up to the hall and when I walk in, I find that I am facing a very large group. They cannot all be our parents. It is an intimidating set-up and Mr

Malinga starts playing to the crowd by introducing my arrival with the terse words:

"Here he is. I have fetched him."

I am not introduced by name, there is no welcome and not a single smile of recognition. The atmosphere is very tense. My unease increases as I sense that I am a pariah in the gathering. It is going to be a very difficult thing to put these people at ease when they are displaying such an unfriendly attitude towards me before I even have a chance to say a word. I can see a table at the one end of the room with a single chair where Mr Malinga has made his way. No one paves the way for me to any place so I find an empty chair, pick it up and carry it to sit next to Mr Malinga. The table is long and we are then joined by four other people who bring chairs with them. They are obviously members of the ad hoc crisis committee. The rest of the gathering must be parents and other interested community members. Apart from the *"Here he is…"* opening, not a word has yet been spoken.

Mr Malinga asks for questions and there is an antagonistic barrage of questions. One of the lady members of the committee next to me, Mrs Ntuli (the mother of Sibusiso), lists them and then I am called upon to respond to each in order.

The first question accuses me of having no real communication with students. So, I stand up and take a deep breath before slowly looking around at each person eye to eye so as to gather my wits. Everything since my arrival has seemed so rushed and almost predestined that I need to calm myself and the audience down. I then start to answer:

"Ladies and gentlemen, this surprises me, for amongst other things I spent two hours with the SRC chairman, David Mokhetsu, in his room on the day they left to come home. I was trying to understand what was at the bottom of the student strike."

David Mokhetsu and another student leader Samuel Letshwenyo are sitting at the back of the room in this meeting, so I say:

"You can ask David Mokhetsu directly now to verify this."

All heads turn to him and he shouts out:

"I am being intimidated by the principal!"

At this point Eugene Nyati, an influential and significant leader in the Soweto community who has been identified by the students to sit in on the crisis committee and who is sitting right next to me, stands up and bangs on the table with force.

"What is going on here? We are told by these two students that the principal doesn't communicate with them and yet he has just told us that he spent two hours in the room with this student to get to the bottom of the matter! I do not know of any other principal in our schools who would go to such lengths to do this!"

145

David Mokhetsu refuses to be drawn in to reply and he continues to claim that he is being intimidated. Earlier, just before my arrival, he had apparently read out a list of demands from an anonymous letter addressed to the parents. I was later told that the crisis committee were shocked at the manner of the reading and threats expressed in the document. David clearly did not expect any backlash. But he is young, and he carries the emotions of the student body who honestly believe they have uncovered some treacherous conspiracy.

Other issues exposed at the meeting are the role of the college's umbrella body LEAF, a number of discipline issues, and the South African Council on Sport (SACOS) affiliation. In response I speak at length on each and the committee openly expresses appreciation at my role in actively and fully attending to each of the issues. Many of the parents are nodding their heads in agreement and I can perceive that their attitudes are changing. Finally, the outcome is a pledge of support from them to assist me to get classes back to normal.

I suggest the formation of an investigation committee comprised of parents and community leaders to look into LEAF and the management of All Saints College so as to dispel the storm clouds of suspicion. This is accepted unanimously and it is agreed that a fact sheet should be produced by LEAF. They also pledge support for a committee that I propose which might be called the Community and Student Affairs Committee (CASAC). This becomes the forerunner of our Parent, Teachers and Students Association (PTSA) which we later form at All Saints.

I am then asked to leave the room and to stand outside while the two students are instructed on their responsibility to relay truthfully to the student body the outcomes of the meeting. The meeting closes and several smiles are directed towards me. I am driven back to the airport by a very sullen and non-communicative Mr Malinga. However, I am feeling much better on this outward journey as I have made a positive impression and helped plot a way forward. I even anticipate a normal start to the next term.

What actually happens later is, in fact, far from normal. It emerges that the two students feel that they have lost face at this encounter with their parents, to the extent that they need to turn it around somehow in their report back to their expectant and supportive fellow students.

*   *   *

One outcome of the Soweto meeting is that a committee of a few parents together with Mr Malinga and Eugene Nyati is mandated to travel to All Saints at the start of the next term to talk to the students and attempt to end the impasse. I agree to collect them in the college's minibus at the airport in East London when they arrive.

I am phoned a few days later by Mr Malinga to say that he cannot come to the meeting. He gives no reason. He goes on to ask if the college will pay for the flight of the two student leaders, David Mokhetsu and Samuel Letshwenyo, to accompany the parent delegation. I cannot see why this should happen because the issues are still unresolved. Rather than challenge the request, I unwittingly agree.

*   *   *

Back at All Saints I call for a staff meeting just before the second term is about to start, to brief everyone in full on the developments during the holiday and particularly the outcomes of the meeting in Soweto. There is a lot of discussion in order to clarify our position and responses to the demands or grievances that were presented to us.

Term 2 start-up day arrives and all the students are back at the college except for the two Sowetans, David Mokhetsu and Samuel Letshwenyo who are due to come with the parent delegation. Meanwhile the student body holds a meeting and decides not to return to classes until their two delegate leaders from Soweto return. On the day, I drive the college minibus to the airport in the late afternoon to fetch the crisis committee delegation and the two students. It is disappointing that the chairman Mr Malinga is not there, and I still do not know why he has not been able to come. I further sense that something is amiss because no one smiles when I find them at the airport arrivals. There is a stony silence for all sixty kilometres of the way from the airport to All Saints, despite several attempts on my part to start a conversation. No one wants to say anything.

When we arrive at the college it is immediately apparent that matters are out of hand. Students come rushing out of the dining hall where they have gathered, and they mob the minibus as it parks. They angrily confront the Soweto committee of parents, banging on the vehicle and shouting accusations at them of having been turned by the principal. Eugene Nyati manages to quieten things by his demeanour. He tells the students that he wants to talk to the principal privately first and then will meet with them afterwards to hear their grievances. I wonder about this. Is there going to be a twist in the tail?

Once in my office, the gloves soon come off. Eugene cuts to the chase and accuses me:

EN: *"Why did you pay for the two students to travel with us?"*

MB: *"Because I was asked to by your chairman Mr Malinga, and I have a question for you. Why is Mr Malinga not here with the committee?"*

EN: *"First, he is not our chairman and next something wrong is happening here. So, Mr Burton we pledge to you that we will get to the bottom of this if you give me the time now to talk to the students – and please recognise that, yes, we are here to find out what's behind all this and returning things to normality."*

The crisis committee delegation and students talk right through the night. I stay away, so I have no idea of what is discussed or what the mood is. More meetings continue through the following day, involving students, staff and parents. Finally, with staff support, I announce a commitment that if students return to classes, we will set aside two hours each afternoon to attend to the listed issues and together we will work towards establishing a community and parent committee through open discussion.

Eugene Nyati, who has been the key liaison person guiding us to this point, together with the other parents, are thanked for their concern and intervention, and taken back to the airport in East London.

*   *   *

We have a short respite and classes do start again. It has been an emotionally draining time through this drawn-out process and I feel really wrung out. But it is not the end. My commitment is to address the issues raised by the students in a full-on meeting every day in our dining hall.

In our first meeting, I stand at the podium with the staff behind me and the student body facing me. Everyone is expectant. A small group of boys sitting on two tables in a back corner of the hall are nudging each other and grinning, clearly enjoying making me feel that I am in the dock. I reckon that they have got me where they want me and now it's up to me to literally turn the tables. I stand at the podium ready to respond. I am not alone this time as I have the backing of the whole teaching staff sitting in a line behind me. The girl students have taken up the front rows of seats with the boys behind them. So, I take my time, shuffle a few pages and then deliberately survey the audience in front of me by sweeping my head slowly from the one side of the hall to the other, looking each student in the eyes, as I had done at the meeting in Soweto. Then I look down at my notes and begin softly.

I start giving a response to each of the grievances on their list and at a critical point a student in the back corner raises his hand. He smiles as those around him do. He has clearly been egged on to interrupt my presentation, but I let him speak out. No need to confront at this stage.

148

"Mr Burton, will you explain to us why you have allowed a girl back who failed her first year to continue through with her second year?"

It is true that we did bend the rules for Desiree Chunku Nkosi and she is aware that she did not pass her M1 year. A special staff meeting had decided that she had lately shown such good improvement that she should be allowed to continue. Chunku is in my tutor group. I reply to the question by saying:

"Chunku is fully aware of her situation and she is so thankful that when she arrived at the start of the year, she promised that she would prove to us that she would cope. She would show us! Which she is doing."

Unfortunately I add:

"You can ask her yourself."

At this point Chunku bursts out of her seat and rushes away out of the door in tears. I am devastated by her reaction and the consequence of what I have done hits me like a sledgehammer. What have I done to her? I am not aware of the level of intimidation that is possibly being played out. What will vindictive students do to her as a possible fingered sell-out? As these thoughts flood into my mind, I start to choke up and my emotions take over. I cannot talk and I start visibly and uncontrollably to sob in front of the whole college.

It is a shattering moment.

I cannot continue so I turn around and walk away from the podium at the front of the hall where I was addressing the meeting, past the row of seated staff members and stand shaking out of public view in a corridor at the side of the hall. A staff member Dominic King comes to me in concern and asks if I am okay. I reply that I do not know what has come over me. It is possibly the culmination of a draining and sustained personal attack on me over the past number of days. I feel that I am now showing extreme weakness in front of everybody. The thought flashes through my mind of what Richard Todd would think of my tearful display if he were standing in the wings. What sort of leadership display is this? I take a grip of myself, mop up and walk back to the podium, determined to get things onto an even keel again. The hall is eerily hushed and I see that the students in the belligerent corner are beaming, elbowing and snickering. They believe they have scored a major and obvious victory in the confrontation and that I have been successfully belittled in front of all. Reduced to tears. I am at the nadir point of leadership, as I have shown that I have wilted under their aggressive pressure.

I step up to the lectern to continue, but before I start to speak, I look down at the front row of girls to see that all of them are openly weeping. Oh dear. That sets me off again with a choked-up spasm but this time there is a roar of laughter from the antagonistic corner which is actually just what I need. It helps me to rally. Whether through anger or adrenaline I will never know, but I handle the rest of the meeting by speaking forcefully and staring down the boys in the corner. There is no doubt in the room at whom I am staring and targeting in my comments that follow. I choose strong words to work through the remainder of the agenda. We close the meeting and I sense that the majority of those who share this emotional time with me understand what has happened. I perceive that the aggressive boys who orchestrated the confrontation are possibly now chastened. Maybe not? I have no idea what the staff feel about it all as I am left to return up the hill with Noreen. Are they shocked? Do they feel that I have failed?

*   *   *

Soon after getting home I walk up to the reservoir at the top of the property to gather myself. I have just been through the humiliating experience of weeping openly in front of the whole school community. I am feeling very low, and that I have failed when it was necessary to show resolve and strength. It is time to phone Franklin Sonn to share my shame with him at breaking down and to confess that I failed at a critical moment. I am feeling very demoralised.

To my huge surprise, instead of commiserating with me, I can imagine him beaming as he says over the phone that what I have done is great. Great? I am taken aback when he says:

"You have shown that you are human and that you care!"

He further reminds me that the shortest verse in the Bible is 'Jesus wept'. I hadn't been able to see it that way, but clearly Franklin is right because the majority of the students start speaking out in favour of returning to classes from then on. Normal staff–student interaction restarts and two days later in an open meeting at the college three Border Education Crisis Committee representatives pledge their future support to help students and teachers to come together. A progressive organisation has been brought into the fold to sensitise all of us together as a college community.

The key lesson that the All Saints staff and I learn from this protracted affair is that the only way to resolve student confrontation is to connect with relevant people or organisations from outside the college. We do not have to stand alone. We are too vulnerable and it is too hurtful. Instead, we will call upon recognised struggle structures. It is a lesson that is useful to remember when future insurrections take place on the campus. Our college experience proves to be a foretaste of a conflict resolution strategy that is to play out on the national stage in years to come.

Really valuable lessons are often born in pain and struggle. The anguishing events of March 1989 produce a number of positive outcomes. At a personal level, I have learned that from weakness can come strength. It was Paul who said in his second letter to the Corinthians in chapter 12 verse 9:

"for my power is made perfect in weakness."

...and Ernest Hemingway said: *"The world breaks everyone, and afterward, some are strong at the broken places."*

Despite my garnering the favour of the progressive anti-apartheid structures and so drawing the wrath of Richard Todd, the next wave of students will again be determined to unseat me. Steeped in conspiracy theory and deeply suspicious of the college's motives, they will again turn on me in a frenzy of deep-seated anger. I know this.

The outcome of this incident has given us a short-lived breather before the next round!

part five

CONTRIBUTING TO THE DEFIANCE CAMPAIGN

chapter 20
Protesting

"One has a moral responsibility to defy unjust laws."

— Martin Luther King Jr

F OR ALL SAINTS COLLEGE, and my role in the liberation struggle, 1989 turns
out to be a watershed year, when we investigate what we are to do to retain
our credibility, and I take the initiative in linking up with the defiance campaign.
We have been aligning ourselves with the progressive structures against apartheid,
so when the Mass Democratic Movement (MDM) calls for peaceful resistance,
All Saints College becomes visibly involved.

On 8 January 1989 the African National Congress declares in a statement that
it is "The Year of Mass Action for People's Power" and proposes a campaign of
militant mass defiance. Later in the month, President PW Botha suffers a stroke
and resigns from the leadership of the Nationalist Party in February. He remains
President of the country and extends the state of emergency for another year.

Later in the year, Botha has a meeting with Nelson Mandela, but he is soon
replaced as President by FW de Klerk, who immediately declares the need for
change. A whites-only election is called for 6 September and then a deluge of
change sweeps the country. Following the release of Nelson Mandela in February
1990, the Rivonia Treason Trial prisoners are also then released; the Congress of
South African Students (COSAS) and the National Education Crisis Committee
(NECC) declare themselves unbanned; the United Democratic Front (UDF) and
the Congress of South African Trade Unions (COSATU) distance themselves
from Winnie Mandela's private militia; and the MDM launches a new defiance
campaign.

*   *   *

As principal of All Saints College it is clear to me that we have to make some far-
reaching decisions. Am I, like most white citizens and especially school teachers in

South Africa, to stand aloof from politics and ignore the call – bury my head in the sand, perhaps with the excuse of protecting the college's income stream? *"I did not realise"* won't cut it. Should I join the white chorus, saying teachers are not politicians and our space is inside the classroom and not outside?

No. This will clearly compromise and threaten our students since their families and communities have expectations that the time is one for sacrifice and that together staff and students should protest with all other schools on the victim side of apartheid's line. We need to make a stand. It is clear to me that I need to heed the national call in some way and join the protests of the rolling defiance programme – to listen to the students, who are much more directly affected by the cruelties of the regime. But how; and will the staff agree?

The risk here is that All Saints College might lose its funding support and have to close its operation altogether. This is plainly a Catch-22 situation. Deep down I feel there is only one choice for All Saints if the college wishes to continue operating in a changing South Africa. We must align ourselves with the MDM's call. But how are we to get there? How are we to achieve consensus decisions on campus and maintain our life-giving financial backing and continuance? The tightrope is taut.

My first step is to consult with the staff and share with them my plan to find out from the anti-apartheid movement what should we be doing. For quite some time we deliberate in the staff room, calmly, without rhetoric or passion. I recommend that students should first be invited to a meeting with the staff. Instead of waiting for them, this time around we should be proactive and take the first step in seeking our way forward. We will try to gain consensus support from staff and students together to connect with a progressive structure and lay our dilemma before it.

We all agree that consulting LEAF to seek permission is not the way to go, as Richard Todd is certainly going to filibuster. We decide rather not to have him say 'no' and then have to go ahead and decide to continue and take action against his instruction. It is best to go ahead first, and plead innocence if he comes down on us like a ton of bricks! With a mandate from the staff, I carry on and call a corporate college meeting to address the issue. Since it is I who call the meeting, I am not to chair it according to our college rules. So, the Students' Representative Council chairman takes the responsibility of directing our deliberations.

The full-house meeting involves both teachers and students. There is a buzz of anticipation and some of the students appear to be a bit confused that the principal is calling a meeting to discuss our participation in the defiance campaign. The room goes disconcertingly silent when I am called upon to explain why I have summoned the gathering. After taking a deep breath, I proceed to inform everyone that there is soon to be a Mass Democratic Movement defiance campaign meeting in Mdantsane (the Ciskeian township on the outskirts of East London, about sixty kilometres away from our college, and second only to Soweto among townships in South Africa, both in size and population). The MDM might be in a position to give us the necessary advice on what we should do.

Not much discussion is needed, as there is nothing controversial in my proposal and the meeting resolves that we send a delegation to the Mdantsane meeting. Its task will be to present the All Saints predicament. Do we stop lessons, lose our income and have to close? Or do we continue lessons and be accused of being on the side of apartheid? We need to try to find a way forward for our institution.

The delegation of five chosen by the meeting includes students Rethabile Mosisidi, Pule Moloabi and Viorety Nkosi, and staff members Peter King and me. We become known as the All Saints Defiance Campaign Committee. Our task is to keep abreast of unfolding developments and to keep the college informed and up-to-date. This is a first time that a committee of teachers and students is paving the way.

On 25 August I distribute a memorandum (see page 157) which the committee has workshopped and developed for students and teachers to discuss together in their tutor group meetings. It encourages students, workers and teachers to support the campaign.

*   *   *

The process of entering Mdantsane Township has to be clandestine. It is in the evening and Peter King and I need to make sure that we are out of sight when we arrive on the outskirts of the township. Entry by our minibus into Mdantsane in the evening can be construed as being politically confrontational because whites are prohibited from entering townships during the government's state of emergency period, which is being fiercely enforced. It is no melodrama, but a serious scenario reqiring us to duck down on the floor and hide from view with a blanket over us. Townships are patrolled by trigger-happy Defence Force personnel in steel-armoured Casspir troop carriers. We make our way cautiously into the township. Fortunately our minibus does not cross paths with any military vehicle in our journey to the meeting and we arrive at the venue without any mishap.

The place for the Defiance Campaign meeting is the church hall at the Anglican Church of the Holy Cross which in itself has a special significance. When we arrive, I am surprised to be ushered onto the stage of the packed church

All Saints Senior College
Ciskei

Private Bag X0053, Bisho, Ciskei
Telephone: (0401) 93081, Telefax: (0401) 91611

All Saints College Memorandum

The newly formed Defiance Campaign Committee wishes to urge all students, workers and teachers to support the defiance campaign clearly and actively so as to reflect our position in relation to the status quo.

In this regard the committee needs to share with you the realities that make it important for people to stand up and reject what is evil, inhumane and unjust. At this time this is done through defying apartheid laws as we have discussed and through taking a stand in words that we reject them. Now is the time for us to actively stand for what is just and humane. We need to expose the evils of the apartheid system and strategies to maintain it.

The realities of our position are as follows:

○ Repression is intensifying – restrictions, banning of organisations, detentions without trial and capital punishment remain a reality in our society – especially in the townships. The "State of Emergency" continues to allow merciless actions by security forces – e.g. harassment, assassination and torture
○ Reforms – contained in the 5-year plan of De Klerk means no big deal to us, as we understand that apartheid cannot be reformed but it must be totally eradicated.

Finally, elections are also meaningless to us – the Black majority in particular, in that they still form part of the system that is meeting repression and exploitation.

The Committee is seeking information about co-ordinated action, it will meet on Saturday at 11h00 and will hold a 'Campaign Meeting' on Sunday after supper. All are urged to attend

M.StJ.W. Burton
Principal

Memorandum outlining the position of the Defiance Campaign Committee and encouraging teachers, workers and students to support the defiance campaign

hall. I wonder just exactly what is going to unfold. I am not sure what emotions are playing themselves out in my mind because I am now openly participating in what could be construed as sedition. I have been mandated by the All Saints community to take this active step of resistance against the government and its volatile defence force. The consequences might be personally calamitous, but there can be no going back. Will this meeting be forcefully interrupted? Might I be arrested and incarcerated? Might there be violence? I do not know if the meeting has been sanctioned or not. I suspect that it has not, as political gatherings are banned under the emergency restrictions and this is clearly going to be a political meeting even though it is a gathering in a church.

Because I have been apprehensive all along, I am positively taken aback when the meeting starts with prayer and there are some hymns sung solemnly and melodiously as can only be done by an African congregation. I am easing into the situation and I cannot help thinking that this is a very far cry from a stone-throwing, anarchistic mob, which is how the press has been describing the resistance movement. Here I am sitting in a church gathering, with all the moral integrity of such an occasion. There are no wild speeches and raised voices, only calm, clear and controlled deliberation. All Saints' participation is publicly welcomed and, once described, our dilemma is promptly resolved because a way forward is soon decided. The consensus resolution taken is that three prominent schools for white boys, Selborne College in East London, Dale College in King William's Town and Queens College in Queenstown, are to be targeted. I do not like this word "targeted". However, I accept that it is not intended with any form of malice in mind; rather I perceive that the whole mood of the meeting is peaceful. I am not sure what I anticipated when we left All Saints. I know that the concern I had had is now partly put to rest. I cannot, however, help thinking that there may be *impimpi* (government agents) in the congregation who could cause much trouble later.

The aim of the meeting, which is stated several times, is to:

"...educate our white brothers and sisters in their schools of our plight in the townships and rural schools, because we are certain that they are not aware. They too are victims of apartheid."

From the body of the meeting Peter King volunteers to draft and print off a manifesto which can be distributed at the marches. He will use the All Saints College's offset-litho printing press to publish these flyers. The manifesto will outline the crisis of teachers and facilities in black schools and point out that white schools are losing pupils. It calls on white schools to open their doors – *"All our schools for all our people"* – and for all who want peace and justice to defy apartheid's discriminatory laws.

The agreed strategy is that participants will meet at selected points in the three different towns. All Saints College is to gather with schools from the townships of Breidbach, Zwelitsha and Ginsberg in front of the post office in King William's Town. We are then to march peacefully to Dale College, which is our targeted school. The march is to be dignified and without the toyi-toying war dance that is usually an integral part of protest marches and placards or posters. Marchers are to be made up of school pupils, school teachers, lawyers from the National Association of Democratic Lawyers (NADEL), and clerics from the South African Council of Churches. In every sense it is to be a peace march.

The meeting in Mdantsane ends in prayer and I am overwhelmed with the decorum and bearing of this first close encounter with the struggle movement in action. I cannot help feeling that despite all the hurt and criminal unfairness that could justifiably have led to outbursts of anger and righteous indignation in this church hall, I am instead experiencing the principled and honourable conduct of an occasion driven by a clear and genuine desire for peace and reconciliation. It is a wonderfully exhilarating release for me that I have been obliged to take such a positive step on behalf of All Saints College and get right into the thick of things. I really feel elevated by such a stirring experience. It is a rare privilege and I am grateful that I was voted into the All Saints delegation, and not left behind at the college waiting for a report back. Of course, I am under no delusions about the seriousness of the matters at hand and the secretive, dangerous terrain that I am stepping into, but I am buoyed up by a sincere feeling of alignment. I believe that what we are doing is moral and right, and I draw strength from feeling that this is the appropriate thing to do. It is in tune with the oppressed masses but it does carry a big red danger signal. *Impimpi* plague these occasions, and follow up with dirty tricks afterwards. The meeting closes in prayer and we make our way carefully and safely back to All Saints.

*　　*　　*

The next day I phone Franklin Sonn, our Trust chairman, to advise him of my intention to join the protest march and that I have informed the college there will be no classes on that day. Teachers and students will be able to participate if they so wish. No one is obliged to march as it is a matter of personal decision. I phone Franklin because I am worried.

Political marches are banned during this South African emergency time and they are usually met with violent and forceful resistance. King William's Town, where we are to march, is not in the Ciskei and so we will be stepping into the lion's den of South Africa without protection. King William's Town is notably conservative and, as mentioned previously, its people voted to stay out of Ciskei. We will not receive any sympathetic support from the citizens of this town. What I am most apprehensive of is my role and responsibility of being *in loco parentis* of our young people. If I lead them into a blood-bath I carry the full responsibility on my shoulders. No one else shares it, and this is very worrying.

Franklin's advice is not just positive. He goes further to tell me that not only should I consider marching with the students but that it is imperative that I lead them. This poses a huge risk, and it weighs heavily on me. My one source of relief is that Franklin says he will back me if anything goes wrong, and as long as I am seen in the forefront of the danger, no fingers of blame can be pointed at me. It isn't my decision alone to respond to the campaign. It is a shared responsibility taken in open and calm discussion. What also weighs on me is

159

that I have deliberately not informed Richard Todd although he is the director of the college. I have chosen rather to confide in the chairman of the Trust.

*   *   *

The day for action arrives. Alongside me, a few other All Saints staff members ferry students to the meeting point outside the post office in King William's Town. We wait quietly near the post office entrance for others to join us. After a short while of standing peacefully, I start to feel very uneasy because I am aware that protest gatherings are banned and are confronted brutally by police and defence forces. Although it is quiet and undisturbed, I am still on edge because violence could erupt at any moment. When I feel that it is nearing the allotted time for us to be marching towards Dale College, I am aware that I am standing close to the leader of the Border Council of Churches, Smuts Ngonyama. I approach him and share with him that it is disappointing that there are so few people gathered around us. There are only about a hundred protesters, almost all from All Saints college. A march with so few will make a very feeble statement.

What we are unaware of is that the South African Defence Force has been active with its Casspirs and troops. They have blocked the routes into King William's Town from the surrounding townships and are using *sjamboks*, batons and tear gas on demonstrators on their way from the surrounding schools in Breidbach, Zwelitsha and Ginsberg. The apartheid forces' tactic of sealing the exits from these places is effective once again. According to *The King Mercury*, the local weekly newspaper, about eight hundred pupils from Breidbach marching to King William's Town are stopped at the Bisho bridge and dispersed. Four hundred pupils from Forbes Grant High School in Ginsberg reach the bus and taxi rank, where they are scattered with tear gas. Hundreds of pupils from Zwelitsha are also dispersed by security forces at the taxi rank.

A police van with police dogs inside is patrolling slowly and menacingly around the town square in front of the post office. Our small gathering is unobtrusively waiting so I ask Smuts Ngonyama if we should start marching despite the disappointing numbers and he agrees that it is time. The surrounding scene is remarkably tranquil during the tense build-up in our time of waiting. So much so, that a young mother unconcernedly pushes her baby in a pram and threads her way amongst us and into the post office to do her business of the day without fear or threat. It is ironic that this is an ordinary working day without danger to her and other citizens, yet here we the protesters wait quietly and anxiously, exposed to potential reactionary violence from the strong arm of apartheid's law enforcers.

No sooner have mother and pram entered the post office than three police vans screech to a halt in front of us. Plain-clothes and uniformed policemen jump out with quirts and batons. The officer in charge announces through a megaphone that this is an illegal gathering and that we have two minutes to disperse. He puts the megaphone down and yells something that sounds like, *"Moer-hulle my boys!"*

The meaning of these words becomes immediately clear as the police forces wade in, striking brutally and indiscriminately at our gathering. The students flee and many are struck and injured in the process.

No-one attacks Smuts Ngonyama or me as the weapon wielding aggressors seem to be focused on attacking only the students and honing in on the screaming girls. The mother re-emerges with her pram at the post office entrance in total wide-eyed bewilderment at the pandemonium around the entrance. She quickly turns around and seeks safety back inside the post office.

All Saints staff members Andrew Stevens and Peter King photograph the wild scenes. It is an extremely risky thing to do, as they are observed doing it and are immediately chased by police. They elude confiscation of the camera by carefully relaying it from one to the other.

Clearly the march has lost any impetus and my main concern now is for the safety of our students. I run to where my Mitsubishi Star Wagon is parked nearby and drive off around town picking up bewildered students, some of whom

All Saints students are attacked by security forces as they collect outside the Post Office ready to participate in a peaceful protest march endorsed by the Mass Democratic Movement as part of its defiance campaign

have been struck by the police and are bruised and bleeding. Once collected, I drive them to a safer place on the outskirts of King William's Town and turn back again to collect more. While doing this, I learn that there is a re-grouping of protesters at the Holy Trinity Anglican Church at the top of the town. So I make for the church and when I get there, I find that the church grounds have armed Defence Force people dotted around. Some with firearms have climbed up trees and there are Casspirs with more troops out on the road. It looks like a siege anticipating a tragedy to be played out.

This is the Anglican church at which I worship each Sunday. In fact, I am a member of the church council and a choir member, so knowing where it is, I enter the church from the choir entrance at the side. A dramatic scene is before me when I walk in. The church's nave is jam-packed with tense, expectant children. Standing in the pulpit and facing the gathering is Archdeacon Patrick Ncaca, who leads a prayer and then a hymn. After that he and a Ginsberg teacher, Khaya Mabece, address the assembly. Their appeal to the students is to stop any further ideas of marching or confrontation as the situation is extremely precarious and we do not want another South African massacre. The two explain that there are Casspirs surrounding the church and shotguns are visible amongst the security forces laying siege. A voice amongst the youth calls out in response:

"We are not afraid of the baton and the quirt! We will not be intimidated!"

At this point I quietly join the congregation from the choir stalls and am soon noticed as I am the only white person in the Church. Khaya beckons me to the pulpit where I am introduced to the congregation as the principal of All Saints Senior College, a comrade and an activist in the defiance campaign. Khaya Mabece then asks me to read a copy of the manifesto that has been prepared by Peter King. All around me there is a gripping tension and an unnerving quiet amongst those who have sought refuge in the church. Some students are noticeably in pain and bleeding. Fortunately, I have a copy of the manifesto in my pocket. I read it out clearly and slowly and this has an important calming effect.

The manifesto opens with a statement of support for the defiance campaign and then declares rejection of apartheid's separated education, outlining the shocking conditions of township and rural schools where subjugation is the hallmark. The solution stated forcefully at the end is *"ALL OUR SCHOOLS FOR ALL OUR PEOPLE"*. I step down and find a place to sit down.

From the pulpit, Khaya then recommends to all that a delegation with one person from each school to represent us should drive up to Dale College. After this is accepted, I am asked to facilitate the process from this point on. It means first phoning Maxwell Anders, the headmaster of Dale College, to ask for his

162

cooperation in allowing a delegation to drive up to Dale and meet him. I am shown to the phone in the church's office and the following conversation takes place:

MB: *"Good morning Mr Anders, this is Michael Burton from All Saints Senior College. I am at the Holy Trinity Church in town and I am appealing to you to recognise that there is an extremely volatile situation here. My request is that you accept a delegation to come and address you and share a message from a written manifesto."*

MA: *"I will do that but there are to be only five in the delegation."*

MB: *"Please don't be prescriptive and set limits. Schools will want to be represented, there are more than five schools here and there is no threat to you or to anyone at Dale College."*

MA: *"Well OK… but if you want to play politics with these people…"*

I leave it at that although I am affronted by his insult of "playing with politics", as well as the offensive reference to "these people". After all, I am not playing with politics but have once more found myself mandated democratically to this responsibility by a gathering. I walk slowly back into the Church to report that we are to be accepted at Dale College. I am then asked by Khaya also to facilitate the process at Dale, together with Smuts Ngonyama, while he and the archdeacon look after the situation in the church. So now I find myself once more being reluctantly elevated from a participating observer to being right up front as an appointed responsible spokesperson. A minibus is filled up with students together with Smuts Ngonyama and me. We drive through town to the school where we are directed to the headmaster's side of the building complex.

Meanwhile the students who are left behind file out of the Holy Trinity Church two-by-two in peaceful procession under the hostile eye of the security forces. An arrangement has been made that a report back will be held at the nearby Victoria Sports ground stadium, where the pupils and their chaperones will gather.

*　　*　　*

Another irony is playing out. My two sons, Andrew and Simon, are attending classes at Dale College at this time. The school has ordered for razor wire to be erected around the premises to protect the boys from a possible stone-throwing mob of rioters. There are five Casspirs on hand. They are parked around the fence to protect the school as a further precaution. Here I am, at the head of the insurgents, a member of what the press has labelled a stone-throwing mob, coming onto the property where my own two sons are paradoxically being protected from their activist father!

The Dale headmaster comes out to meet the delegation, unable to hide his edginess as he ushers us into the President's Room. This is the school's showcase of the time with portraits of notable people such as Ian Smith, the former Rhodesian Front leader, looking down on us. Mr Anders invites the group to sit down around a long table. I introduce our delegation:

"Mr Anders, thank you for receiving us. We come in peace. These are young people from schools around our area and they wish to share their school circumstances. First prize is that you will call a school assembly now and allow each of them to address the assembly. Second prize would be for us to address your teachers and/or your prefects."

I then briefly describe the shock and horror that we have experienced as police have aggressively brutalised our young people while they were standing peacefully in front of the post office. After my introduction, what I have just said is then supported by a report from Smuts Ngonyama who is representing the Border Council of Churches.

Mr Anders then asks if he might hear what the student delegation members have to say. One by one the students speak and at the end he responds that he has never before been so positively moved by such articulation from young students. However, he explains that he is in no position to grant us the audience that we seek since he is bound by recent government regulations which require permission from the Education Department's inspectorate for anyone to address the school. These are difficult times. He makes a commitment that he will attempt to get such permission as soon as possible. Meanwhile he keeps a copy of the manifesto that we give him with a promise that he will circulate it around the school. The delegation accepts his explanation. I share with Mr Anders that it is my responsibility from now on to liaise with him on behalf of the MDM and to report any developments. Satisfied that we have achieved all that we can at Dale College, our delegation is ferried to the Victoria Sports Grounds for our report back.

*   *   *

The turnout on the field is massive, reportedly over twenty-five thousand people fill the stadium and the packed sports field below. As soon as our delegation arrives at the ground, we are loudly heralded by all who are gathered there. We are escorted to the centre of the stadium where a sound system has been assembled. Khaya Mabece opens the proceedings by presenting a full account of the day's earlier experiences. Speaking in isiXhosa and English he recounts how events have played out through the morning. He is followed by Smuts Ngonyama who further describes events that unfolded, starting with the police charge into the small crowd that had collected outside the post office. Then comes my turn and I am referred to for the first time publicly as "Comrade Mike". I even hear some ululating as I step up to the microphone.

The scene below and around me is intimidating and I am filled with trepidation standing above this huge crowd to share the outcome of the Dale College meeting. It is the largest gathering I have ever addressed and there is no time for stage fright even though I have no script to follow. I explain as carefully as I can how we met the headmaster who has given us an assurance that he will arrange for us to address his school in the near future. Again, I read out the manifesto that has been prepared for the occasion. It is all that I can do to appease the expectations and emotions of the people who have experienced so much unprovoked torment.

Once my report is delivered and people eventually disperse with the promise of the follow-up, I go with the rest of our delegation to the offices of Smith and Tabata in town. There we brief the National Association of Democratic Lawyers and hold a press conference. At this meeting, delegates from each school and members of the Standing for the Truth Campaign, some parents and Border Council of Churches representatives offer reports to members of the press in a cramped room.

After that, because the headmaster of Dale has said that he needs to consult with his school council, I decide to call in to meet with the chairman of this council, Mr Neville Woolgar. He is an influential local lawyer and personal friend. I start to share with him the events of the day and show him a copy of the manifesto. I then find out that he fully understands the situation and actually witnessed the police brutality in front of the post office, which he could see from his office window. He gives me the assurance that he will do everything to get the Dale headmaster and other council members to accept and accede to the very reasonable requests that we have expressed.

*   *   *

Two distressing issues then follow. The first relates to the Holy Trinity Church where the protesters fled to after the police had broken up the marches and the second relates directly to the headmaster of Dale College.

At the morning service on the Sunday afterwards, as the church council member who happened to be present at the event, I am called up to the pulpit and asked to explain to the congregation of the church what took place on that fateful day. So I share the circumstances that I witnessed in the church to dispel the rumours that I am told are being aired – that communists took over our church and sang revolutionary songs and shouted slogans. I clarify forcefully that there were no songs or slogans aired but rather that the church was a tranquil refuge for shocked and injured schoolchildren. The only singing was a beautifully sung mournful hymn. I further point out that inside our church it was peaceful and that Archdeacon Patrick Ncaca led us all in prayer and talked of reconciliation rather than confrontation. I emphasise that our church has been the place where a potentially disastrous massacre was changed into a peaceful ending without any bloodshed which was just a heartbeat away. I ask:

"*What better use for our spiritual home to share peace and worship?*"

...and I ask the mantra that I often set for myself:

"*What would Jesus have done?*"

I add that it is disappointing that Dale College missed a chance to show reconciliation there and then. At Queens College in Komani the headmaster, Mr Dudley Schroeder, understood and accepted the situation. He invited a hundred people from the crowd to address his school in contrast to the restrictive regulations that were quoted to us by Mr Anders and that prevented us from sharing our message with Dale College.

A short while after my report to a somewhat shocked congregation, I am informed by the rector, Reverend Hornby, that I am no longer welcome to use the pulpit at Holy Trinity Church. Clearly, I have stepped on too many reactionary toes in my address. I hear that people are saying "*we don't want that communist on the hill to address us*". Their comfort zone has been disrupted by what they perceive to be a revolutionary invasion and because they are set in their ways, they are unlikely to change their views.

Days go by and the Dale headmaster stays silent. After nearly two weeks have passed, I phone him to ask what is happening and he questions the hurry as he only intends to meet his council at the end of the month. Of course, he has just left us waiting while we were promised an immediate answer and he has not shared with me or any of us why he is being dilatory. My predicament takes a sinister turn when I am informed by Mluleki George, the United Democratic Front leader, that there is a perception building up amongst the people that I had deliberately stepped into the church on that day so as to subtly suppress the momentum of the protest. This is a dangerous perception that has apparently built up amongst those whom I represented as honestly as I could.

I need to do something to reveal the truth and Mluleki suggests I prepare a letter, on a Mass Democratic Movement letterhead provided to me, in which I ask the Dale College headmaster to explain the tardy response to our requests after his earlier promises to attend to the matter immediately.

We never do get the audience that we seek nor do we receive an answer to my letter. Wider political developments and events have taken centre stage. However, by showing my hand with the letter, which has been sanctioned by the MDM, I am personally let off the hook.

It has been a very difficult and nerve-wracking time for me to live through. It is a momentous and watershed time in the history of All Saints Senior College though. As principal I have nailed my colours to the mast and I have drawn the college down a definite line of future action. At a special assembly on 29 August, I report back to the college and explain my role in the events.

The weekly, *The King Mercury*, publishes a report on 30 August with the heading "*Four injured in defiance march*". The report explains how the police used tear gas, stun grenades, batons and quirts after the gathering for the march was declared illegal by the police command.

Whispers and Shouts, the student newspaper at All Saints, publishes an interview with me on 1 September. It is headed *Personal Questions on the Defiance Campaign*:

Reporter: "*In one or two words, what contribution did the events of Monday the 28th and the Defiance Campaign give to All Saints?*"

Mr Burton: "*An opportunity to publicly affirm our stand as teachers and students in response to the national call against the oppressive laws that govern our country's education.*"

The All Saints staff then sends a letter of concern and objection signed by all to the Minister of Law and Order, Mr Adriaan Vlok, pointing out that our students were brutalised whilst causing no provocation. The letter is acknowledged in a dismissive one sentence statement but there is no follow-up response of any sort. Not that we really expected one.

* * *

I am fortified by a letter written by our Trust chairman, Franklin Sonn, which validates all our endeavours to make All Saints a significant institution in the anti-apartheid movement.

The watershed year of 1989 ends with a national assembly, which advertises itself as an assembly of people of our country that will be truly democratic in its character and objectives. This is the "Conference for a Democratic Future", held at the University of Witwatersrand on 9 December. The aim of the conference is to address key issues, including a programme of mass action to end apartheid, engaging the attitudes of people on questions of negotiations, and a call to the international community to play a role in ending oppression and exploitation in South Africa.

The unifying perspective is declared as: "one person–one vote" in a democratic

Letter of support from the chairman of the trust, Franklin Sonn, endorsing the stance of All Saints College as a part of the anti-apartheid movement

country; the lifting of the state of emergency; the unconditional release of all political prisoners; the unbanning of all political organisations; freedom of association and expression; press freedom; and a living wage for all. All of these noble intentions are universally upheld and I feel privileged to have been invited to be part of the Border delegation. The conference boasts a total of four thousand six hundred delegates in all.

When I get back after the conference, I report to the All Saints community that it was a momentous occasion and an honour to have been invited to participate, albeit in a passive role. Particularly pleasing is to have been approached by and to have talked with former All Saints College students who were there. Rudolf Mastenbroek, President of the National Union of South African Students

(NUSAS) at Stellenbosch University; Dumas Nxarane from the University of Fort Hare; and Natalie Zimmelman on the SRC and NUSAS Committee at Wits University. They were all delegates at this conference. All Saints College was well represented, which should have dispelled any view that our anti-apartheid stance has been a token one. We are now contributing on a national scale and finding some of our alumni fulfilling Richard Todd's dedication statement of "*to those who may lead and serve*", engraved on the college's foundation stone. It makes me feel good to report this to him and the trustees.

All Saints is one of 2 100 organisations represented. It is an impressive and massive display of national solidarity. My input at the conference is to record our identification with the struggle in using our college campus as a venue for activities such as regional workshops for the constitutional guidelines proposed by the African National Congress, Standing for the Truth workshops, launching the National Sports Congress, the annual general meeting of the United Democratic Front, and restructuring the National Education Union of South Africa (NEUSA) which was later to become the South African Democratic Teachers' Union (SADTU).

*   *   *

The volatility of All Saints College with me at the helm can be stressed by comparing these events taking place in 1989 with those that are to happen just two years later in 1991. Because our senior college offers a two-year academic course, we have a student body that is very different every two years. Deep suspicion is widespread and regular justification becomes necessary.

In 1989 I am publicly declared an activist and a comrade in the struggle against apartheid – which brings a potential threat from those who uphold apartheid. All Saints is recognised in our region as standing firmly against apartheid. Yet, just two years later in 1991, I am set up to be killed by a sector in the student body who are convinced that I am an enemy agent working for apartheid and that All Saints is a Joint Management Centre.

It seems that every year I have to start out on a new tightrope with new perils as a new bunch of students start importing their conspiracy theory questioning and resistance. The risks that I am being forced to take on and off the campus don't seem to mean much to the new intakes. Perhaps, apart from the political dimensions, they are wanting to assert themselves as leaders. Franklin Sonn warns me:

"Michael, if young leaders are being attracted to All Saints, don't expect them to behave like sheep."

The pendulum swings fully from one side to the other in such a short time. Yet I am only a teacher who has been thrust under the spotlight and I cannot claim to be a proactive and deliberate political activist.

Richard Todd, however, is of the view that I am pursuing my own political agenda at the expense of his special school.

chapter 21
Marching

"Non-violence is the greatest force at the disposal of mankind. It is mightier than the mightiest weapon of destruction devised by the ingenuity of man."

— Mahatma Gandhi

DESPITE the intense repression of the state in the late 1980s, including mass detentions, the restriction of political activity and a ban on all media activity, the state has not been able to crush resistance. In 1989 there is a strong revival of anti-apartheid activity. It begins in jails across the country with political detainees embarking on a hunger strike. This leads to the government's releasing a large number of these detainees, largely to avoid an international outcry. This inspires further resistance to the state.

The United Democratic Front (UDF) is one of the most significant anti-apartheid movements. It comprises 400 church, civic and student organisations with a membership of close to 3 million. Through uniting different organisations such as trade unions, the aim of the UDF is to make South Africa ungovernable, thereby crippling the apartheid system. The UDF is launched in 1983, and begins its work by promoting protests and boycotts amongst its members. A year later, the "Township Uprising" breaks out, resulting in a partial state of emergency being declared. This is extended to a full state of emergency by 1988.

The UDF then starts to form closer links with the Congress of South African Trade Unions (COSATU), and formalises their association in 1989 with the launch of the Mass Democratic Movement (MDM). This is a loose alliance of anti-apartheid groups that come together in 1988 when the apartheid government places restrictions on the United Democratic Front

On 2 August 1989, the MDM organises and implements its first major national campaign since the start of the state of emergency. Campaigns differ in each region, but acts of civil disobedience are generally encouraged throughout the country. Permission for the MDM to stage protest marches is granted and marks a major turning point in the apartheid government's reaction to anti-apartheid movements.

*   *   *

Response to the call for defiance by the MDM gathers momentum throughout 1989. Soon after our participation in the planned peaceful march that was viciously halted by a police attack on us in September 1989, I take a leading role in further non-violent protest.

On behalf of the MDM, an application presented in my name is made to the King William's Town municipality to hold a release-our-leaders protest march.

The protest identifies five areas of concern. The state of emergency; the unnecessarily violent suppression of orderly protest; the continued imprisonment, banning or restriction of leaders of the South African people; all other apartheid laws and institutions; rejection of forced incorporation into homelands.

It is a massive protest. The King William's Town Borough Council could not have foreseen the scale of the response. A *Daily Dispatch* newspaper report estimates the number of participants at more than thirty thousand. Our call for action is supported by the Border Council of Churches and the Standing for the Truth Campaign, the National Association of Democratic Lawyers, the Mass Democratic Movement, as well as the National Medical and Dental Association.

Permission from the local authority for the (release-our-leaders) procession to go ahead

A portion of the protest in King William's Town, estimated at over 30 000 people calling for the government to "release our leaders"

*   *   *

Because All Saints has taken an active lead in promoting this protest march in King William's Town, I phone Franklin Sonn in Cape Town and invite him to support our protest march as the chairman of our Board of Trustees. Without hesitation Franklin accepts willingly.

His flight from Cape Town arrives just in time for me to collect him at the airport. We join the march when it is halfway on its route through King William's Town and we are immediately marshalled to the front.

The march ends at the Holy Trinity Church at the top of the main road through to Stutterheim. A small delegation of leaders is mandated to go forward to the police station a few blocks on. I am included in this delegation together with Franklin Sonn, since we are in the front line of the protest march.

When we arrive at the police precincts our leader, the Rev Bongani Finca, presents a statement to the Special Branch representative Mr Flippie Fouché.

Before he presents the protest statement, Bongani Finca says that he has a personal statement to address directly to the receiving officer. He stands before Mr Fouché, looks up at him, and tells him of an incident in Stutterheim a week earlier when pupils and priests were silently and peacefully protesting about their abysmal conditions. Archdeacon Patrick Ncaca, a senior church member,

The front line of the mass protest march showing Franklin Sonn and Mike Burton (with white jackets) with clerics

Rev Bongani Finca addressing security police outside the police headquarters

From the left with his back to the camera Flippie Fouché, looking up at him Rev Patrick Ncaca, above the hailer Mluleki George, holding the hailer Rev Bongani Finca and on the right Franklin Sonn

was forcefully struck whilst in an attitude of prayer by a member of the South African Defence Force (SADF).

Bongani Finca then says some remarkable words:

"Go tell your president that we are prepared to forgive you ... but first you must ask for forgiveness".

Mr Fouché mumbles something but is unable to utter anything meaningful in response. This cameo moment is described by Franklin Sonn as a high point in his struggle experience. He sees extreme significance in what is being played out. The reason this is so significant to Franklin Sonn is that he likens it to the occasion when Jesus stood before Pontius Pilate. All the trappings of power rest with the state official who is rendered speechless by this simple but profound statement while the real power in this case is with the priest who has been struck standing in front of the Special Branch officer.

The outcome is that I, through the facilitation provided by Peter King and Sindisile Maclean on our staff, and thereby All Saints College, have successfully organised and led a peaceful mass demonstration. The College has become a catalyst for public resistance. Crisis is transformed into opportunity. The challenge of what we can accomplish – presented at the start of the year – has been responded to. All Saints and I are poised for future actions of resistance and later for actions of reconstruction towards a democratic state for South Africa.

*   *   *

The defiance campaign is halted in mid-September when the government, with FW de Klerk taking the lead, agree to enter into a new era of constitutional negotiations with the ANC. The defiance campaign has shown the South African state that it is possible to resist apartheid and bring about change. Very shortly after the defiance campaign, De Klerk unbans the ANC and other political organisations. He also releases Nelson Mandela from prison.

chapter 22
Transforming

"The wings of transformation are born of patience and struggle."

— Anonymous

I N THE HISTORY of the anti-apartheid movement, 1989 is a watershed year. It is also a year that marks changes in the structure of the All Saints Trust. The political environment has changed dramatically since 1986 when the Board of Trustees was established. Although it consisted of business people and people with special support skills, none have been involved with the anti-apartheid movement. In 1989 it becomes necessary to transform the Trust.

Up until this year, Richard Todd has been solely responsible for nominating suitable trustees. They have been excellent people who have helped in the running of the college and have been given portfolios of responsibility. An example is Dr Tim Ndaki, who reports on medical and nutrition matters at the college. Tim and I get on very well since he is the choirmaster at the Anglican confregation where I am a member of his church choir. Another example is Stewart Dorrington, who is responsible for keeping the King William's Town golf course in good condition. His portfolio is to monitor the developing fields and grounds of the All Saints College estate. Chris Perry is a Johannesburg businessman who takes a legal interest and Louis de Waal shares his business acumen.

It seems to me that it is important that our Board of Trustees should represent more of an understanding of the anti-apartheid movement, especially since the MDM declares this as a year of defiance. For this reason, I start promoting names of people who are sympathetic to the struggle. As the college principal my status on the Trust is as an ex-officio member and therefore I have no vote but can put forward names. In 1989 Franklin Sonn is the chairman of the Trust. He is supportive of my suggestions and he understands my motives. I visit local trustee Stewart Dorrington at his office in King William's Town and talk through the names before I forward them for him to consider and propose on my behalf. It seems better that I do not actively table my recommendations, and Stewart is prepared to do it.

The first person that we agree upon is Sue Power from the Black Sash. Stewart adds Jannis Sephton, who runs a farm school at Barkly East. We both agree that since just over half the students at the college are girls, it is important and about time to have some female representation on the Trust. They are proposed accordingly and are accepted unanimously.

Then we promote Lex Mpathi, Greg Fredericks, Gideon Sam and Mthobi Tyamzashe, all of whom are actively involved in transformation for a post-apartheid South Africa. When Stewart tables these names at the Trust meetings, they are accepted without dissent. Richard Todd shows by his silence and his body language that he is annoyed at the transformation that is happening.

* * *

By transforming the membership of the Board of Trustees, we have built a sense of reassurance that as any conflicts arise, I now have a group of people to whom I am accountable who will listen with understanding. I feel a big sense of release. From the beginning, the trustees have been handpicked by Richard. They consequently feel an allegiance to him and his views on the management of All Saints. I am happy that there is now a balance of trustees who can look after our college's business along with those who understand the political environment in which we are trying to operate.

The Board of Trustees is joining me on the tightrope!

* * *

After Franklin Sonn's tenure as chairman of the Board has ended, I appreciate the support of the two chairmen who follow him, namely Stewart Dorrington and Jonathan Clark. Everyone at All Saints owes a great debt to the strength of character of both these leaders. When we appear to be floundering against an onslaught from our umbrella body LEAF and its director, Richard Todd, they are steadfast in their integrity and resolve to keep us afloat.

Stewart Dorrington the Chairman of the All Saints College Trust at a time when the funding tap was being turned off

Stewart Dorrington is a businessman and managing director of a King William's Town leather tanning company. He lives in the same street as Richard Todd, and they are firm friends from the start. They take regular walks together in their home suburb. From the start Richard shares his vision and thoughts with Stewart Dorrington. In 1987 Richard invites Stewart onto the All Saints Board of Trustees. At the time Stewart holds the high office of chairman of the Rhodes University Council in Grahamstown, so he is an eminently suitable trustee and he takes up the position conscientiously. He is also well versed in the undercurrents of political unrest and although he lives in a conservative white neighbourhood, he is sensitive to the aspirations of oppressed people.

Stewart is our Trust chairman from 1992 to 1994, at a time when the students became most aggressively rebellious. He supports my consultative management style. He knows it puts me at loggerheads with Richard as LEAF director, who demands a more autocratic approach.

Stewart Dorrington writes to me:

"As one of the Trustees of the All Saints College and having lived through the very harrowing experience of recent student unrest with you, I would like to go on record as saying how tremendously impressed I have been by the courage and fortitude you and your staff have shown through this unfortunate period in our history.

That we come out of it a stronger and healthier college with a much sounder appreciation of the problems that lie ahead of us in the 'real' South Africa cannot be doubted. In my opinion you take full credit for having guided the college through this crisis and I hope that you will receive recognition for this from the LEAF organisation. Any normal being would have collapsed under the strain."

As it turns out I never do get the recognition to which Stewart Dorrington refers. In fact, quite the opposite, for in November 1993 I received a summons by fax from the LEAF chairman, Ronnie Napier, to go to Johannesburg to account for myself and explain why I have "stepped out of line".

The implication is that I have allowed an insurgency on the All Saints College campus which, as a result, puts a financial strain on the college and puts the LEAF umbrella body at risk. I am being set up as the scapegoat for Richard's inability to sustain the support of funders. I am seen by him to be the weak link and so he demands that I toe Richard's line:

Ronnie Napier writes:

"I would therefore ask you, please try to cooperate with Richard Todd as national director and try to resolve (your) differences without delay .... I am appalled at your failure to understand this."

Stewart Dorrington is sufficiently perceptive to see what is happening and he plays a very important role as the All Saints Trust chairman in protecting me from the wrath directed at me by his former close friend Richard Todd. He meets Richard and the LEAF Trust at a quarterly meeting in Cape Town, raises the question of the principal being summoned and makes it clear that the LEAF chairman and national director should rather travel to Bisho to meet All Saints trustees and staff. This never happens.

When the inevitable divorce from LEAF comes in 1994 and the funding tap for the college is turned off, with staff being given immediate notice by Richard Todd, Stewart Dorrington brokers a deal with the Ciskei Government for funding support to keep us going in the interim. He is able thereby to rescind the shocking notice given by LEAF.

*   *   *

When Stewart Dorrington retires as the chairman of the All Saints Trust, the college is not yet in the clear. He hands the baton to Jonathan Clark, who plays an equally important role of taking the Trust and the college into the next phase of our development. That is, to establish an Educational Resource Centre providing support to teachers and twelve hundred students in township and rural schools in the district.

Jonathan Clark the Chairman of the All Saints College Trust at a time when the college transformed itself into an education development centre under his leadership

Jono Clark was invited to join the Trust at a time when the relationship between Richard Todd and me was at its nadir. His understanding of All Saints College's situation is astute and incisive. His lawyer's mind can cut to the chase. He writes:

"All Saints, in my mind, is probably remembered more for its ironies, where one consequence was intended but another one resulted. And it happened time and time again.

For example, the land was given by Sebe believing this would generate some bright, politically-correct, middle class black kids. The money for the building was given by the mining houses for the very same reason – they wanted black skills, because the unions were putting pressure on them.

But in truth what came out of it were politically agile, smart kids who weren't going to put up with the expectations of governments and weren't going to go along with the expectations of the sponsors and the people who provided the land. So, the

179

outcome was poles apart from what was intended.

Then we have one of the icons of the century, Nelson Mandela, who arrives in the new political dynamics and says: "Free education for all." Up until that date the mining houses felt some sort of social obligation to contribute. Certainly, on the overseas market, they were being watched on their social contributions so they felt they could make contributions to black education, which was a very good thing. The day Mandela said 'free education for all' they all breathed an enormous sigh of relief and said they don't have to subsidise the school any more.

Richard Todd was the one who put Burton in charge – another irony. He thought Burton would be just the right guy. And here was a person who moved with the times, who was flexible enough to see what he had to do. And if he hadn't done it like that the school would have closed."

Jonathan Clark sees us through the final breakaway from LEAF. He supports the necessary transformation of our operation from being a school for a few to a wide-ranging resource centre for underprivileged schools in our province.

He tells an amusing story of what happened when we sought advice from one of the prime initial donors, the Anglo-American Chairman's Fund:

"The time came when we realised, we had to sell the college at Bisho. There was no option, we had to sell it. We realised about R11 million or R12 million. But the money had initially come from Anglo-American and so we felt we should go back to them and say: 'We've now sold the buildings that you gave us. We've got the money. Do you want it back?' So, we wrote a letter and we got a reply from Clem Sunter, then chairman of the Anglo-American Chairman's Fund to say; 'Thanks for the thought but come up and discuss it.'

We also said we need some of his wisdom in scenario planning... I and Mike Burton went up there and we were treated to this wonderfully sumptuous environment, with a lunch, good wine, etc.

He (Clem Sunter) said he'd given out many millions of rands in terms of donations – but never in his born days had any one of them come back afterwards and said: 'Do you want your money back?' and he split himself laughing. He thought it was so funny. We had a wonderful lunch and he endorsed our plans going forward and that's where it ended.".

chapter 23
Supporting

"People must not give in to hardships of life. People must develop a hope."

— Steve Biko

AT A MORNING tea break in June 1992, Joan Schmidt, our college secretary, informs me that three members of the Parent Teachers Association of Charles Morgan Primary School in Ginsberg township, which is across the Buffalo River from King William's Town's central business district, request a meeting with me and they are waiting outside my office. The chairman introduces himself as Thobile Maclean. He is the brother of Sindisile Maclean who has been on our All Saints staff since 1990. Charles Morgan Primary School counts among its alumni Stephen Bantu Biko. I learn later when Thobile replaces Sindisile on our staff in 1993 that the Maclean brothers had worked directly with Steve Biko at his clinic before his untimely and brutal death at the hands of the security police.

The plight of Charles Morgan Primary School, which is in a dreadful state of disrepair, is described to me fully. I am informed that a protest march to the Department of Education and Training (DET) in King William's Town is planned for Wednesday next week. They ask me if I and All Saints will support the march. I pledge my personal support and inform the three PTA representatives that the opportunity will be offered to the staff and students at All Saints College.

I consult with Sindisile Maclean. I let him know that while I intend being part of the demonstration, I wish to walk within the body of the march and not at the front. This does not happen. Once more I find myself marshalled to the fore and with linked arms I am again in the front row of the marching mass of protesters. As the only *mlungu* (white person) I am again sticking out like a sore thumb. Every time that I am in the front of a mass protest march, I realise that it is not a wise thing to do at this volatile time.

The route is from Ginsberg to the DET offices in central King William's Town but when the march reaches the circle near the centre of town, it is halted by the police. We are told that only a delegation of leaders will be allowed through the town's business district. The body of marchers is to proceed to the Victoria sports grounds and wait for a report back of the outcome. I try to melt into the body of the crowd, but am in too prominent a position to be allowed to do this. Thus I find myself holding a banner which had been planted in my hands by one of the smiling marchers and am now part of the delegation leaders advancing on the DET offices with the objective of moving in and occupying them. Things happen quickly and there is no way that I can step back. I just hope that I will not be required to address anyone as my participation is one of support and not one of being directly affected.

While I am standing at the doors of the DET offices I am aware of a somewhat bemused crowd of mainly white, probably conservative, townsfolk – onlookers on the other side of the road, just standing around. Alan Hatley, a friend and quantity surveyor in the All Saints Senior College construction is in the crowd of spectators. He breaks away crosses the road and comes up and asks me what I am doing. After I briefly explain the issues around the protest, he congratulates me with a thumbs up and a supportive smile before walking away.

However, over his shoulder I detect a plain-clothes police officer filming us and his camera is clearly focused on me. The clandestine photographer stares at me with malevolence. This is a chilling and a threatening reminder that I am treading on very dangerous grounds as the SADF's dirty tricks brigade is still very active and it is naive to think otherwise.

Two completely different responses to my standing here.

We find the offices of the DET are locked. The officials are away for a lunch break. I think they knew what was coming their way and chose a pathway of discretion as the better part of valour, and have simply slipped away rather than face the heat. This tests the patience of the demonstrators, so occupation of the offices is achieved by breaking in. Forced entry is not good and not what I had agreed to support. Once inside the building, it seems to me that the occupation of the offices is rudderless and chaotic. However, eventually the grievances are presented and our report-back satisfies the crowd gathered at Victoria sports grounds. The march has achieved its objective of informing the DET and the public of the Charles Morgan School's predicament.

Fortunately, this time I am not drawn into having to say anything to the crowd. One positive outcome is that the Mayor of King William's Town, Bev Radue, publicly embraces the Charles Morgan cause and promises his support and determination to resolve the problems facing the school. As their mayor, he is in a position to make educational facilities equitable within the city. He manages to bring government attention, and the consequent remedial repair action, to the school. Repairs are effective and the school is once more in an acceptable condition.

*　　*　　*

Not long after the repairs and extensions are completed, and along with Bev Radue, I am invited to a celebration function at the school. The down side for me is that I am asked to make a speech. Again, what to say?

I decide to revert to being a geography school teacher and tell the story of what I announce as *A Parable of the Rock and the Sand*. For my presentation I bring two props – a largish piece of granite and a small plastic packet filled with sand. After introducing myself as a geography teacher I hold up the piece of granite and say:

"This is granite and it has three component elements – easily seen because each has a different colour, and each has different properties. These are the dark specks of mica, the white specks of quartz, and the light grey specks of feldspar. Bonded together they form a rock which is almost indestructible – granite.

Rocks are common objects known to all of us. They can be picked up and used as weapons in resistance to apartheid."

I show an iconic picture that encapsulates the struggle. It is of township youths hurling rocks in frustration against the might of the South African Defence Force (SADF) in the form of its casspirs. I draw attention to this evoking the biblical account of how David felled Goliath in a similar one-sided battle by using a small rock and a sling. I hold up the rock and mimic throwing it, saying that rocks are sometimes used as weapons against injustice.

"Apartheid has separated out those elements in granite through its segregation policy, and has entirely misunderstood the effects of weakening the rock... because the result ... [and I pour out the sand onto the table in as dramatic a way as I can] When separated out, rock turns to sand, and the Bible tells us that the wise man built his house upon the rock and the foolish man built his house upon the sand."

I go on to explain that when the floods rose, the house on the rock withstood the danger while the house on the sand was washed away. In this way apartheid as a policy is built on sand and has no foundations to withstand the flood of opposition.

"The message for the future, however, is for us to move away from using rocks as weapons to destroy something that we hate. This change is not easy because throwing in anger releases emotions. The change now must be to use the rock to build something which we love ... our future."

I point out that this is much less immediate and much less emotive. Building is often a slow struggle of hard work with little direct satisfaction, but the final result is critical for a new South Africa.

I conclude by saying that again the Bible gives an important message for the future because Christ is described as the cornerstone of the church and Peter "the Rock" is given the responsibility to build the church.

My sermonising address is well received and a hushed but smiling silence follows. A Xhosa man dressed in traditional finery calls out. He is an *imbongi* (poet and praise-singer). He moves into the centre and amongst other things calls out that I really am an *umfundisi*, both teacher and priest. It is a rare honour and occasion for me.

chapter 24
Massacre

"Gqozo and De Klerk have the blood of Bisho on their hands. De Klerk and his puppets must go! Forward to an Interim Government."

— Communist poster

I N SEPTEMBER 1992, all the ingredients are in place for a confrontation that will lead to bloodshed on the doorstep of our college. The Bisho Massacre shakes us to the core. Journalists have information two days before the event that indicate preparations for a massacre are happening. It is clear that journalists also know much about the deployment of forces.

Prior to a planned protest march on Bisho, the ANC sends a memorandum to the government requesting that the regime of military leader Brigadier Joshua "Oupa" Gqozo be replaced by an interim administration that will allow for democratic reforms in Ciskei. This is rejected by President de Klerk on the grounds that Ciskei does not fall under South Africa's jurisdiction. The ANC retaliates by organising a mass protest march on Bisho with the aim of ousting Gqozo.

Gqozo is seen on television on the day before the event warning that he will do everything in his power to prevent the march advancing into Bisho, and he does not deny that this will include meeting the marchers with force. The misinformation that he has received, described as a security report, informs him that the ANC's military wing Umkhonto we Sizwe plans to overthrow his government. He is clearly frightened by this and is preparing a siege strategy.

Led by top ANC officials including Chris Hani, Cyril Ramaphosa, Steve Tshwete and Ronnie Kassrils, a group of some 80 000 people gather on the outskirts of King William's Town. They are ready to march up to Bisho to demand an end to military rule and the re-absorption of the so-called black homeland into South Africa. At the artificial border point between Ciskei and the rest of South Africa, razor wire has been erected, blocking the entrance to

Bisho. When the marchers try to cross Ciskei Defence Force lines, Gqozo's soldiers are instructed to open fire. What happens this day is recorded in history books: how the crowd is fired upon, and unarmed protesters killed.

*   *   *

My role in this horrendous event starts when I make a written statement to our students on the day in which I express my and the staff's concern that the march will meet with violence, and that our students therefore are not given permission to march in protest.

After I distribute this notice and address the students about my fears of impending violence that could lead to the of loss of lives, I invite an SRC delegation to come with me in an early morning reconnoitre of the area where the march is to take place later in the day. As we drive through Bisho we see soldiers and the gun emplacements being made ready. Further down the road on the edge of King William's Town we come across the gathering marchers. We talk to Smuts Ngonyama and he introduces us to some of the leaders in the front. They are Cyril Ramaphosa, Ronnie Kasrils, Steve Tshwete, and Chris Hani.

When we arrive back at the college, we present our situation report to the college. Our SRC vice-chairman, Tando Bonga, recalls the events afterwards:

"Mr Burton said, 'Guys don't get me wrong. I won't allow you to go on the march but I will give you a vehicle to the march, because if I give you permission your parents will come to me and say you are a very irresponsible parent. As a responsible parent I won't allow you to march, because I have seen this guy Gqozo on TV promising violence.'

Me and Mr Burton and Mr Maclean we drove the students there and we came back.

Then during lunch Mr Burton, a very grim-faced Mr Burton came to me and said, 'Tando, I've just heard over the radio there's been some shooting: we need to go there and make sure we collect our students.'

We drove together, four or five of us, but we didn't find any students. We drove around the back roads to King William's Town to the hospital. Then we went to the morgue, you can't believe what happened.

The scenes were not beautiful. There was blood all over. We looked for our students and we could not find them. I saw someone I knew who had passed away, who had been shot.

Luckily there was no one at the college who was injured there. And I remember very well that I could not eat after that. The whole day I could not come to terms with what had happened. But luckily All Saints had prepared us for that moment later in life, because we can take a decision to do something, but we must take responsibility for what happens. I say thank God that happened the way it happened, because Mr Burton said 'I'm not going to give you permission to go there; the kombi is there – we will take you there'.

It's a way of teaching you lots of things, it's not running away from responsibility. It's actually giving you a choice.

Life is all about choices, the choices you make. I made the choice of going to All Saints and I am happy with that."

My own memory of the incident and its aftermath is that I count the visit to the hospital, to look for any of our students who may have been amongst wounded, dying and dead, as one of the most shocking of all the experiences I have faced in my tenure as principal of All Saints Senior College.

Peter King gives his account of events:

"I went to Bisho in the morning to get permission to be part of the march on the basis of being a freelance photographer. Walking out of the civic facilities were the Minister of Law and Order, Vlok, and the Deputy Minister of Defence of South Africa. And that was the morning of the Bisho massacre. I made that statement to the commission of inquiry and nothing ever came of it but the South African security forces were certainly present. Later I was between the Ciskei troops and the group of leadership of the marches, on the side of the barbed wire that is the present Fort Hare side. There were a whole range of senior South African peace monitors positioned between the marchers and the Ciskei troops. The main group of leadership remained on the road and a splinter group of the marchers with Ronnie Kasrils leading went through the stadium and went through a gap in the fence which would have been either deliberately or negligently left open by the security forces. The security forces, who had been lying in the grass at that particular opening, fired on them. I personally know that they were lying in the grass because when I joined the marchers from the All Saints' side, I saw them, they took lateral positions, lying down with their rifles on tripods. When they opened fire the troops who were in the Fort Hare property also opened fire on the marchers who were still on the road and so the troops were firing from two different directions.

Fortunately, none of the monitors were killed, but 29 other people were killed, 28 of them marchers, one of them a Ciskei soldier who was shot by his own colleague. The helicopter was on the ground and when the marchers moved from the road towards the stadium the helicopter took off and proceeded to circle. It was a matter of two minutes from the time that it took off to the time that firing started. I did not notice what the helicopter was doing. It's a very sobering experience to be under fire. Most of the peace monitors who had been immediately in front of the barbed wire and between the barbed wire and the leadership corps, were lying flat. I happened to be next to them and most of them tried to find shelter adjacent to the troops' vehicles so the chances of being struck by the odd stray shot would be minimised.

Based on what I know from the commission of inquiry and my own eyewitness impression, I believe that the firing on the north side started when the troops saw the marchers coming towards them. I personally believe it was an ambush. At the time the security forces said they'd come under fire and responded with fire. They searched for days for any sign that supported the theory that they had come under fire and there was nothing whatsoever.

Those who were in the line of fire and escaped with their lives were fortunate because they fired for, according to the commission of inquiry, 90 seconds non-stop, with semi-automatic rifles. It's something you do not forget. I did realise immediately that it was an occasion of huge gravity and I lay as flat as I could as did all the other people around me who were in the line of fire. I did hear bullets going over my head. It wasn't heroism or stupidity; you just don't believe that people would open fire on you; maybe naive."

*　　*　　*

According to the Truth and Reconciliation Commission of South Africa, Colonel Mkosana had instructed forces to open fire and later Rifleman Gonya had fired a grenade launcher. The ensuing bloodshed resulted in the death of 28 marchers and one soldier. Over 200 activists were injured.

The Goldstone Commission was appointed to investigate the massacre. Justice Richard Goldstone condemned both parties for their role in the violence. The Bisho Massacre resulted in FW de Klerk and ANC President Nelson Mandela entering a new phase of negotiations. They signed a Record of Understanding on 26 September 1992, which paved the way for the resumption of hitherto stalled formal negotiations in 1993. In 1997, a monument to commemorate the role that the marchers play in the struggle for freedom is erected on the site of the massacre.

*　　*　　*

Immediately after the tragic events of 7 September, the countryside around us becomes unsafe, and safety becomes uppermost in our thoughts.

A report in *The Weekly Mail* by Claire Keeton records:

"A wave of conflict between villagers and troops has turned Ciskei into a virtual war zone in the wake of the Bisho massacre, sending hundreds of refugees flooding into surrounding towns."

We hear news reports indicating that youths are being attacked and whipped by soldiers. Since the massacre no young people are safe on the streets of Ciskei. The South African Democratic Teacher's Union (SADTU) spokesman, Mxolisi Dimaza reports:

"Since the Bisho killings students from 7 to 21 years old are fleeing their homes, and random assaults are taking place on school premises in areas such as Zwelitsha and Phakamisa".

Our reaction at All Saints is first of all to recognise that normal schooling is simply not possible. Our safety and protection cannot be guaranteed on our property, so we make plans to end the term. Parents are asked to confirm with us that the region is peaceful again before students should return to school. To cover myself and the Trust, I needed to seek legal advice and as a result a leaflet was sent to parents:

"We accept that we are all affected by the political happenings in the region, which may again heighten, but believe that we must not lose sight of the need to follow through the scholastic programme for the year.

But we wish to be clearly understood that college activities will be continued under the following conditions and understanding:

A. We restate that scholars are admitted entirely at their own risk;

B. Scholars will be requested not to participate in political activities;

C. We will require commitment to the scholastic endeavours;

D. The academic staff commits itself to ensure the successful completion of the year."

part six

BUILDING FOR THE FUTURE

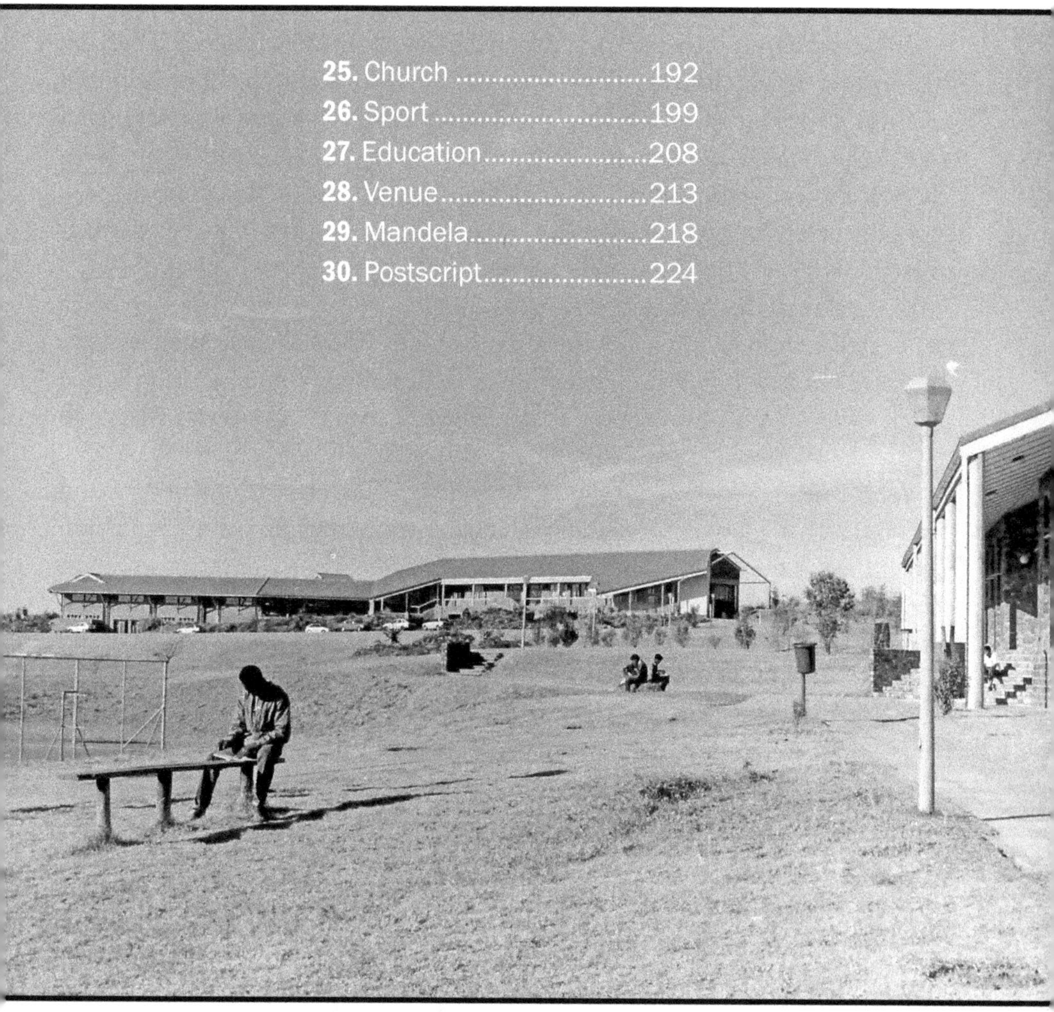

chapter 25
Church

"Stand up for truth, regardless of who steps on it."

— Suzy Kassem

IN THE ACTIVATION OF a defiance campaign against apartheid from a church platform, 1989 is also a watershed year.

The campaign is initiated by and launched at the Convocation of Churches held in May 1988. The Convocation, to which all churches and church groups in South Africa are invited, resolves to develop effective non-violent actions in the face of the deepening crisis in the country caused by the apartheid regime. The aim is to end the apartheid system by putting pressure on the South African government to abandon apartheid and to participate in a negotiated settlement to establish a just, non-racial and democratic society in South Africa.

In the face of the deepening crisis the churches feel that they have no choice but to stand for the truth and witness against the evils of the apartheid system. They feel obliged, in the face of suffering, victimisation and oppression of the people of God, to be in compassionate solidarity with the people as well as to oppose the apartheid system and the related regime.

Whilst being aware of the general mandate of the church to work for and towards the Kingdom of God, the immediate and specific goal of the campaign is identified as the establishment of a non-racial, democratic, unitary, free South Africa. The church is clear in its goals, which are the unbanning of peoples' organisations and the returning of exiles, the release of all political prisoners and detainees, and the abandonment of apartheid.

It is agreed that all this will be done with the goal of a negotiated settlement in mind. The churches see this as the only way in which the destruction of life can be reduced. They feel that there is no alternative way in which a total destruction of South Africa can be averted. The Convocation of Churches invites all Christians in the country and all peace-loving South Africans to participate fully in a campaign of "Standing for the Truth".

As mentioned previously, I am a member of the King William's Town Holy Trinity Anglican church council. We receive an invitation to attend the annual general meeting of the Border Council of Churches to be held just outside King William's Town at the Horseshoe Motel, on the road to Stutterheim, to address the church's stand against apartheid. The invitation notes that discussion on the Standing for the Truth Campaign is on the agenda. Christopher Harper and I are the two delegates chosen by our council to represent our church. I suppose this is appropriate because my portfolio on our council is Justice and Reconciliation.

Ironically, during these days of apartheid even our churches have their subtle divisions. Although churches claim to be open to all races, the mainly white clerics in our area belong to a grouping calling itself the Ministers Fraternal while the mainly black clerics belong to the more politically active South African Council of Churches. I therefore anticipate attending a meeting with mainly black clerics.

One white priest who crosses this delicate divide is Bishop David Russell and I get to know him through the Standing for the Truth Campaign. I draw a lot of moral strength from David Russell's brave stand.

*   *   *

Entering the Horseshoe Motel's meeting room and once more sitting near the back, intending to be on a listening brief, I do not expect to become involved further than this.

Ntombazana Botha, who is sitting close by, is not known to me at this time. She has been prominent in forming the United Democratic Front and is working in the offices of the Border Council of Churches. Ntombazana later becomes the Deputy Minister in the Department of Arts and Culture in 2004. As I sit here, she passes me a note encouraging me to particpate in the meeting and put my name forward to serve on one of the standing committees.

The meeting opens by looking back at the year's activities from the launch of the Standing for the Truth initiative at the Convocation of Churches. The campaign is resolved to develop effective non-violent actions in the face of the deepening crisis in the country caused by the apartheid government. The aim is to put pressure on the South African government to abandon apartheid and to participate in a negotiated settlement in order to establish a just, non-racial and democratic society.

It is noted that many actions in the defiance campaign have taken place in our region in a short space of time. There have been actions by students, parents

Handwritten note from Ntombazana Botha to Mike Burton in a meeting of the Standing for the Truth campaign led by the South African Council of Churches

and teachers in Fort Beaufort and Stutterheim. There is action in hospitals where black patients move into white sections and ask for treatment. The date for student protest marches targeting schools – Selborne in East London, Dale in King William's Town, and Queens in Komani – is planned for 29 August. There are also to be protest marches in September in East London, King William's Town and Stutterheim.

When it comes to electing officers, I try not to be noticed but my name is forwarded by someone, possibly Ntombazana Botha, to sit on the executive of the Standing for the Truth Campaign. I am not at this meeting as an observer this time, but as a mandated participating member from the King William's Town Anglican Church, so I cannot protest or make any attempt to withdraw my name.

As it turns out, and much to my misgiving, I am elected. This is the second anti-apartheid committee onto which I have been elected – one for sport and now one for church. Both are focused on preparing for a new South Africa. It seems that I am being drawn into a network of planning the way forward for a post-apartheid era on two fronts.

*   *   *

Not long after this, on 8 October 1989 I am one of the delegates from the Border region who participate in a national workshop held at St Peter's Lodge, Rosettenville. Our elected committee members for the Standing for the Truth Campaign are Rev B Buckley (Chairperson), Rev Hartland, Sr Marcella, Mr M Burton, Rev Ntisani and Rev Ngqono.

The aim of the workshop is to evaluate the churches' Standing for the Truth Campaign in the light of the defiance campaign. Early discussion identifies certain expectations and aims. Most of the delegates want a clear vision of what "Standing for the Truth" means, its theological implications, the mobilisation of the grass roots, and communication between structures.

As the defiance campaign gathers momentum events such as the assassination in May 1989 of David Webster, a leading activist in the Detainees Parents Support Committee, forcibly strike home to me that there is a very serious threat for me in being identified as a participant in anti-apartheid activity despite the moral high ground that can be claimed.

The meeting in Rosettenville recognises that the marches have led to huge gains, such as reforming structures and deepening links between such organisations as the Congress of South African Trade Unions, the United Democratic Front, the South African Council of Churches and the National Education Crisis Committee. The campaign is seen as an action campaign where people are not afraid to expose apartheid as being alive and well.

A focus is on the illegitimacy of the South African government and a stance that the church has a duty to work for its downfall. This is considered to be beyond a civil rights struggle. The campaign has to be clear on what is being defied and why. Simply summarised, it is to remove the apartheid regime by peaceful means.

The facilitator of the Rosettenville workshop is the Rev Frank Chikane. From 1987 he has been the secretary general of the South African Council of Churches. It is from this platform that he presents to us the international perspective, and he outlines the historical development of Standing for the Truth . There is no debate about violence:

"...as Christians we cannot be violent, and the Church does nothing violently."

Frank Chikane continues:

"The Church must lead in the non-violent struggle to get rid of the apartheid system. We need to explore the 80% political space that is not part of the armed struggle – we need to fill that 80% of space, fill it with non-violent action and if it is filled then the 20% armed struggle on the other side collapses."

I embrace the notion that the Church must take the side of the people.

An unexpected highlight of this gathering is the arrival of Walter Sisulu immediately after his release following twenty-six years as a political prisoner. Walter Sisulu is an anti-apartheid heavyweight who has been severely punished together with Nelson Mandela and other Rivonia Treason Triallists. He had been sentenced to life imprisonment in 1964. With other senior ANC figures, he served most of his sentence on Robben Island. Now in October 1989, he is released, and on the day of his release he joins us at Rosettenville.

Two years later, in July 1991 Walter Sisulu was to be elected ANC deputy president at the ANC's first national conference after its unbanning.

In this, his first port of call after his unbanning, his address at our national workshop at St Peter's Rosettenville supports Rev Frank Chikane's main message, which is that violence is unnecessary in effective resistance.

*   *   *

Back from Johannesburg I find my work cut out for me. The Rosettenville experience has been euphoric, but now the nuts and bolts are going to be most demanding as I once again question my role in this puzzling time while apartheid is going through its final death throes.

My twin responsibilities on the committee are to co-ordinate the Standing for the Truth Campaign in education and to facilitate the return of exiles, known to all as the returnees. These two commissions are huge and I have no sub-committee with which to work. I discover that there is a repatriation forum which has been elected earlier but I am not part of this. In addition, both of these tasks are potentially political dynamite for me to head up, especially from a racial point of view.

The repatriation of exiles carries big issues not least of which are the attitudes and expectations of those returning, as opposed to those who have faced the dangers of remaining behind. They appear to be antagonistic towards each other. The returnees expect red-carpet treatment on their return and this is a red rag to the bull for those who have braved it out back home. Those who have stayed feel that exiles have been living in luxury outside South Africa and deserve nothing special on their return. Another issue is the continuing education of their children, many of whom can only speak the language of their country of exile.

Other key issues include employment and accommodation. These are too much for me to head up so I withdraw from this responsibility.

With education I am involved with the People's Education movement and fulfil my Standing for the Truth portfolio there.

*   *   *

Nearer to home, we have a crisis at Nkqonkqweni, a village very close to All Saints College in the Peelton district. A number of our support staff employees live there and they report to me that the Ciskei Defence Force is uprooting them and forcing them to relocate far away near Komani. Entire families are being forcefully carted away and their houses demolished.

In response, a meeting is called at the Holy Trinity Church in King William's Town. I am at this meeting when the Nkqonkqweni refugees put their case to the church gathering. They inform the meeting that their homes have been bulldozed and that they are desperate.

I do not have prior consent from the All Saints College Trust or the college community to make any sort of offer, but I am moved to invite refugees from the forced removals to take shelter in our college squash courts and to provide them with mattresses and blankets. This is the weekend before the matriculation end-of-year examinations and I do not want to disturb the students. I point out that while we can offer limited shelter, we cannot protect anyone from the Ciskei military forces.

I am acutely aware that by offering the college and taking this stand, I am openly confronting the state of Ciskei for the first time. I now need to seek approval at All Saints because the students must participate in a decision that involves so much risk. When I report back at All Saints, the students overturn my offer to the Nkqonkqweni community to provide shelter with mattresses and blankets in our squash courts. Instead, they offer the use of their rooms in the residences saying that they will share with each other. The arrangement is not long-lasting, as the refugees are soon all moved to the Roman Catholic Church Hall in King William's Town.

During this time of upheaval, Peter King and Raj Kurup, teachers at All Saints College, are approached by a distraught woman whose two children are missing. They drive her in the college's minibus to Peelton right next to Nkqonkqweni. This search is in defiance of the emergency regulations. They are fired upon by security soldiers with automatic rifles, then arrested and detained. They are threatened and receive a verbal warning including one directed against me.

"You tell Mike we know him. He is MDM. We will come and clean him out."

For a while now I have regularly been getting threatening phone calls that link me with Smuts Ngonyama and Mluleki George. Franklin Sonn raises the issue of my family's safety on the campus at a Trust meeting, and points out that we are particularly vulnerable. He suggests special security measures. They never happen because the open 167 hectare campus is almost impossible to secure without huge expense.

At this same time one of our support staff, Willy Gqitani, who lives in Nkqonkqweni, is arrested and detained. I spend a whole day at the Zwelitsha police station, eventually securing his release because no reason could be provided for his being taken into custody.

*   *   *

Three years later, in 1992, the people of Nkqonkqweni are eventually returned home and I am invited to participate in their welcome home celebration. At All Saints we prepare a photo montage of the forced removal times for their rural centre and I am asked to give a long speech at the party. In response, the headman of the Nkqonkqweni community makes it clear that they are adopting All Saints College as part of their community.

Mike Burton presents a collage at the celebratory function to the Nkqonkqweni community when they returned home after having been evicted by Ciskei police and sheltered at All Saints

chapter 26
Sport

"Our young democracy witnessed the ability of sport to act as a catalyst to bring people together, share excitement and build a nation."

— Steve Tshwete, Minister of Sport, 1995

"**N**O MAORIS, NO TOUR"
This had been the response in the 1960s to South Africa's National Party government on the occasion of Prime Minister Verwoerd's political interference in dictating who can and who cannot play against the Springbok rugby teams on the basis of their race.

That was the beginning of the unravelling of the apartheid juggernaut. Sport, and particularly rugby, is the catalyst for this unravelling. South Africa had been effectively removed from most international sports by the early 1970s. The country was barred from the Olympic Games in 1964 and 1968 and expelled from the Olympic movement in 1970. South Africa had moved itself into a position of isolation from the rest of the sporting world by adhering to its discriminatory stance.

Rugby has had an almost mystical significance and importance to Afrikaners in South Africa and the Nationalist Party was substantially Afrikaner, to an extent that the *Daily News* reported in 1976 that "Rugby is the Afrikaner's second religion".

Expulsion of South Africa from international competition in rugby could not be tolerated by those in power and so two years after Hendrik Verwoerd's assassination, Prime Minister Vorster's government bends the rules and dramatically allows New Zealand to send Maoris on forthcoming rugby tours. But the tours do not run smoothly. They are marred by much-publicised vehement demonstrations and growing sanctions movements.

Politics and sport are never far removed from each other. Cricket is an embodiment of colonial England across the British Empire. It forms a formidable weapon of British soft power in incorporating other nations into the British fold. The game and its English values are found in the Caribbean, India, Pakistan, Bangladesh and Sri Lanka, despite the populations there not being white. Consequently, the cricket boycott against South Africa, while important, was felt most keenly in the English-speaking white community. It is not a top priority for the predominantly Afrikaner Nationalist government.

* * *

I experienced the wrath of sport boycott protests at first hand when I was at Oxford University as a student, also being a regular member and captain of the Oxford University Cricket Club (OUCC) First XI at that time. The intended Springbok cricket tour of 1970 had been cancelled as a consequence of the protests. Different sectors of the British population got involved in protesting against the Springbok tour. Nineteen-year-old Peter Hain emerged as the chairman of the Stop the Seventy Tour campaign in Great Britain. He had lived in South Africa until his parents, anti-apartheid protestors, had been expelled from the country because of their political activities. He got involved in anti-apartheid protests in Great Britain and was given the nickname 'Hain the Pain' during his organising of the campaign to stop the 1969–1970 Springbok tour.

According to the intended itinerary, a match at Oxford was set as a tour opener. An immediate consequence was that one night our cricket ground in the University Parks at Oxford was dug up with a deep trench right across the pitch so that it could not be played on. I was in the Oxford University Cricket XI to play against the South African touring team and was naturally disappointed that the game was rendered impossible. I was looking forward to taking the field against many of my former 1963 South African Schools XI team mates who were now due to represent South Africa on the tour. They were Barry Richards, Lee Irvine, Mike Proctor and Hylton Ackerman. But it was not to be. In addition, my Eastern Province team mates Arthur Short, Eddie Barlow, Graeme Pollock and Peter Pollock were to be coming to play at Oxford.

The Oxford University authorities decried the action of damaging our pitch as the work of vandals, but making fields unplayable was happening all around the country. It was part of the campaign orchestrated by Peter Hain to stop sporting tours from South Africa coming to England. Protest marches and civil disobedience such as spraying sodium chlorate on fields soon led to barbed-wire protection on grounds and other emergency measures.

This was no environment for a cricket tour. The Cricket Council called the tour off with deep regret, following an official and strongly worded request to do so from the British Home Secretary. Politics and sport cannot be separated. The MCC regretted the discourtesy to the South African Cricket Board and went on to say that they deplored the activities of those who were intimidating. John Vorster, South Africa's Prime Minister, was predictably angry.

"For a government to submit so easily and so willingly to open blackmail is to me unbelievable."

Ali Bacher, South Africa's captain, was more resigned:

"I regret the manner in which politics have become involved in cricket... [but] unless we broaden our outlook we will remain forever in isolation."

*　　*　　*

Now nearly twenty years on, in 1988, I am nominated and elected to the executive of the Border Senior Schools Sports Union (BSSSU) as vice-president. I have an important role to play as a white person on the side of non-racial sport in its move to unify with all-white apartheid establishment sport. My portfolio is cricket unity.

In November 1989 the Border Senior Schools Sports Union aligns itself to the Mass Democratic Movement and seeks affiliation by stating in a general council meeting that we unanimously endorse our support for the defiance campaign which is taking resistance to new heights. We are invited to the inaugural meeting of the interim National Sports Congress Border.

In February the next year this body calls a meeting for teachers and students to reject apartheid sport and the entire infrastructure of the apartheid government. The meeting announces that there are plans to officially launch the National Sports Congress Border in April.

The Border region is paving the way for the country to follow with a national launch. The BSSSU is in the forefront of promoting non-racial school sport in our Eastern Cape province and even in the country. I am inadvertently a cog in the decision-making structure at the schools level. These are heady days as we see further events unfolding.

It is all a far cry from Richard Todd's opinion that I should ensure that the role of the college in sport should be neutral and that I should stay out of controversy. Franklin Sonn, however, is very supportive of our direction as it means that the college is becoming more and more relevant in the eyes of the struggle community. By being elected as the vice-president of the BSSSU, I am almost paving a way for All Saints College to become increasingly prominent and politically acceptable as a model for a post-apartheid South African school through sport.

My role is being shaped by fast-changing circumstances and a decision to follow the counsel of leaders in the struggle. I did not seek this path, but soon I find myself in the forefront of what is becoming an avalanche of change.

*   *   *

All Saints now participates in regional competitions under the BSSSU. On the national scene, the yet-to-be-launched National Sports Congress (NSC) is gaining popularity as the legitimate sports unity movement. The BSSSU moves from its SACOS affiliation to the NSC in November 1989 and it hosts a landmark event in April 1990 under the NSC banner.

*   *   *

On Saturday 21 April 1990 the BSSSU hosts the first-ever open non-racial National Schools Athletics Championships. It is held in the Bisho stadium under the umbrella of the National Olympic and Sports Congress. The list of participating units includes Border, Port Elizabeth, Uitenhage, Western Cape, Northern Transvaal, Southern Transvaal, and Transkei. There are teachers, athletes and spectators filling the ground and its grandstand to overflowing. Thousands of people are crowded into the space. I am there as the acting-president of the BSSSU, which is the host union. Our president, Greg Fredericks, is in Israel so it is my responsibility as the vice-president of the host structure to make the welcoming address.

I am sitting in the pavilion next to Smuts Ngonyama from the NSC Border waiting for the opening ceremony to start up. Smuts is first called to the microphone and he announces the official opening. He says that the gathering is to participate in the creation of a new schools sports federation which will be rooted in the masses of the country. It will be genuinely non-racial and guided by the noble principle of democracy. We must be led by tolerance, discipline and co-operation if the NSC is to achieve its objectives.

Now comes the moment for me to welcome everyone on behalf of the BSSSU, but there is so much movement around and such an excited buzzing of noise after his speech that I ask Smuts how am I to get everyone's attention?

"Simple Mike. Just go down to the microphone in the front, raise a clenched fist and shout out Amandla!*"*

This word, used by the African National Congress and its allies, is the popular rallying cry in these days of resistance against apartheid. The leader of a group calls out *Amandla!* and the crowd responds with *Awethu! Amandla!* means

"Power to the people!" and *Awethu!* (literally "ours") is the crowd's affirmative response.

Well, I do as he suggests. For the first time, I raise a clenched fist and shout *Amandla!* into the microphone. I get such an overwhelming *Awethu!* in response, that I repeat my *Amandla!* several times. We are now all ready for my welcoming address. It flashes through my mind in the moment before I launch into what I am going to say, just what my family, my school and university friends and my colleagues would think if they could see me rallying a crowd in this manner? Here I am standing up as Comrade Mike with raised clenched fist calling out an anti-apartheid rallying cry. Is this the same person that they know? What would Richard Todd think if he was sitting in the crowd? Well, I can't hold back now.

After my dramatic *Amandla!* call, I welcome everyone to the historic occasion and point out that the intention of this gathering of athletes is to defy apartheid. I emphasise that the purpose of this meeting is to compete with each other and not just against each other. I share the anecdote of an athletics meeting for intellectually disabled that I know of. As the children are running around the circuit, the leading child trips and falls. The others in the race all stop and help him up and the race continues. It is a short speech but it has a positive effect.

Alfred Mkhonza is an All Saints College student who shines at this athletics meeting by winning all his races and setting really excellent records in the 100m and 200m sprints, outperforming all his opponents. The next year, Alfred goes on to break the Under-19 100m and 200m records in the National Athletic Championships held at the Pilditch Stadium in Pretoria. Previous records of 11,06 seconds and 22,72 seconds are significantly reduced to 10,67 seconds and 21,82 seconds respectively. He is then chosen for the Junior Olympic trials.

Earlier in the year I had had a preview of Alfred's sprinting prowess – in unusual circumstances. He is in my tutor group at All Saints College and we are spending a weekend hiking on an Amatola mountain trail. For most of the time Alfred is lingering at the back of the group, sometimes dropping way behind. It is clear that backpack hiking is not his favourite outdoor activity. Then all of a sudden like a bolt of lightning a blur of movement shoots past the rest of us. Even with backpack and hiking shoes Alfred probably covers a hundred metres in under eleven seconds. And the reason? He had come across a snake on the path in front of him, and leaped over it and careered on past us at breakneck speed!

* * *

After the athletics events of the day, officials gather in the Arts lecture theatre at All Saints College. It is the most convenient venue as it is less than a kilometre away from the Bisho stadium, and an interim South African Senior Schools Congress (SASSCO) is launched. In this way our College is the venue for the start of what later becomes the United Schools Sports Association of South Africa (USSASA). It is the recognised post-apartheid umbrella body for school sport administration. At the meeting I am elected to the executive committee of the interim SASSCO, together with John O'Connor who is on our All Saints staff and Greg Fredericks who is now a trustee at our college. Once more All Saints Senior College is stamping its footprint on South Africa's transformation to democracy.

What amuses me is that the newspaper reporter refers to me as Mr Button. He does not know that isiXhosa speakers find it difficult to pronounce the 'ur' in Burton and tend to shorten the vowel to either Mr Betton or Mr Button. I have recently found out that my nickname amongst the All Saints College students is *Iqhosha* which is the isiXhosa word for a button. Mr Iqhosha – Mr Button, that's me!

*   *   *

The next significant sporting event in which I take part is the launch of the National Sports Congress at the St Francis Centre, Langa, in June 1990. I attend as the BSSSU delegate. An All Saints College minibus takes me and other Border delegates all the way and through the night to Cape Town for the occasion. We arrive at our hotel destination in Bellville in the late morning. At the launch, the welcoming address is delivered by Mluleki George who is the convenor of the interim committee of the NSC. Many international messages of support are then read. The keynote address is given by Steve Tshwete of the ANC executive. He is later to become Minister of Sport in South Africa's democratic government. Mluleki George is to become the national president of the NSC, Smuts Ngonyama the treasurer and Mthobi Tyamzashe the general secretary. All of these sportsmen are from the NSC Border. It is a grand occasion. I am prompted by the Border delegates to ask a question from the floor, which I do. I cannot remember the issue or what I asked, but I do remember the amused reaction of my colleagues at my audacity in speaking out from the floor. Was I set up? I don't think so, as nothing untoward came of my utterance.

From August 1990, All Saints College becomes the venue for most NSC meetings. On the NSC Border senior executive are four representatives closely linked to the college. They include All Saints College trustees Mthobi Tyamzashe and Greg Fredericks, our college's Sports Master Sindisile Maclean, and myself as the college's principal. I have been elected to the position of Senior Vice-President of this senior sporting body.

Our focus is on unity in school sport. On behalf of the BSSSU, and as chairman of this unity policy meeting I am required to address members alongside other speakers coming from the African National Congress, the South African Democratic Teachers Union, the Border Education Crisis Committee and the Congress of South African Students.

*   *   *

From here we move into action. In March 1992 Telford Vice writes in *The Daily Dispatch*:

"Unity in schools cricket on the Border is around the corner – and cricket is leading the way. Three meetings have been held between the establishment Border Schools Cricket Union (BSCU) and the National Olympic and Sports Congress (NOSC) affiliated non-racial Border Senior Schools sports Union (BSSSU). These have produced a set of resolutions and a joint statement of intent as well as a high-profile steering committee to work towards full integration between black and white schools."

The first unity meeting is held at the Malcolm Andrew sports pavilion at Dale College in King William's Town. I arrive with our delegation and as the nominated spokesman. On the other side of the table, I know almost everyone from my own earlier cricketing career. Peter Haxton was captain of the Rhodes University XI back in the 1960s with me as his vice-captain. I also played against him for Eastern Province when he was in the Border provincial team. I taught geography to David Alers at Plumtree School in Zimbabwe and was his cricket coach in the late 1970s. Henry Breytenbach was the Border Schools Manager at a Nuffield cricket tournament when I was the Zimbabwe Schools Manager. Colin Winchester was at Rhodes University with me. So I knew them all.

As chairman of the Border Schools Cricket Union (BSCU), Peter Haxton opens the meeting by welcoming our delegation and inviting us to join the Nuffield structure. He describes it as being a very well-run and respected organisation with a long positive history and tradition. I, of course, know all this as I played in two Nuffield tournaments in the early 1960s as a schoolboy and was a Zimbabwe team manager at a tournament in Durban in 1977.

My reply is:

"Thank you for inviting us to join you but it can't work like that. The only real solution is that both organisations must disband and re-form as a single unified schools cricket body."

Asking them to disband is a controversial stand against establishment structures. However, from our side it is the only way that we can broker a win–win outcome and not always be passengers in the future. Clearly the move carries with it a number of difficulties but the negotiations are carried out in a positive spirit. We eventually decide to unify under the banner of the National Olympic Sports Congress and on Friday 20 March 1992 we launch the united non-racial schools' cricket structure in the Border. We are the first in the country to reach this landmark stage. An outcome of this meeting is that I am then elected as the chairman of the new executive committee.

Ted Allen writes a newspaper article under the heading *"Another first for Border cricket"* and he records.

"The managing director of the united Cricket Board of South Africa, Ali Bacher, who was unable to attend the launch yesterday, congratulated the Border Cricket Board on the occasion of the unification of cricket at schools level. 'This is a great occasion for the future of cricket for all cricketers in South Africa but for your area it is very special that the BCB lead the way, being the first to achieve unification of cricket at schools level,' he said."

That is not to be the end of my responsibilities for I then find myself at the helm as I go on to be elected as the co-president of the newly formed united South African Schools Cricket Body together with Andrew Layman from Glenwood High School in Natal.

One of my first responsibilities as co-president is to attend a cricket net for the newly elected Coca Cola Under-19 South African cricket team. Since I was a spin bowler in my days of playing cricket, I am asked to link up with cricketing icon Jackie McGlew who is looking after the spinner's net and to help with a bit of coaching. Jackie asks me to take a special interest in one young player from the Western Province.

This young player's bowling style is bizarre and defies any advice that I can proffer. He holds the ball between his thumb and forefinger, and then seems to push his one ear down towards the ground, lose sight of the wicket in front of him and throw his arm over his back. How it lands where he wants it to challenges logic, and then after it lands it seems to weave some sort of magic that bewilders the most seasoned of batsmen. I say to Jackie McGlew that there is absolutely nothing that I can suggest as the boy's bowling action is so convoluted that it is best to leave it altogether as is. It seems to work brilliantly as the batsmen who are used to something more conventional are totally bamboozled. The boy's name is Paul Adams and he later becomes a senior South African test cricket player. He is described as a left-arm chinaman bowler with a unique bowling action and he has a very successful test and one-day international career. In cricketing terms, Paul's eccentric bowling style reminds me of Dick Fosbury, who revolutionised the high jump event in athletics with an eccentric unique back-first technique, now known as the Fosbury Flop. The styles of both of these sportsmen seem to defy logic, but each of them gains amazing results by stepping outside the box.

Unfortunately, I cannot continue the responsibility of an almost full-time sports administrator that being co-president of South African Schools' Cricket demands of me, as I have so much to do as the principal to keep All Saints Senior College on track. I withdraw from the National Olympic Sport Congress as I feel that my task is completed. I was part of brokering a successful process of unity in school sport and now it is time for proper full-time sports administrators to take over.

When I had taken up the reins as principal at All Saints College, I had no idea that one path of my journey would lead me to such an elevated position and through so much off-the-campus sport involvement just six years later.

chapter 27

Education

"For the times they are a-changin'"

— Bob Dylan

'Last year the students' slogan was *'Liberation now, education later'*.
At the December conference this was changed to *'Peoples' Education for Peoples' Power'*."

— Ihron Rensburg (NECC Secretary, May 1986)

Education had been the direct cause of students being at the forefront of protest against apartheid. The demand for democratic people's education had begun in the 1950s in protest against the Bantu Education Act of 1953. This Act legalised several aspects of the apartheid system and enforced racially separated educational facilities.

In June 1955, the Congress of the People had met in Kliptown, Johannesburg, and had drawn up the Freedom Charter for the democratic South Africa of the future. The demands of the people for an alternative to the National Party's apartheid power were collected, debated and expressed in this charter.

In the 1980s, the anti-apartheid struggle's educational and political goals had become clearer, with the demand for "People's Education for People's Power", which had eventually emerged as a concept, vision and programme of action out of the education crisis of 1985. It was based on a rejection of apartheid education and was epitomised in the ongoing school boycotts of 1984 and 1985. Subsequently, it begins to develop further to envisage education for the majority of the people – students, parents, teachers and workers. Students, teachers, and parents had begun to question what a different, alternative education system would be like. What would be its underlying principles? What would be its method and content?

Student struggles and their rejection of Bantu education in the 1980s becomes linked with demands and campaigns concerning everyday issues that confront communities. In this way the student struggles are connected with community, workers', women's and youth organisations. Students develop an understanding that educational transformation requires societal transformation. After a period, the intensified and sustained boycotts lead to concern amongst parents and teachers regarding the future of their children and students. A 1985 Soweto Parents Crisis Committee Conference passes a resolution on a conditional return to school to use schools as the beginnings of People's Education. People's Education can be described as a deliberate attempt to move away from reactive protests around education and to develop an education strategy and contribute to laying a basis for a future, post-apartheid South Africa.

"Down with gutter education!"

The apartheid policy of Bantu schooling as low-level, or gutter, education has been aimed at directing black or non-white youth to the unskilled labour market so as to ensure continuing white control and prosperity. The anti-apartheid struggle rejects this inferior education designed to ensure domination of one sector of the population through the subjugation of the majority.

Education is not apolitical. People's Education is both an educational and a political programme. The struggle for alternative education is part of the political anti-apartheid movement for a democratic, non-racial South Africa.

People's Education aims to prepare all in the community for full participation in a democratic society. It depends on and promotes the unity of different sectors of society – parents, teachers, students and local communities. It has to be controlled democratically by and in the interests of the majority of the people.

The National Education Crisis Committee transforms itself into the National Education Co-ordinating Committee. It believes that People's Education and People's Power are not incompatible but rather are intimately and reciprocally linked. In the wider context of the NECC movement, People's Education can be regarded as the working out of the educational consequences of the Freedom Charter, which is an expression of the will of the people. A very important demand is for the establishment of organs of people's power such as Parent-Teacher-Student Associations (PTSAs) and Student Representative Councils (SRCs).

*   *   *

In the Eastern Cape an ANC Education Conference is held in April 1991 at the University of Fort Hare in eDikeni. As principal of All Saints I am invited to attend and at one stage find myself being promoted to be the chairman of a commission to develop Peoples' Education in our region. I decline such a huge responsibility as I do not feel that I am sufficiently conversant with the issues. Following this preparatory conference at the University of Fort Hare, a number of members of a shadow desk are tasked with following up on a research programme motivated by the National Education Co-ordinating Committee. I am elected to be a member of this commission. The major objective is the development of an alternative policy framework on education for a future non-racial and democratic South Africa. A key question to be addressed is the link between academic, technical and vocational education in the context of People's Education.

The first main aspect of the policy debate is about education control. This raises questions of Who? How? and Why? Should there even be control? and What do we mean by control? A second key aspect is the content of education, which raises the questions of What should be learned? and Why. Finally, the question is How should education be financed? These are profound questions for us to grapple with and try to unravel.

I accept a position on the shadow desk working group or Education Commission and, together with MJ Fuzile, Ray Tywakadi, Nezi Jordan, Eldred Fray, Nosimo Balindlela, and Gideon Sam, we set about the task.

Education negotiation for People's Education takes on a visible national perspective at the National Education Conference (NEC) which is convened the next year in March 1992 in Broederstroom, outside Pretoria, by the Education Delegation. The Education Delegation had been formed by Nelson Mandela in 1991 to facilitate direct negotiations with the state in order to address the crisis and challenges in black education. The NEC calls for People's Power based on the principles of People's Education.

I am not able to do much on this committee other than read the literature, attend meetings and participate in the discussions, which are based on readings from the national movement and elsewhere. I simply do not have the time to research further.

However, as part of small delegations, I do find myself travelling to places like Butterworth (now Gcuwa) and eDikeni. My task is to participate in meetings with teachers in these areas so as to brief them, as well as to discuss issues around changing responsibilities and disciplines in the new democratic South Africa which is on the horizon.

The future of the People's Education for People's Power movement seems to get diluted and a bit lost with the national level negotiations for South Africa's new democratic government. As a result, the political and educational ideal of People's Education for People's Power appears to give way to democratic elitism in post-apartheid South African schools. Its implementation faces daunting difficulties and is seen as a massive struggle between the state and black communities for the control of schools. The capacity of teachers to cope with People's Education innovations is questionable. For many teachers, their own education, training, experience and organisation do not provide them with the confidence or resources to drive radical changes. The implementation of People's Education seems to be a step too far.

One major need is for consultation, organisation and establishment of supportive structures. It demands that parents, teachers and students work closely together to produce the resources and attitudes to learning that are necessary. These are not easily found.

*   *   *

In May 1993 Education Providers are invited to a meeting by Gideon Sam of the Independent Teachers Enrichment Centre (ITEC) in East London. The purpose of the meeting is identified as "Towards a Regional Education Forum". It is specifically to address the development of Science, Mathematics and English in our region through In-Service Education and Training (INSET); to draw together institutions that have the capacity to deliver on INSET and to determine what they are prepared to do; to form a linking network and forum for participating institutions and organisations; and to investigate accreditation and evaluation of all INSET work.

I accept the invitation and attend on behalf of the All Saints Trust. From this beginning in August 1993, a three-day conference is organised to establish an educational forum of deliverers and coordinators from the formal and non-formal sectors. Other aims include refocusing education towards constructively addressing the needs of the region, facilitating a sense of ownership, belonging and accountability, and providing a platform from which education and training reconstruction can begin.

I am elected as a member of the conference planning committee and am quoted by *The Daily Dispatch* (6 Aug 1993) as saying:

"This region's major resource is its people. If we sit back now, we will fall behind. The region must see that its primary target is the development of its people."

The conference is titled "Education in Transition: Towards a Regional Education Forum" and the guest speakers invited are John Samuels and Franklin Sonn. In his keynote address, Franklin Sonn calls for a new culture of responsibility and discipline instead of the mobilisation which has been used to overthrow the apartheid regime.

The overall aim of the conference is to address the reconstruction or transformation of education and training in the Border-Kei region. The objectives are to determine clear strategies to resolve the deepening crisis in education, address the issue of governance or control of education and training in the region, and resolve the issue of fragmentation in the Border-Kei region. In other words, to find ways of co-ordinating all education and training efforts and initiatives in the region; and generate policy options to address the multitude of issues pertaining to education and training.

The Border-Kei Education and Training Forum is founded on 4 November 1993 and it has working groups in different sectors. I am elected as the coordinator of the working group that focuses on secondary education.

By the end of the year the regional body resolves to link up with the National Education and Training forum (NETF). The groundwork is completed for a founding document to be launched on 18 November 1993.

chapter 28

Venue

"It's a very special venue, and a very special time."

— Matthew Hayden

T IS MONDAY 8 June 1992, and today I must go up to my office early. Half
an hour previously I have been asked in a telephone conversation with our
new Trust chairman, Stewart Dorrington, to prepare an inventory of how the
college has been used by outside organisations. I need to justify how I have been
allowing what I have described as progressive structures to meet outside school
hours on our premises. Stewart needs to know who they are and what were they
trying to achieve so that he is fully informed ahead of the next Trust meeting.

I sit down at my desk and pull out my files to put together a record. I am
happy to build an impressive array of organisations that have met, planned and
strategised for the new era in South Africa's political evolution by using our
facilities. The issue is that this is flying in the face of apartheid and brings a
risk with it from the security and defence forces. I am comfortable that the
meetings are peaceful. They are planning for the future and not plotting sedition.
However, I am uncomfortable that mischievous leaked misinformation could
lead to violent invasion of our property.

So I turn through the pages and see that in 1990 we hosted a People's Education
Workshop with papers on the National Democratic Struggle (NDS) focused on
the role of students and teachers and on People's Education, an African National
Congress executive meeting and an ANC Department of Education women's
section.

In 1991, a plethora of meetings and workshops were held at All Saints
and in the current year a whole lot more. Not all represented banned political
organisations. The common thread had been preparation for a post-apartheid
time to come. While all these off-campus organisations are using our property
in this manner and bringing much acclaim from the surrounding community for

213

the role that we are playing, I know that Stewart's motive for asking me for this inventory is because we both anticipate some sort of disagreement from Richard Todd representing our umbrella organisation LEAF. I want to build an argument that in no way do these activities impact negatively on the normal college modus operandi. The student body is indeed comfortable in seeing what is happening and they have responded by making sure that they work well at all available times.

Stewart has just confided in me that I am to be accused by Richard Todd of being an absentee headmaster. This is something Richard intends tabling at the upcoming meeting. Stewart needs to cover all bases. He wants to ask me to step aside at the meeting and allow him to answer any finger pointing that might be directed at me. I take a deep breath because I resent the allegation of being described as an absentee headmaster, as I do not consider that I have at any time neglected any of my school duties: my ire is rising. Stewart recognised thta I might respond with righteous anger, as I believe that I have been gaining legitimacy and acceptability from our students and the struggle community, and our examination results have been soaring. I perceive that Richard's charge is going to be that I am using my position to further my own agenda at the expense of the school. My counter argument would be that more than once I have heard the accolade from community members that:

"All Saints College is our beacon that is showing us the way."

But Stewart wants me to stay out of it and not rise to provocation. He is probably right and I trust him implicitly. In the All Saints venue file, I find a paper in which Gideon Sam has written everything that I need to show Stewart. These are words written by a member of our board of trustees and therefore I cannot be accused as being the source:

"What we were doing in the sports movement was saying to ourselves: we are preparing ourselves for an Eastern Cape government that is going to come after this government... And it was in that context that All Saints was the place where we all came together and worked on these issues.

Thanks to the kind of leadership we had on the Trust as well as [on] the staff, because we never had a situation where we got onto the campus and half the teachers were saying that this is not a political rally, or this is not a political school. They understood, I must say in that regard that Michael was very fortunate to have the right staff – people who understood what it was all about and how we had to prepare our children to be well-educated in preparation for liberation.

What remains very strong in my memory is from a sporting perspective, because I am a sports person. We were looking for answers to many of the challenges we had in sport. And I think critical to our success of what we have now in sport – although there are still many other challenges – was the fact that at All Saints we had put together the entire cabinet for a new Eastern Cape government. We knew who the people were who we had to put in particular positions. And that kind of coming together of minds from throughout the area to congregate in that hall, to say if this happens, then this, if you move there and you move there…We knew what was going around us. In other words, our activities were not delinked from the other activities of the day.

Hence All Saints whenever there were big marches, All Saints was part of them. We never, even as board members, raised our eyebrows to see that there's that person, what's he doing in the march? Because we understood that you had to be part of the people and their struggles if you were situated in that part of the world. It would have been a disappointment to us as leaders at the time if we had a situation where we had this island of excellence which had no link to the struggles of the people.

Hence all we had to do when we got onto the campus was interact with the staff; interact with the students and hence the students had a very wide experience because of the activities that were taking place there and because of their leaders who were participating in most of the activities of the day.

I am sure when you talk to most of them that kind of experience is not any experience that many of the children at Selborne or Cambridge or Stirling experienced at that time.

All Saints was a mixed society, a sort of a microcosm of what we believed would be an ideal South Africa in which we lived together and studied together.

It was very difficult in apartheid SA and worse in the homelands to gather freely, to get together. You were always afraid that you would be disrupted by homelands police, or that there would be so many spies within your meeting. And so, you knew that even going into church what would that say? Because you were actually exposing the minister and his congregation to become the bad boys and girls of the Ciskei government. You also knew that a church that allowed this free thinking and this kind of meeting to come into its premises it would actually become marked, the minister would take a lot of intimidation…

Getting a place like All Saints, it was like: 'Don't touch! Leave them alone. They have…' I don't know how to describe it but there was this aura around All Saints. It was like: 'Guys, leave that place alone, that's not just a place you go into and disrupt their activities. It's a school. It's one of a kind. You can't just go into that place and disrupt their activities.'

Hence meeting at All Saints, you felt so relaxed, so very relaxed, that you could go to All Saints and be accepted, and be welcomed onto the campus and be given the space where you could sit and discuss and have the time to do the things that you wanted to do.

Now many people will not realise even how difficult it was to get to a venue. Now I remember in the old days, that for us who were in Alice, if you come to All Saints *you were a homeland citizen with a blue ID so that going to King, the SA police could stop you and say you are not supposed to be here. So, going to Mdantsane you had to go through Fort Jackson and there would be a roadblock there to check whether you were actually entitled to get in. 'Do you have your blue ID?'*

So, when we think about where we are today and the role that was played by institutions like All Saints, many people will not realise what it meant to us in the liberation movements to have sanctuaries like All Saints when you could go to and have freedom to talk about and to decide without worrying that somebody was going to come in and crash into the hall and disrupt your activities. And that is why when we think about all these things today, people must always remember how difficult it was to do certain things and respect the privilege of what we have today. Not many people think about where we are today and where we come from.

Hence, sometimes I say to students today, I say: "You are privileged, especially if you are a university student, you are very privileged, if you are a college student, because come to think of it there are millions out there who don't have the privilege, and it was worse in the days before we had the freedom that we've got today.

It's those kinds of things we've got to bring across to people: let's respect what we have now because if you lose it now and you go back to where we come from it will be worse. No doubt about it. It was a hard world.

In the years between the unbanning of the liberation movements and the first democratic elections, All Saints was a regular venue for all manner of conferences and workshops preparing for change – 28 are on record most of them organised by old friends and allies of the College."

I feel that my case can be closed with my inventory list which identifies the organisations that have used our facilities and what they discussed. At all times we are covered by insisting the registration form records the organisation's title, the meeting's agenda and the details of attending delegates at every meeting. These are then shared with staff and students each time. It is important to be transparent.

I attach a printed copy of Gideon's writing as an appendix, put it all in an envelope, get into my car and take it to Stewart in King William's Town where we talk it though. When I drive back, I feel comforted that Stewart Dorrington is fully behind me in our attempt to legitimise All Saints within the struggle as an education institution while maintaining an extremely successful academic record despite the political distractions that come with the times.

While I feel comforted that All Saints is playing such an important role in the planning for a brighter future, I am still apprehensive about how things might work out with Richard Todd. It is still fresh in my mind how we were opposed to each other because I had linked All Saints with progressive structures in order to resolve a wild-cat strike at All Saints. He came at me aggressively at the Trust meeting, planning to suggest his inability to access funds was directly due to my management of All Saints. But he lost ground badly when Franklin Sonn banged the table and harshly put him in his place. Might he still be planning some sort of revenge?

chapter 29
Mandela

"Lead from the back — and let others believe they are in front."

— Nelson Mandela

THERE IS an excited buzz around the college. We have just heard that Nelson Mandela, recently re-instated as president of the African National Congress, is attending a meeting in our lecture theatre today, Sunday 9 August 1992. He will be arriving any minute now. All our students and most of the teachers rush to the administration block with me to to greet him as he arrives. This is a big surprise and a huge occasion. We mustn't miss our chance.

The motorcade arrives and stops on the road just below my office. Nelson Mandela steps out onto the very ground where only a year earlier our rioting students had held our alumni hostage and I'd faced their wrath. This visit is a vindication; proof that they were wrong when they set out to prove that our school was linked to the repressive apartheid government. Nelson Mandela's presence endorses that our college has contributed both academically and to anti-apartheid resistance.

Now, so soon after that frightening time, the leadership of the ANC has chosen our college as the venue for an important Tripartite Alliance gathering. Our own staff member, Sindisile Maclean, has guided the motorcade right up to our steps. He beckons me down onto the road as Nelson Mandela with other ANC leaders including Steve Tshwete, Saki Macazoma and Jessie Duarte, start climbing out of their vehicles and walking up to our entrance. I'm welcomed into the throng.

If Nelson Mandela is endorsing us with his presence so soon after his release from incarceration, surely now even the most cynical or suspicious of our students have to recognise that All Saints has "arrived", politically.

My heart is in my mouth. This is an unbelievable honour bestowed on our institution. Many people might ask the question why did Nelson Mandela come to All Saints College so soon after he was freed? The answer is because

Nelson Mandela arrives at All Saints to attend a Tri-partite Alliance meeting held at All Saints College. Mike Burton is the back left wearing a white polo-neck shirt

All Saints has proved itself to be an institution that both responded to the call for defiance and further supported the anti-apartheid struggle by opening its doors to progressive structures to plan for a democratic time to come.

I rush up a side path so as to get ahead of the visiting group. I want to get in front of Madiba so that as he enters our foyer, I can formally welcome him to the school. I am not sure what to say but clearly, I must describe who we are and what we are trying to achieve at this place. What an opportunity.

Nelson Mandela stands before me, his calm eyes fixed on mine. When I mention that we are part of an umbrella organisation, the Leadership and Education Advancement Foundation (LEAF), I can see that he wants to respond. I stop and he surprises me and the gathering in the foyer by making a short impromptu speech. Peter King has the presence of mind to turn on the tape recorder he carries with him. Madiba's topic is leadership. Steve Tshwete tugs at his

Mike Burton welcomes Nelson Mandela in the foyer of the administration building

219

leader's elbow and whispers in his ear, reminding him that all the delegates are waiting for the important meeting to be started. Nelson Mandela looks around, enjoying the occasion. He is not to be hurried.

"I would like to tell you a story which I've related a hundred times," begins Madiba, *"But it's appropriate enough to repeat here, because it's a story that relates to the impression of a young person about me. Shortly after I was released, I visited Harare, the capital of Zimbabwe, and I became friendly with a young lady of thirteen years. We were conversing one day, and she said to me, 'Do you know what the children in my school think of you?' I said, 'No.' She said, 'They say that when you were young, you were very handsome.' But then the sting came: 'But now you are old and ugly.'*

I don't know what you think of me, but since that day I have wanted to wear make-up, so that I could look as I was in my younger days!"

Madiba laughs, enjoying this self-deprecatory recollection. He laughs easily and it is infectious. His audience relaxes.

"It is always a pleasure for us to exchange views with young people. It is always said that young people are the leaders of tomorrow, and that is true, but you have to be in prison to understand the importance of friends, of support, of solidarity for your cause. When we realised that we enjoyed the support not only of the general masses of the population, but in particular of the youth, we knew that whatever might happen to us as individuals, the struggle for freedom itself was assured of success, because a cause which is supported by the youth can never fail. I have said several times that amongst you here are going to be the leaders of the community. There are going to be leaders of political organisations, ambassadors who are going to represent us in foreign countries, there are going to be members of parliament who are going to make our laws, there are going to be Prime Ministers, there are going to be Presidents. It is in that capacity that we regard you, because the leaders of tomorrow must be young people who are fully equipped.

It is no longer sufficient to have a first degree – to have a BA or BSc – now you require senior degrees – masters degrees and doctorates. As we have pointed out before, what happens in Iceland immediately becomes known in the Cape Peninsula. The world has become very small, and you are not only going to compete with your white counterparts in this country, who have got better opportunities for education. You are going to compete with the entire world. You are going to represent us in world bodies – the United Nations, the Security Council, and so on. You must therefore equip yourself to ensure that you are able to lead and serve this community. You can only do that by ensuring that you have the highest qualification."

He takes a break and looks around at the young audience hanging on his every word:

"It is a tremendous inspiration to us that we have the support of young people. Whatever happens to us as individuals, we are assured that the struggle itself will

prevail. We have now reached a critical moment. It is clear to us from everything that is happening that we are on the verge of getting our freedom, and we would like you therefore to support us. And the best way of supporting us is to ensure that at the end of the year you pass your examinations. That is the significance of this institution, as well as all centres of education.

I must again tell this story, which I've told several times. I went to India in October 1990, and I was interviewed by twenty young people who were selected all over India. They put questions to me which indicated that they had a full grasp of what is happening in this country. They asked me about the various black political organisations in the country, the reasons why there is no unity, the strength of the government and its agencies, and after very detailed questions – even allowing for the fact that they will have been briefed by their teachers – the amount of knowledge that they had about South Africa was a challenge to our own young people. When we were the same age, we were unable to know even about the existence of the African National Congress, but today children miles away from our country, between sixteen and eighteen years of age, were asking me detailed questions about my own country – the population, the size of the country, the temperature and climate – all those details which we must know. At least you must know how large the population is, how many so-called Coloureds in this country, Indians, Africans, Whites, how big the Cape is, the Orange Free State, the Transvaal and so on, when Winter comes – because these things are different depending on in what country you are. You must be able to have this basic information."

He once more stops as his entourage is urging him to finish and move on to the important meeting that is waiting for him. But Madiba is enjoying sharing this time with us and he carries on:

"You must realise also that we are very proud of you, and we wish you well in your examinations. We hope that you people are going to help us to realise our dream to have an effective voice in the running of our country.

One day in the thirties I was walking through town in Umtata, where I was born. Suddenly the whole street came to a standstill because a chap was crossing the street, and somebody said to us:

Do you see that man crossing the street? That man has studied and studied and studied, until he passed this standard called 'Matriculation'. And we all stopped and looked at this man because he seemed to have come from another world. And even the way he walked - he walked like a man who had passed matriculation.

We do want you to pass your examinations and to have your degrees, but the best way to use your degree is to be able to mix with your people, because you are acquiring this education in order to be able to serve your people."

Then he closes by sharing what a leader should not be and what a leader should be:

"*Some time back in the fifties I was invited to a ceremony – two teachers had got their first degrees, and the main speaker was Dr Phathudi, who became the Chief Minister of Lebowa. He was an inspector of education for a long time. In the course of his remarks, he said to these graduates: 'Now you have passed your BA in one of the best universities in the country – the University of the Witwatersrand. You are now leaders, and the task of a leader is not to listen to the ordinary people – you must instruct them. You must not fear deciding and giving your instructions to the people below you. That is the task of a leader.'*

Well, that is exactly the opposite of a leader. A leader is a man who doesn't announce himself, who doesn't boast of his qualities, who is able to bring himself to the level of his people, who puts his people in front. When there is danger, he leads; when you celebrate victory, he is behind. When a person looks after sheep, you drive them to the front – you are behind them.

You let them graze. If you wanted to lead them to a particular area in the veld, you are behind them – you drive them along to that area. At sunset when you have to bring them home, you go around them and drive them back – you are behind them. That is how you serve your people – you are always behind them, but when there is a danger then you go to the front line – you share the same hazards with your people.

We have the hope that we have a new generation – a generation that is going to regard itself as part of the masses of the people. Just remember as you work hard on your studies that that is what we expect of you. It is one of our greatest moments that we are here, and we will look back on it with very fond memories. Once again, we wish you well in your exams.

Thank you."

All Saints students welcome Nelson Mandela and he is clearly delighted

Nelson Mandela is then led away. He disappears into the Tripartite meeting and a loud roar greets his arrival there. He is back where he should be and we have enjoyed our magic moment, so I turn around and slowly walk away. I'm not in a hurry and I decide to climb up to the reservoir where I first sat on the day of my arrival at this place. Back down on the plinth at the base of the great water tank once more I gaze out at the scene in front of me and mull over the dramas that have been played out at this remarkable place. It is a special, brief moment to reflect on what I have learned in my time here. I feel a warm glow as I know now that despite the torment that has come with the events as well as all the distressing misunderstandings and suspicions, it has all been worth it.

All Saints has come of age and has at last been recognised as a legitimate and successful educational institution in the struggle against the apartheid regime. It is the culmination of a what has been a precarious journey for me. To have Nelson Mandela visit the college today for this occasion is the endorsement of my realisation that I have successfully walked the All Saints tightrope. It has not been easy. With Mandela's visit to All Saints everything has come together. I have walked the delicate tightrope and am safely at the end of the journey.

I sigh and get up and walk down to my home as my little Jack Russell dog runs up and joins me and then happily prances in the grass. I am at peace with All Saints and all the lessons that I have learned at this special place.

chapter 30
Postscript

"Falling leaves hide the path so quietly."

— John Bailey

WHAT HAPPENED to All Saints and LEAF after 1992? The simple answer is that the funding taps were closed off. The questioning of the financial sustainability by the staff in the days of our initial induction foretold the inevitable demise of All Saints. As it became more and more difficult to source funding the issue became who was to blame.

Unfortunately, the life-span of LEAF and its colleges was ephemeral at best. Too much reliance on finding money annually was placed on the herculean efforts of one person, the director. He never wanted to share this responsibility. He kept it close to his chest. It was his vision and his responsibility. The model was flawed as there was no back-up endowment or team involvement. His success bubble burst soon after 1992 brought democracy to replace apartheid.

Ironically, while the political changes of 1992 in South Africa seemed to be painting such positive and colourful broad sweeps they led to sponsors both within the country and abroad withdrawing one by one from initiatives like ours. They reined in their funding support and redirected it to various government departments where it was swallowed up in the newly elected democratic government led by Nelson Mandela. It was a time when all non-governmental organisations faced a sudden support drought. Many dried up altogether and had to close.

All Saints Senior College was a founder member of the Southern African Association of Independent Schools (SAAIS) and the consensus prophetic opinion among the members of SAAIS was that the LEAF long-term vision was unworkable in practice. And that was how it worked out.

The end for All Saints was abrupt and uncompromising. At the start of October in 1992 I, together with the All Saints staff, was given an impersonal notification of less than one month's notice by the LEAF Bursar, Mike Rochfort.

We would all receive no salary in November nor in the future beyond. In the written communication – for which there had been no prior warning or consultation – there was no reference to any terms of retrenchment. It was just a flat dismissal. Richard Todd was quoted in *The Daily Dispatch* on the 10 October as saying:

"To my knowledge these letters warned the staff that if no alternative funding could be found, they would be out of work as the College would be closed or sold."

We then found out that Richard Todd had flown in to Bisho and negotiated with Minister Jacobs in the Ciskei government to sell All Saints College to the Bantustan administration for R20 million behind our backs. This was a desperate move of his to sell one college, his All Saints flagship, so as to keep the other two LEAF colleges afloat.

Richard Todd was distraught. His strategy, to keep afloat the colleges located nearer South Africa's financial heartland where funders could easily visit, was completely without regard for the futures of all at All Saints. When his negotiations with the Ciskeian government reached an advanced stage, the All Saints Trust heard about them and intervened. The Trust chairman at the time was Stewart Dorrington. To save the situation, he played a master-stroke based on a major oversight by Richard Todd.

The oversight was that when LEAF was launched in 1987 Richard Todd had left the All Saints Senior College establishment and its assets in the ownership of the All Saints College Trust. In hindsight he should have transferred the ownership to LEAF as the umbrella body. But he didn't. For whatever reason, whether it was owing to the cost implication of transfer or some lapse, he now did not have the jurisdiction to negotiate a sale of the college. He was only one member of the All Saints College Trust and the deal with the Ciskeian government was called off.

The downside of this confrontation was that, whilst beforehand the income from LEAF had been precarious, it was now totally withdrawn. We were to be punished. LEAF acrimoniously turned off the funding taps for All Saints College. Parallel with the funding failure of his grand scheme, Richard Todd's bitterness towards me intensified. He projected all the shortcomings of his vision leading to the demise of All Saints and LEAF onto me personally. I was the cause as, in his view, I had failed dismally as a headmaster. The nadir of our personal relationship was reached when he wrote to Ronnie Napier, the LEAF chairman, in 1992:

"I have now had a guts-full of Burton and really would like to end altogether any association of any sort with him. I am not quite sure what steps to recommend – whether he goes or whether I go or whether LEAF gently withdraws from All Saints.

Michael Burton has become a problem that I can no longer handle and a person with whom I no longer wish to have any contact at all. He ruined more than half of 1991 for me and has done a similar job on the whole of '92. I am not prepared to take him on again in 1993."

With the failure of LEAF and its inability to continue sourcing funds for our college, Stewart Dorrington approached the Department of Education and Culture in the the Eastern Cape province for support. At the same time, we investigated transformation of our *modus operandi* to extend our community interaction programmes into a resourcing and development programme. Neither of these initiatives could save the day.

Our separation from LEAF, together with my dissociation from Richard Todd, close the pages of this story of my time as the principal of All Saints Senior College. Gideon Sam wrote:

"After all is said and done, the demise of All Saints can be written as one of those tragedies of our society. I think when the history of All Saints has been written, that final sentence will probably be: Oh, what a tragedy that it never continued because it had the road ahead."

However, for the All Saints College Trust the pages were not closed. Later the All Saints College Trust transformed itself under the leadership of its new chairman, Jonathan Clark, into the All Saints Education Development Trust. It sold the College and its campus to the University of Fort Hare and relocated its activities to the Sacred Heart Convent in King William's Town.

I was then appointed as Director of the All Saints Education Development Centre. For the next ten years, the remaining All Saints College staff and I supported over a hundred deprived senior schools as well as over twelve hundred students and teachers in our province with a variety of resources and programmes. Arguably All Saints as a resource centre played a much bigger and more valuable role in the development of this neglected corner of South Africa through engaging schools in a co-operative effort.

But that is another story, and it is worth telling.